SERVICE OPERATIONS MANAGEMENT

SERVICE OPERATIONS MANAGEMENT

Neville D. Harris
Head of Department of Management and Administration
Newcastle Polytechnic

CASSELL

To Helen, in loving appreciation of her
enthusiasm and encouragement

Cassell Educational Ltd
Artillery House, Artillery Row
London SW1P 1RT

First published 1989

ISBN 0–304–32217–2

British Library Cataloguing in Publication Data
Harris, N. D. (Neville Dale), *1935–*
    Service operations management
    1. Service industries. Management
    I. Title
    338.4

Typeset by Fakenham Photosetting Ltd
Printed in Great Britain at the Alden Press, Oxford

CONTENTS

041824

v

PREFACE

The major thrust in management development during this century has been within the manufacturing sector, and examples of techniques which have been developed in this environment are readily available. I find much greater similarity in outlook between managers working in very dissimilar product manufacture, like soft drinks and electronic components, than between managers in the non-manufacturing sector. In management development programmes for local authorities, for example, the very many different professionals, although working for the same employer, appeared at first to have little in common. Thus in dealing with solicitors, librarians, civil engineers, park managers and those from social services, the central illustrative theme of management designing, producing and selling a product range was not relevant. All managers have responsibility for *resources* of some kind – even if it is only their own time – and the theme of this book is to identify techniques that can be of value to all types of managers, enabling them to identify their responsibility for resources and to be more effective in the task of managing. The need to recognise that a service system of any kind needs care in design, operating and 'selling' is one that could be pursued with advantage in non-manufacturing. In some service sectors such as retail, travel, hotel/catering and finance this is done, and because of many specialised texts covering these areas, my examples are by and large culled from less obvious customer-conscious areas of service.

Over the last fifteen years publications on the manufacturing management theme – usually referred to as 'production management' – have attempted to widen their appeal and have used the term 'production and operations management' and latterly 'operations management'. Although these often specifically refer to the 'service sector' in the initial chapters, as the book develops so the examples become more manufacturing biased and in many we are, like so many of the early production texts, thrust into the metal-cutting environment of an engineering works and are up to our ankles in swarf! The study of management, and in particular manufacturing management, owes a great deal to the pioneering work of engineers, and the unique illustrative material deriving from batch production methods which spawns models of production planning and control, economic ordering, and even revolutionary means of enhancing productivity through group technology, etc., is a gift to the lecturer. However, not only is there a large manufacturing segment which does not relate to engineering, most importantly there are many different activities which are in non-manufacturing where the basic production management techniques in some cases need to be modified and adapted so that the learning and application is eased.

Another feature of management texts produced over the past few years is to separate the people resource, and produce books on 'human resource management' or personnel. Likewise, the books on manufacturing management have avoided most people issues and concentrated on the resources as if they were all as malleable as materials and as programmable as machines. Although I do not intend the personnel aspect to be a dominant theme in this text, it will be seen as a major resource by many from the 'service sector' and the personal and interpersonal skills of the manager will be a decisive issue in effective resource utilisation.

SERVICE

Service Operations Management is intended to cover all work activities that are not strictly manufacturing. Because of the nature of operations management it is most likely to be concerned with the delivery of a service in which the customer or client is closely involved. Examples given are almost bound to be incomplete, but the reader has to ask if the area in which they are involved is more concerned with the provision of a service rather than the creation of a product. A more precise definition of the various types of operations is provided within the text, but at the outset it is only necessary in broad terms to identify the degree to which the activities managed are concerned with services rather than products.

The type of service that springs readily to mind is those provided by the public sector – health, social services and local authority services generally, including schools and colleges, refuse collection, planning, and recreation such as baths, parks, etc. The list provided by the above two major public services, health and social services, is endless. However, within such activities there are elements of manufacturing, such as the provision of meals to patients in hospital, to those in residential care and to school pupils. Some local authorities may have their own printing unit, which has exactly the same problems as that of a private sector printer in terms of output.

Another set of service providers are in the private sector, some of which are taking over on contract the equivalent services in the public sector such as cleaning, laundry and building maintenance. In the private sector it also is possible to include a variety of personal services such as hairdressing, hotels and restaurants, retail services to the home, garages, and financial services such as banking, insurance and building societies. Many of these have very specific management problems based on the technology of the service, but the analysis of management within a service provision will apply equally to such areas.

Manufacturing industry will account for a large proportion of service activities in terms of support to the manufacturing itself – transport and distribution, office services, maintenance, etc. – and managers in these areas have to consider carefully which sector they identify with. Many books have been exclusively concerned with problems associated with managing a manufacturing unit, regardless of the type of throughput. This has led to a concentration on output of concrete saleable products. The service manager is dealing with a variety of unpredictable demands, and customer satisfaction is much less easily gauged.

OPERATIONS

This book fills the gap between the many texts concerned with operational practice within manufacturing and those concerned with the service sector which tend to be concentrated on strategy and marketing. The aim of the book is to provide for the operations managers within services activities a number of approaches to the identification and solving of problems that are within their control, so that the operation can become more effective. It does consider the essential quality of service, and shows how conventional operational techniques can be applied to advantage.

MANUFACTURING AND SERVICE INTERFACE

A major reason for writing this book is to show how, at an operational level, many of the techniques that have been developed in manufacturing can be readily translated to the service sector. The more the two sectors are linked in this way the more management will be seen as a means of 'crossing the divide'. The differences can thus be minimised.

The need for managers at all levels to be able to identify problems in all sectors, regardless of 'technology', is critical for our future, and the mixing together of headteachers, hospital unit managers and retail managers with production managers is likely to be greater in future development programmes. These ideas have been recorded and developed as the following references indicate:

Armistead, C., Johnson, R. and Voss, C. A. (1986) Introducing services industries in operations management. *International Journal of Operations Management*, **6**, pp. 21–29.

Institution of Industrial Managers (September 1986) *Qualification Courses for Managers – Regulations and Syllabus*. Series 5A, Part C, Subject C3/C6 – Operations Management. Ealing: IIM.

Killeya, J. C. and Armistead, C. G. (1983) The transfer of concepts and techniques between manufacturing and service systems. *International Journal of Operations Management*, **3**, pp. 22–28.

Voss, C. A., Armistead, C. and Johnson, R. (1985) *Operations Management in Service Industries and the Public Sector*. Chichester: Wiley.

ACKNOWLEDGEMENTS

I am fortunate to work with colleagues who have creative minds, and who have inspired me with their research and interests. Also I have been able to work closely with many of them in developing ideas for learning which have combined their specialist knowledge with my own. The effect of this is to have material which quite rightly is 'owned' by several people.

Also in my life in faculty I have amassed a number of papers, some of which had no author's name. Many of these ideas will have found their way into this book and I, therefore, owe a debt of gratitude to all those whose ideas I could not separate or whose only reference would be 'anon'.

However, there were many whose specific contributions can be identified, in particular, Brian Day, Department of Management and Administration, Newcastle Polytechnic, who wrote the whole Chapter 8 on quality and reliability.
The others are:

George Boak, Northern Regional Management Centre, Washington, Tyne & Wear, for the time demands quadrant in Chapter 14.

John Bothams for examples of operating systems in Chapter 1, teamwork activity in Chapter 11 and leadership in Chapter 13.

Kathleen Bothams, Project Worker, Northumberland County Council, Social Services Department, for research work into service marketing which was summarized in Chapter 3.

Bob Cruickshank, independent consultant, for the ideas in Figure 4.2.

Ian Fatherley, Depot Manager, Scottish & Newcastle Breweries, for the ideas on effective teamwork in Chapter 11 and work on structured task management development in Chapter 12.

Alan Fendley, Deputy Head of Department, Department of Education, Newcastle Polytechnic, for help with Chapter 12.

David Milmore for ideas for Chapter 2 on organisations.

Terry Miskell for ideas on planning methods in Chapter 3.

Eddie Palmer, Training Manager, North Tyneside Social Services Department, for developments in Chapter 14.

Dr Vas Prabhu, for help with resource problems in Chapter 10.

Alan Ray for ideas on capital assets in Chapter 9.

Alex Skedd for help with Chapter 7 on materials management.

Professor John Webb, ex Polytechnic of Central London, for ideas in Chapter 6 on layout and handling.

Those people whose jobs are not identified are all members of the Department of Management and Administration, Newcastle Polytechnic.

I am indebted to the following editors, publishers and copyright holders for permission to reproduce significant quotations or illustrations or to adapt material:

David Charlton, editor of *Management Services*, for use of Robinson (1987), 'Productivity in the retail' (Chapter 1); Turnbull and Shaw (1987), 'Leisure services and new technology' (Chapter 1); Brown (1976), 'Organisational relationship charts' (Chapter 2); Hamill (1985), 'Salesmen, supervisors and small offices' (Chapter 5); Sussams (1984), 'Vehicle replacement' (Chapter 9); Harris (1976), 'Management services and professional staff' (Chapter 14); and Neale (1970), 'Developing a change strategy for an organisation' (Chapter 11).

University Associates International Ltd, for the organisational blockages list (Table 2.2) and Figure 12.1, quoted from Woodcock and Francis, *Unblocking Your Organisation* (1979).

Mrs Di Southern of John Wiley and Sons Ltd, Chichester, for Table 4.2, examples of some questions on 'client management', from Normann, *Service Management; Strategy and Leadership in Service Businesses* (1984).

The Controller of Her Majesty's Stationery Office, for Figures 6.1 and 6.2 and Table 6.1, from *Materials Handling: An Introduction* (1978) and *Materials Handling for Senior Managers* (1982).

Tony Crabtree, Market Analyst, ICI, for the public house layout planning example in Chapter 6.

Malcolm Peel from the British Institute of Management for Table 11.2 and the quotations from Rawlinson, *Creative Thinking and Brainstorming* (1970) in Chapter 11.

Croom Helm Ltd, for figure 12.3, from Broussine and Guerrier, *Surviving as a Middle Manager* (1983).

Sidgwick and Jackson Ltd, for Table 13.3, from Le Boeuf, *How to Motivate People* (1984).

Harper and Row Ltd, for permission to use material on managerial roles in Chapter 14 from Mintzberg, *The Nature of Managerial Work* (1973).

Whilst I am grateful for all the help I had from all the above, any mistakes or misinterpretations must be entirely my own.

I would also like to place on record my thanks to the many services, organisations and people within them that I have been able to work with as a consultant and from which many examples have been developed. Also ideas have been gleaned from the course members on all types of programmes that we run in the Polytechnic. Some have developed excellent assignments, projects and placement reports within the service sector which have been of inspiration.

Neville D. Harris

1

WHAT IS OPERATIONS MANAGEMENT?

INTRODUCTION

Until the early 1970s, the major impetus of management writing assumed that readers were in some way connected with manufacturing or production, and the functional area was referred to as 'production management'. Because many of you reading this book do not necessarily work in the manufacturing sector, it is more appropriate to use the term 'operations management' to cover the major resource management within an organisation.

To explain how this term is used and its full interpretation within the book, let us first turn to organisational objectives. These will enable us to see clearly how operations management makes a contribution to the organisation and enables us to specify what the objectives of operations management are.

ORGANISATIONAL OBJECTIVES

One definition of management is:

> The process, activity or study of carrying out the task that a number of diverse activities are performed in such a way that a defined objective is achieved – *especially* the task of creating and maintaining conditions in which desired objectives are achieved by the combined efforts of a group of people.

> (*French and Saward, 1975*)

Two phrases are important to us in the above – first, 'defined objectives', which indicates that management is a purposeful activity. Objectives are not always written down by organisations, and very often are quite diverse. An attempt to tie top management down to specific objectives may be very difficult in practice, and in some cases these are only thought through and articulated after a number of years of activity.

Secondly, 'performed in such a way' implies that performance of the organisation, department, section and individual is crucial to achievement. We are, therefore, concerned with effective performance. Much of this book is targeted at the improvement of performance, which is the real essence of management.

ACTIVITY

Write down what you perceive as the objectives of your own organisation. Then consider the

1

objectives of your own department, or unit within the organisation. How can your achievement of these objectives be measured?

To help in this you may need to think of the following:

1. How would excellent performance in your department be recognised?
2. How would a poor performance in your department be recognised?
3. Do your objectives relate to:
    (a) costs
    (b) quality of service
    (c) customer or client satisfaction
    (d) time
    (e) employee relations
    (f) public concern
    (g) share of the market
    (h) profits (or staying within budget)
    (i) effective use of resources
    (j) development of new products or methods, or type of service
    (k) or simply perhaps – survival?

These are all areas in which *objectives* can be set. In some commercial organisations, the need to make a profit is undoubtedly a dominant objective which in turn leads to considerable concern with costs. However, the other objectives must never be forgotten and it can be concluded that a measure of managerial effectiveness is getting the balance right between these many, sometimes competing, objectives.

CASE EXAMPLE

If you are from the non-manufacturing sector you may feel that the profit motive of the production sector is sometimes too dominant, but in the service sector there is a tendency to forget economic performance. In a recent contract with wardens of residential houses for the elderly, after a detailed discussion in different small groups, the aims listed in Table 1.1 emerged as the warden's *perceived* objectives.

You will note that these are concerned with 'client satisfaction' and 'staff development'. No mention is made of such factors as costs, resource utilisation, etc. Now, in omitting these, the wardens are not to be blamed since the organisation they worked for had not provided them with any objectives at all. But there is a need again to stress this balance.

It will help in the remainder of this book if you find out all you can about your own organisation's objectives and also those of your 'operations' department. You may wish to review these critically in the light of the subsequent discussion.

Table 1.1 Aims of residential units for the elderly.

Clients

To provide a secure environment (therapeutic community) where the quality of life for residents is enhanced through:
(a) Tender, loving care
(b) Warmth
(c) Social activities
(d) Self-help and determination
(e) Respect for residents' privacy
(f) Avoidance of mundane routines and institutionalisation
(g) Support and understanding of physical and psychological needs
(h) Maintaining of functioning ability

Staff

To encourage staff in self-development:
(a) In active social involvement with residents such that trust can be gained
(b) In involvement in decisions which effect them and the home

To promote further training for all staff, namely:
(a) Improve standards of in service training
(b) Improve team spirit between all grades of staff
(c) Promote skills to deal with physical care
(d) Encourage attitudes conducive to the task
(e) Promote demonstration of affection
(f) Encourage new ideas which lead to action

OPERATIONS MANAGEMENT – A DEFINITION

Initially the term 'operations management' was coined to embrace those activities linked to production – such as design and distribution – and the term 'production operations' was used in 1971 to move away from strictly manufacturing problems.

Other opinion leaders have indicated an interest in other systems, e.g., hospitals, office procedures, supermarkets, and use 'operations management' to cover all 'systems of men, materials, capital, equipment, information and money, to accomplish some set of objectives' (Vollman, 1973). A more specific definition appeared '... concerned with the design and the operation of systems for manufacturing, transport, supply or service' (Wild, 1977) and more succinctly '... producing a product or providing a service' (Hill, 1983).

Many of the more recently produced books have tried to cover – in one volume – the manufacturing (products) and service industries. As a result the majority of examples come from production, and this does not help understanding if you are in the service sector. This book is intended to rectify this bias and provide examples with which you will more readily be able to identify.

Slack (1983) suggested that operations management:

1. Is the central function of most organisations.
2. Generally has responsibility for the vast majority of the organisation's resources (particularly the people resource).
3. Is a pervasive activity.
4. Is the area within the organisation where many social and technological changes are taking place.

Whilst some functional specialists in manufacturing such as marketing, personnel and finance may not agree fully with the above, in the service sector, these are likely to be justifiable statements.

Finally, there follows a definition which encompasses many of the above ideas:

> *Operations management is the management of a system which provides goods or services to or for a customer, and involves the design, planning and control of the system.*

THE SYSTEMS APPROACH

Already reference has been made to balance in objectives and the above definition uses the word 'systems'. This word, or more particularly the approach, must inform the rest of this book so that we do not fall into the trap of solving a problem in part.

To illustrate this, here are two examples:

1. Some organisations request training programmes for supervisors on the exercising of managerial skills such as team leadership, time management, etc., and yet the way in which these same supervisors are treated by top and middle management indicates that such development can never be properly implemented. The whole 'system', including top management, needs exposure to development rather than just the supervisors.
2. The approach to management techniques has been very much 'flavour of the month' and any new technique or approach is seized on as if it was some panacea. Without the proper support, extremely effective techniques will flounder. During the 1960s a variety of approaches to payment by results were used in local authorities, and the only ones in which there was organisational success were those in which properly planned implementation ensured that it was part of a total payment system, and which presented effective information to support the weekly results.

The thrust that must be continually sought, and which will be emphasised throughout the text, is that of the systems approach – to avoid analysis of part systems in cause–effect terms, and to take a much broader view of the problem. The total systems of which the above problems were a part will, if examined, provide alternative solutions which are more likely to meet the organisational objectives. Thus an operations manager will be concerned with the linking together of money, staff, machines and material resources, information, methods, clients, etc. To look at any one in isolation provides a limited solution to the problem unless it can be shown clearly that the part system is the area which, if improved, will enhance the quality of the whole system.

CATEGORISING OPERATING SYSTEMS

The service sector and the manufacturing sector have so many overlaps, it is useful to provide some categorisation. As Normann (1984) suggests, 'The distinction between manufacturing and service companies is . . . hazy. Is IBM selling goods as services? Is

Volvo being a service company in so far as a good deal of its product is being leased out?' Normann goes on to identify the essential characteristics of service:

1. *Intangibility*, i.e. concepts rather than things. A haircut, a service of the car, information – these cannot be stocked, and whilst they include tangible parts, e.g. food in a restaurant or goods in a shop, the act of purchase or consumption is intangible. Fitzsimmons and Sullivan (1982) further suggest that there is difficulty in measuring output from service organisations since numbers of clients does not take account of quality of service.
2. Service often requires acts and interacting which require social skills and the arranging of 'social events'. This leads to –
3. The production and consumption occurring simultaneously with the customer being a part of this process as in a supermarket, bank, college, etc.

In looking for ways of improving 'the service', more involvement of the customer is often of benefit to both the customer and the service organisation. The considerable increase in open and distance learning is a good example: the customer (student) takes more responsibility for his or her own learning which should result in greater satisfaction. For this to be successful a lot of time and money needs to be spent on designing the system.

Fitzsimmons and Sullivan (1982) add to the above the time-perishable capacity, i.e. the bus seat not occupied, the hairdresser without appointments, the hotel room without a guest, etc. These are missed opportunities. Chase (1980) suggested that the level of involvement between the services can be high ('front office') or low ('back room'). Many offices in local authorities may have a limited involvement with clients (planning, environmental health, etc.) whilst some members of the department are with the clients (public) a great deal of their time. Similarly, in the supermarket there may be as many people in the stock room and offices as in the shop itself.

Whilst the above are very effective in differentiating service from manufacture, it is possible to go further. Wild (1977) suggested a number of categories for 'operating systems':

1. Manufacture
2. Supply
3. Transport
4. Service

Manufacture

Manufacturing means *making* something. So, in the car industry, iron, steel, plastic and other materials are used to manufacture cars; in the kitchen of a hotel, food ingredients are mixed, flavoured and cooked in order to manufacture meals. This involves a change in the *characteristics* of the original raw materials – shape, texture, chemical composition, etc.

Supply

In a supply operating system, however, the goods are in the *same* form at the end of the operating system as they were at the beginning; a shop or a mail-order company would fall into this category. It is *ownership* or *possession* which changes during a supply operating system.

Transport

This means that someone, or something *belonging to someone*, is moved from place to place. The change here is *location*.

Service

Here someone, or something belonging to someone, has something done to or for that person or things. The changes here will be more varied. For example, the provision of personal services such as by a dentist, optician or hairdresser, normally involves some change even if it is just peace of mind. Sometimes the change may be that the person now has certain information or access to information that he or she did not have before. So, we could say that a reception desk or a telephone exchange are also service operating systems.

Subsystems

Most organisations are combinations of systems rather than fitting simply into one of the four categories mentioned above. Each of these parts which make up the whole system is called a *subsystem*. For example, a mail clerk in a large organisation (it might be manufacture, supply, transport or service) who goes around delivering mail is acting as a transport system.

ACTIVITY

Think about a take-away restaurant where meals are cooked for customers to take away and eat off the premises. While customers wait for their orders they can watch the television or read the newspapers. Which categories of operating systems can you identify here?

First, there is the cooking operation which is *manufacturing*. The selling operation is *supply*, and the shop-front television, papers, seating and atmosphere is *service*.

It is important to be able to untangle the different operating systems which make up most business organisations because each subsystem will have its own objectives (not always stated) and these may conflict with the objectives of another subsystem. This lies at the root of many departmental conflicts.

ACTIVITY

Fit your whole organisation into one of the four categories manufacture, supply, transport or service which you consider to be dominant. Which category does your own department, section or work area fit into?

Types of production

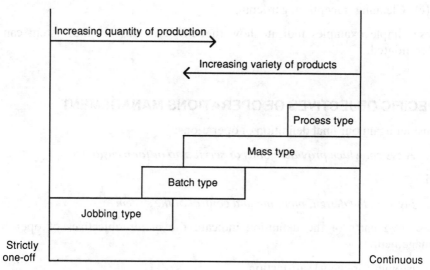

Figure 1.1 The production continuum

A production firm and its operating subsystem

This section illustrates how the subsystems interact, and also indicates the 'service' part of production.

1. *Manufacture*. This is perhaps the principal function of the operating system, with the overall purpose of producing goods. Manufacturing methods are usually classified as follows:
   (a) *Process* – involving continuous production of a commodity in bulk;
   (b) *Mass production* – similar to process, but usually associated with motor car and domestic appliance manufacture;
   (c) Batch production – for discrete items manufactured over a given period, the set-up then being changed to accommodate a batch of different items – similar to mass production but insufficient continuity of similar items;
   (d) Jobbing – strictly one-off items made to a customer's order.
   These methods are illustrated in Figure 1.1.
2. *Transport*. The prime function is to change the location of items of manufacture. Within manufacturing organisations, transport systems may be used for:
   (a) Issue of raw materials to commence manufacture;
   (b) Movement of work in progress between manufacturing departments;
   (c) Removal of completed items to finished stock department, and for disposal of waste materials, etc.;
   (d) External to the organisation – onward to distribution.
3. *Supply*. Internal stores department where stocks of raw materials are kept until required by the manufacturing function, stores of spares for machines, finished goods stores or warehouses, etc.
4. *Service*. Usually covers such functions within the organisation as:
   (a) Maintenance

7

   (b) Welfare facilities, medical and first-aid services
   (c) Cleaning, reception, gardening.

These simple examples indicate how the different parts of the system can be differentiated.

SPECIFIC OBJECTIVES OF OPERATIONS MANAGEMENT

Consider again our final definition of operations:

> *A system which provides goods or services to or for a customer*

and

> *involves the design, planning and control of the system*

These two parts of the definition indicate the *major* objectives of operations management:

1. Customer (or client) satisfaction
2. Resource productivity

These objectives are to some extent in conflict and an acceptable level of service must be provided by designing and planning the system of delivery accordingly.

Customer satisfaction

The extent to which the customer is involved in the system has profound effects on that system: generally it adds to the complexity and the need for the system's flexibility:

1. The more time the customer spends in the system the less fixed is the process which can be used. For example, in a school or a hotel there is a high customer contact and the process by which the customer is served needs to be more flexible than in, say, manufacturing large quantities.
2. It is much less easy to predict the demands on the capacity of a system with high customer contact. There can be sudden surges of customers for meals, for example.
3. There is a much greater need for staff to be skilled in handling people, both staff and customers.

As customer contact is decreased the process can be made increasingly efficient. A good example of how the system can be designed to reduce customer contact, and yet provide a satisfactory service, is any 'fast-food' outlet, where the menu is limited but service is fast and cheerful. Similarly we might consider the difference between the 'village stores' type of shop and a supermarket.

The customer's effect on objectives

Deciding who your customer is is an important stage in working out what your operating system is trying to do – in other words what your objectives are. Determining your objectives in the light of your customer's needs is crucial to good management but it is often not understood or is overlooked.

There is a true story of a bus company executive who, when being interrogated on television about buses running late, said: 'The buses would run to time perfectly if it were not for the passengers at the bus stops.'

This may sound ridiculous, but many systems seem to operate with equally ridiculous objectives.

ACTIVITY

Assuming you are reading this text as part of a management development programme (i.e. a college course, a company programme or for your own benefit), who are the customers (eventual beneficiaries) of the management development?

1. Obviously you, the student.
2. Possibly you will have thought of your employer.
3. Closer to home are your family, if you paid for the course out of the family budget. They should benefit directly from your increased competence and confidence.
4. A major part of the costs of setting up a management learning programme may have been paid for by a management or supervisory institute, and so they, having an interest in your qualifying, can be regarded as a customer.

Though not customers in our terms there are other people you may have thought of who should benefit. It is necessary sometimes to consider such people in designing an operating system:

1. There are your staff who will benefit by your increased management competence.
2. Society in general should benefit either directly through a better product or service, or indirectly through a general improvement in standards of service and competence.

All the customers identified above expect something from the management learning programme as they do from any operating system. This puts us in a position to identify the first objective of an operations manager:

> *The operations manager should provide customer satisfaction by providing the right thing at the right price at the right time.*

We can all think of times when an item we wish to buy was not in stock, or a meal was too expensive, or a bus was late. Any of these situations means total dissatisfaction.

Resource productivity

Almost anything is possible given unlimited resources. But managers have a responsibility to keep costs down by careful use of resources. So the second objective is:

> *The operations manager should ensure the effective and efficient use of all resources.*

We can call this *resource productivity*.

What exactly do we mean by 'efficiency' and 'effectiveness'? We can see what they mean and the difference between them from an example. Suppose a supervisor from a production line needs some packaging. He goes to the stores where he has to remain waiting to be serviced for some time. Thus production, which costs £100 per minute, is held up. He is kept waiting because the storeman is counting brass washers which are worth £5 per 1,000. He prides himself on his accurate record-keeping and knows exactly how many of each item he has in stock.

It *is* 'efficient' to keep very accurate records, but equally it is 'ineffective' not to serve the customers while the storeman is counting washers, because the washers are of relatively small value and production time is far more expensive. That is not to say that having a stock of washers is not important – this is why we said it was efficient because production could be held up if the storeman ran out. There needs to be an effective as well as an efficient system for reordering washers which helps the storeman achieve the result he is supposed to achieve – keeping the production line supplied and running.

Balance

The operations manager has to reconcile the conflict between the demand for customer satisfaction on the one hand and making the most effective and efficient use of resources on the other. If there is no time constraint on when the product or service is required, then there is time to organise the resources efficiently and effectively, time for working out the best way to do it for the least cost. Such a situation is rare – it is quite difficult to find an example. Imagine you have a plot of land and are building, in your spare time, a bungalow to retire to. You will have the time to organise materials and the building to produce an excellent home with the least cost. However, if there is a sudden need to complete the bungalow within a month, costs will rocket and you will have to put up with whatever materials and labour are available.

So, we can say that time constraints mean:

1. some resource productivity is lost in order to give customer satisfaction, *or*
2. some customer satisfaction is lost in order to achieve better resource productivity.

There has to be a trade-off between the two: operations management is about managing that trade-off.

ACTIVITY

Consider your own organisation in terms of the balance it achieves between customer satisfaction and resource productivity.

CASE EXAMPLE

Although the major objectives of operations managers are those of resource productivity and customer satisfaction, the other objectives listed on page 2 are not ignored. To illustrate this, let us consider the case of the fleet manager.

A bus company recently decided to change its organisational structure and set up the idea of 'fleets' – a set of 30–40 buses covering a distinct set of routes. The key person in this would be the fleet manager. This post is a very good example of an operations manager, and Table 1.2 demonstrates the way in which this links in with our ideas so far.

Table 1.2 Duties and objectives of a fleet manager.

Duty	Objectives
1. To be responsible for the management of a specific group of drivers and their performance	Worker productivity
2. To be responsible for monitoring and reporting on the quality of operation for a specified fleet relating to: (a) Vehicle standards (cleanliness, destination equipment, vandalism and accident damage) (b) Level of service (frequency and capacity) (c) Roadside furniture (d) Appropriateness of vehicles and routes (e) Roadworks, diversions, etc. To develop liaison with the engineering department as appropriate	Equipment productivity and quality and reliability – customer satisfaction Public responsibility and time
3. To assist drivers in the performance of their duties, through motivation, communication and welfare, and to encourage and evaluate comments and suggestions from the group	Links with worker productivity indirectly but also employee relations
4. To develop and sustain good public relations by communicating to individuals, groups and market influencers regarding current service and to identify and report potential customer travel requirements	Customer satisfaction. Share of market Development of new 'products'
5. To ensure that current publicity material is displayed in vehicles and other appropriate locations and to ensure out-of-date and damaged publicity material is removed	Share of market Public responsibility
6. To report on potential means of increasing total revenue which consider both appropriateness of fare structure and numbers of customers	Profitability/costs Customer satisfaction Development of new 'products'
7. To detect and deter fraud	Profitability/costs

RESOURCE MANAGEMENT

All organisations need to manage their resources and the type of organisation often determines how the activity can be distinguished. Figure 1.2 clarifies the contextual location of operations management within the total operations system. In this figure we show the major inputs to any system:

1. *Skills* – which can be manual, cerebral or managerial
2. *Physical assets* – machines, vehicles, computers and office machines, etc.
3. *Information* – which is the life-blood of most organisations. This can include

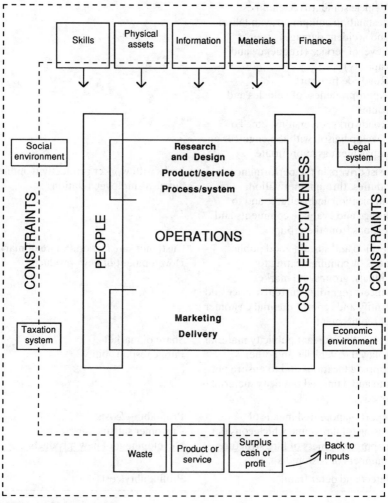

Figure 1.2 The operational system
Adapted from Harding (1986)

information about the market, about the methods of being most effective in operations, about advances in appropriate technology.

4. *Materials* – which will vary in importance. For a supply organisation they will be in its very *raison d'être*. For a service organisation, like a travel agency, the materials will be office supplies, travel brochures, tickets, timetables, etc.

5. *Finance* – which is an obvious need for all organisations.

These feed into the system which comprises research and design.

Operations, marketing and delivery enable the conversion process to take place and the output of the system to be identified, which will be either product(s) or service. It will also produce some waste and possibly some financial surplus or profit.

The operating system is seen to be governed by two major factors, people and cost effectiveness. The diagram also shows the types of constraints that affect all types of organisations: the legal and taxation systems and the social and economic environments.

Resources

In Figure 1.2 you will note how all the resources of an organisation are brought together, namely skills, physical assets, information, materials and finance. You will note also that materials management is linked closely to operations management, though some writers would include it as a subdivision of operations. In manufacturing, operations or production is conversion of materials, whilst in transport and supply the materials are moved/stored.

Departments and functions

The manner in which the various subdivisions of operations management manifest themselves will depend very much on both the size of the organisation and whether it is in manufacturing, transport, supply or service. To illustrate this let us consider the functions in turn, and then place them in 'type of organisation' context.

Research and design

In manufacturing, a research and development function may be a major influence in the production process. This is easily seen in the pharmaceutical industry. In other firms the design function is predominant, particularly in engineering, clothing or furniture. This design does not just concern itself with the product, but also the process of manufacturing – in engineering, for example, a lot of effort is currently being put into designing advanced manufacturing systems which encompass the use of robots etc.

Differentiation between R&D and design is difficult, and for practical purposes the process is a continuous one in terms of what occurs. Some firms choose to distinguish the functions, but essentially the research leads to development for manufacture, which requires design of the product in some cases, and certainly of the system for production.

The 'design' for the product can be in the form of drawings, formulae, patterns, recipes, models, etc. For example:

13

1. In a manufacturing organisation producing, for example, clothes or curtains, a lot of effort needs to be expended in designing a method of manufacture which is cost effective, can be operated by the staff and can function within the other resource limitations that a firm may have.
2. In a transport organisation the research and design effort will be very much encompassed within operations management. It will include, for a bus company, the detailing of routes, fare structures, timetables and coping with a variable demand.
3. In the supply area such as a shop, design will be concerned with the layout, the display and what to sell. It may include consideration of different hours of opening and the effect of the possible revision of Sunday trading laws.
4. In a service organisation such as a restaurant or an elderly persons' home, the system of operation has to be designed as well as the training of staff. This will include duty rotas, how to deal with emergencies, accounting for supplies, etc.

Operations

This is where the actual activity takes place. Manufacturing is very visual and most people have mental images of factories producing goods for sale. In transport, the movement of buses is the operation, whilst in supply, it can be seen as the goods are stored, moved or handed over from one person to another. Finally, in the service sector the work of a garage, hospital or restaurant are suitable examples of the operation.

Marketing and delivery

These two areas need to be distinguished. Marketing will include such activities as promotion, pricing, public relations, marketing research, selling and after-sales service. All types of organisation are involved in these to some extent. For some the major effect of marketing is the manner in which the customer perceives the delivery of the product or service. This is particularly noticeable in transport (bus passengers), supply (shop customers) and service (hotel guests). With manufacturing industry, on the other hand, the product does not normally reach the customer until some time after manufacture, and very often via a supply and/or transport agency.

The delivery function is concurrent with the operations function in all types of service organisation – in fact for some 'transport' organisations delivery *is* the operations function.

OPERATIONS MANAGEMENT PROBLEMS

A major difficulty with operations management is to keep the two areas of customer satisfaction and resource productivity in balance. The operations manager will be concerned with the following specific goals on a day-to-day basis:

1. Cost
2. Quantity

3. Quality
4. Time

Each of these could, by its very nature, pull against the others. High quality could reduce quantity of activity and thus increase cost. Low cost could affect quality, whilst meeting time deadlines could mean extra resources and this could increase costs. Many of the problems that occur within the operations area concern themselves with 'trade-offs' between these aspects which link back to our original definition of customer satisfaction and resource productivity.

The problem areas fall into the following categories:

System design or re-design

This is concerned with establishing methods of working, with the environment and with the layout of physical facilities. It can be seen as a continuous process, since the demands made on the system will change, technology will change and thus most systems are capable of being improved.

Examples are one-man buses, supermarkets, self-service restaurants, airline terminals, etc. All of these are the results of a detailed planning of a proposed system or a revision or improvement of an existing system. Perhaps they have come about as the result of a gradual evolution.

Capacity measurement

This answers the question: How big should the system be? It relates to the number of people to be employed, number of machines and other facilities related to customer demand. We need to know for production how many to make and thus how big should the facilities be. Similarly other areas need to find out in some way what demand is likely to be made on the operation. This is not always easy since it is often seasonal or has peaks and troughs. Sometimes the demand on the facilities just cannot be met, for example when they are in the hands of a health authority which has limited resources.

The capacity problem also is concerned with *balance* between different resources. For example, have we got a sufficiently responsive repair workshop to keep our fleet of buses operating?

Utilisation of resources

How do we schedule our work to ensure the greatest utilisation of men, machines and materials? This is part of a continuing central activity which ensures that, despite changes in demand, there is an optimum use of all facilities. It may often require a considerable amount of re-scheduling by managers based on current information and part of the system design will have to allow for this.

Quality and reliability

This aspect is equally the concern of the provider and the customer. We need to determine the level of service and how reliable it is. The operations manager needs to

15

ensure that quality and reliability are built into the system and that the cost of this is not excessive.

These four areas are the main ones that create problems for operational activities and in subsequent chapters we shall explore how these can be effectively planned and controlled. The four areas very roughly equate to:

Cost	– System	– What will it cost?
Time	– Capacity measurement	– When can we do it?
Quantity	– Utilisation	– How many?
Quality	– Quality	– How good?

They do not remain in watertight compartments. They are all part of a total system and changes in one area will naturally affect others.

THE SCOPE OF OPERATIONS MANAGEMENT WITHIN THE SERVICE SECTOR

To justify the detailed work in the remainder of this text the following short extracts from various articles underline the need for the operative area to be seen as vital.

> This review of productivity in the retail has concentrated on high tech topics to emphasise how the business of volume retailing really is big business where people have to matter because without them there is no business.
>
> Less spectacular but equally vital work is being carried out to improve working methods on the fresh fish counter and in the meat preparation room. Problems common to all business, such as cleaning, cannot be overlooked as improvements are always possible. In a retail empire a small saving in one store becomes a major benefit when applied company wide. Staffing levels are still higher than strictly necessary, notwithstanding the constraints quite rightly imposed on productivity by the demands of quality service. Staff will be of a higher calibre in future with greater product awareness and better commitment to serving the customer. In the final analysis it is the customer who pays the wages.
>
> The modern superstore should combine the service and convenience of the cornershop with the very best quality and choice in an environment that will make shopping less of the chore it so often is now.
>
> *(Robinson, 1987)*

The following extract is from an article which explained how Scottish & Newcastle Breweries' subsidiary Thistle Hotels needed to reconsider traditional attitudes and transform the service it offered to guests.

> But once these policies were in place, management still wanted something to raise standards of service into line with the new furnishings and fittings, and to involve employees in the business.
>
> By coincidence the Kensington Palace Thistle in London was housing seminars expressly designed for service sector personnel. Based on a

programme developed for SAS, the Nordic airline, these were provided by an outfit called Scandinavian Service School which had already been retained by British Airways. 'The ideal course for the service industry', uniquely shaped to develop social skills. So Thistle signed up the trainers to conduct repeat performances throughout the organisation, involving all 3,380 odd employees, managers and managed full-time and part-time.

(Foster, 1987)

There is abundant evidence from all sectors of the service industry that the application of new technology plays an important part in the financial health and survival of companies both up front, in customer contact, and behind the scenes in administration. Many service industry companies including those which provide leisure on a commercial basis have successfully educated themselves to adopt new technology and to adapt to the change it creates. They have also educated their customers from all socio-economic groups to do likewise and to enjoy the benefits of quicker more convenient service.

(Turnbull and Shaw, 1987)

In addition to the above specific examples from retail, hotel and leisure there is today a continuing debate about local authorities, education and the health service, all of which have relevance. Perhaps the twin objectives of resource productivity and customer satisfaction can be explained by this quote from Richard Harbottle, who said, as he assumed the post of Chairman of Northumberland Health Authority, that his aim was:

to make the National Health Service in the county work as efficiently and waste free as possible, while trying to maintain a proper service to patients.

References and suggested reading

Adam, E. E. and Ebert, R. J. (1978) *Production and Operations Management*. Englewood Cliffs, NJ: Prentice-Hall.

Barnt, S. E. and Carvey, D. W. (1982) *Essentials of Operations Management*. Englewood Cliffs, NJ: Prentice-Hall.

Bennett, D. J. and Lewis, C. D. (1980) *Operations Management*. Englewood Cliffs, NJ: Prentice-Hall.

Brown, R. G. (1971) *Management Decisions for Production Operations*. Hinsdale, IL: Dryden.

Chase, R. B. (1980) A classification and evaluation of resource in operations management. *Journal of Operations Management*, **1**.

Chase, R. B. and Aquilano, N. J. (1973) *Production and Operations: A Life Cycle Approach*. Homewood, IL: Irwin.

Constable, C. J. and New, C. C. (1976) *Operations Management – A Systems Approach through Text and Cases*. London: Wiley.

Dilworth, J. (1983) *Production and Operations Management Manufacturing and Non-Manufacturing*. New York: Random House.

Emery, F. E. (1969) *System Thinking*. Harmondsworth, Middx: Penguin Management Readings.

Fitzsimmons, J. H. and Sullivan, R. S. (1982) *Service Operations Management*. New York: McGraw-Hill.

Foster, G. (June 1987) How Thistle was grasped. *Management Today*, pp. 68–69.

French, D. and Saward, H. (1975) *Dictionary of Management*. London: Pan.

Harding, H. A. (1970) *Production Management*. London: Macdonald & Evans.

Harris, R. D. and Gonzalez, R. F. (1981) *The Operations Manager – Role, Problems, Techniques*. St Paul, MN: West Publishing.

Hill, T. (1983) *Production/Operations Management*. Englewood Cliffs, NJ: Prentice-Hall.

Hughes, C. (1985) *Production and Operations Management*. London: Pan Breakthrough.

Miller, J. G. and Graham, M. B. W. (1981) Production/operations management: agenda of the 1980s. *Decision Sciences*, **12**, pp. 547–571.

Normann, R. (1984) *Service Management – Strategy and Leadership in Services Business*. Chichester: Wiley.

Robinson, H. K. (April 1987) Productivity in the retail. *Management Services*, **31** (4), pp. 8–11.

Schonberg, P. J. (1985) *Operations Management – Productivity and Quality*, 2nd edn. Plano, TX: Business Publications.

Slack, N. (1983) Operations management and curriculum design. *Management Education and Development*, **14** (1), pp. 19–32.

Turnbull, L. and Shaw, N. (June 1987) Leisure services and new technology. *Management Services*, **31** (6), pp. 20–22.

Vollman, T. E. (1973) *Operations Management*. Reading, MA: Addison-Wesley.

Wild, R. (1977) *Concepts of Operations Management*. London: Wiley.

Wild, R. (1985) *Essentials of Production and Operations Management*, 2nd edn. Eastbourne: Holt, Rinehart and Winston.

2
THE ORGANISATION AND THE OPERATIONAL UNIT

INTRODUCTION

In glancing at the bookshelves on management in any library, apart from books about the whole of management, 'organisation' is seen to be the next most popular topic. In this chapter it is not intended to summarise all of organisational theory, but to concentrate on those aspects of organisation which can be influenced by the operations manager: how his own unit is organised and how he can best survive organisational change. The underlying theme is *analysis* of the organisational information which should help the operations manager to learn about the organisation and how best to make changes.

Organisations are created, or have evolved, in order to meet needs that cannot be met by individuals or small groups. Obvious examples are the newspaper and television industries, or any modern convenience dependent upon mass production – cars, frozen food, pharmaceuticals. Others which affect all people are government agencies, local authorities and hospitals. All these are big enough to form a critical mass of expertise and attempt to operate by taking advantage of 'economies of scale'.

Such organisations have a common feature of size so that it is virtually impossible for all members to know each other. In developing an organisation the following steps will need to have been taken:

1. What activities need to be conducted by the organisation and grouping and structuring them will have been determined.
2. Roles will have been devised and allocated to individual members arising from the above grouping.
3. Accountability will have been assigned to groups and individuals for effective performance.
4. A set of rules, procedures and methods of working will have been determined, including communication, decision-making, and conflict resolution. You may find that in one organisation a whole series of committees and working groups are formally convened to aid communication (as in local authorities and education) whereas in others the division is based on smaller, independent units which allow more autonomy of operation.

The rules, procedures and methods of operating in organisations are often referred to as 'the system' and can, in some instances, lead to bureaucracy and a feeling of oppression by some of the members of the organisation. However, there are also a number of very good examples where organisations have been able to develop effectively their human constituents so that 'excellence' is created and members feel a sense of pride in belonging to the organisation.

In the analytical approach to organisation that can be taken by the operations manager the following are of use:

1. A review of the current structure of the whole organisation from the point of view of whether it achieves its purpose effectively.
2. A review of the organisational structure of one's own section/division/unit.
3. Concern for the human factors in the organisation – how do staff view the organisation and what lessons can we learn from those views?
4. An ability to influence the organisation with regard to developing a corporate culture which in turn can lead to 'excellence'.

These then form the structure of this chapter.

ORGANISATIONAL PURPOSE

Management is a purposeful activity; it is operated through an organisation, which in turn needs to be linked to objectives. The organisation can be regarded as the 'framework for managing' and if it gives the impression of being distorted or unbalanced it is unlikely to aid the effectiveness of this process.

Organisational analysis of any kind is complex and can rarely be done effectively by one person. In some cases the main problem is the attitudes of people (see below), but in others it is possible that the organisation is using a type of structure which is no longer appropriate since so many changes have taken place since it was first designed.

CASE STUDY

In some instances the customer or client satisfaction objectives of operations management can be severely impaired if the organisation is wrong.

DAVID CANTER

Lessons from King's Cross

The inquiry into the King's Cross disaster is now dragging into its second phase. The debate over the fire's cause and spread has given way to a catalogue of recriminations against London Underground's management and staffing. It is therefore easy to forget that the King's Cross deaths, like those at Bradford City football ground and other disasters, were a reflection of a deteriorating relationship between users of a service and those who provide it.

Our research into human actions in fires has revealed two recurrent failures that turn dangerous situations into disasters. The first is the failure to heed early warnings of danger. The second is the public's misplaced reliance on instructions from improperly trained staff and officials.

These fractures in customer–staff relationships worsen an emergency in a situation already ruptured by a lack of concern for its users. If fires are so commonplace, as it is now emerging they were in the Tube, then a whiff of smoke is treated by everyone as of little note and so disregarded until it cannot be ignored.

And if staff and public regard each other with distrust, then, in an emergency, all rely on whatever police officers happen to be available to take protective action, although they may not have the detailed knowledge needed.

Our studies of behaviour in emergencies for car-carrying trains that will travel in the Channel tunnel have shown similar questions must be asked of that underground system. Will Eurotunnel's designers think more of their passengers than their profits?

Will they create an environment for the traveller in which any threat will be noticed well in advance of reaching dangerous proportions? Will they create a relationship between staff and public that ensures mutual respect, so they can help each other during danger? These should be the central questions to which the King's Cross inquiry ensures an effective answer.

David Canter is Professor of Psychology at Surrey University. He is presenting a paper on behaviour in emergencies at the British Psychological Society in Leeds today.

(*Source: The Observer*)

In order that you can more effectively judge your own organisation a brief review of the various approaches to organisation follows, from which you can ascertain which features are apparent in your own organisation.

The classical or scientific approach

The approach concentrates on the following problems:

1. Determining organisational objectives and deducing from these a detailed description of the work to be done.
2. Grouping activities into sections, then sections into departments and departments into administrative units.
3. Delegation.
4. Specifying responsibility or accountability for performance.
5. Establishing formal relationships among employees so that each knows his position.
6. Organising work at the 'sharp end' whether it be office, factory or hospital ward.

The human relations school

This is often subtitled the behavioural school since the emphasis is on people's behaviour. It arose partly as a backlash to the classical school since it was felt that this approach ignores the emotional aspects of human nature. There is a recognised difference between the objectives of people and the organisations they work for.

The human relations approach is an attempt to define a social environment that stimulates people to strive for overall objectives. Hence it tries to create an organisation which:

1. Achieves objectives while satisfying its members.
2. Encourages high productivity and low absenteeism.
3. Stimulates co-operation and avoids industrial strife. (It is not suggested that all minor conflicts and disagreements are to be avoided – some disagreements ('constructive' conflicts) are inevitable and healthy. The aim is to avoid creating situations where people constantly work against each other ('destructive' conflicts).)

In this approach the study of organisation becomes wholly the study of behaviour, of how people behave and why they do so. Its exponents hope to predict behaviour within different organisations and to provide guidance on how best to achieve the organisational arrangements that evoke co-operation. More specifically, the approach has been concerned with the effect of organisation on:

1. Individual and group productivity
2. Individual development
3. Job satisfaction
4. Supervisory and management behaviour

The systems approach

The systems approach emphasises that for any investigation there is an appropriate system to be studied, and the purpose of the investigation decides both the extent and limits of the system and the appropriate subsystems. The organisation of the enterprise is a means to achieving its objectives. Thus the organisation system must embrace both the enterprise itself and that part of the external environment, for example the market, that impinges on objectives, so that these can be set as a basis for organisation. The subsystems chosen centre on the main decisions to be made to accomplish objectives. The organisation should be designed to facilitate decision-making, but since decisions depend on information and information on communication, the organisation is built up from an analysis of information needs and communication networks. Decision-making is chosen rather than activities or departments because it is through the process of decision-making that objectives and policies are laid down and actions taken that result in company success or failure.

The systems approach to organisation consists of the following steps:

1. Specifying objectives
2. Listing the subsystems, or main decision areas
3. Analysing the decision areas and establishing information needs
4. Designing the communication channels for the information flow
5. Grouping decision areas to minimise the communication burden

Contingency approaches

A contingency approach builds on the diagnostic work of the systems approach in order to determine the most appropriate organisational design and management style for a 'given set of circumstances'. It takes into account the following variables:

1. The external environment
2. Technological factors
3. Human skills and motivation

and develops a structure which is the best combination.

The result is a mix, using approaches as appropriate from the other schools. This may require organisations in the public sector, for example, to rethink some of their structures as the authority becomes more accountable following a move towards privatisation. Highly technical divisions (say computing or management services) may need to have a very much more organised structure than, say, a large services department, and so the approach to organisations should attempt to identify these factors rather than to impose a similar modelling for all parts of the organisation.

In viewing some of the more successful enterprises it is obvious that part of their success is the creation or development of a structure in which people feel that they 'belong' and in some cases have even had some role in developing.

There are a large number of reasons for organisations to change at present – slimming down, technology, changing objectives, mergers, internal developments at different rates, markets and client demands, etc. It is rare that organisations remain constant for very long, and even though wholesale changes are not common, departmental changes can be fairly frequent, and it is this area we need next to address.

An example of a different type of organisational structure that has recently emerged is that of the *matrix organisation*, in which the hierarchical 'family tree' of most organisations is replaced with a feature in which some managers report to two bosses rather than one, creating a dual chain of command. Figure 2.1 illustrates such a matrix organisation for a retail store.

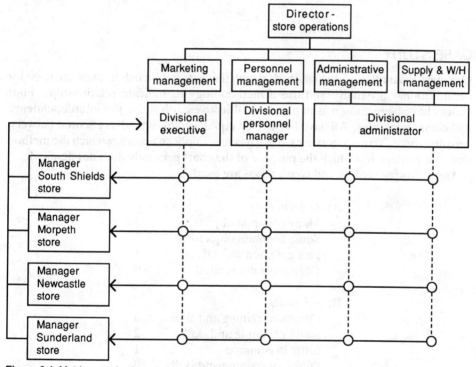

Figure 2.1 Matrix organisation: store management

The illustration shows a local 'division' of several stores, with a central divisional executive team providing specialised help in marketing, personnel and administration (finance and supplies) which is appropriate for that type of firm.

ORGANISATIONAL RELATIONSHIPS

Some operations managers may have a number of divisions or units reporting to them each headed by a manager or supervisor. These sub-organisations may be inherited and not ideal, and the opportunity to change them may occur when a manager leaves or gets promoted.

It is important to review the structure in a rational manner, and in order to help in this a technique called *organisational relationship charts* can be employed. These charts have been developed from *layout relationship charts* used to identify the best arrangement of sectors in the physical layout of an office, stores or workshop (see Chapter 6). These in turn were probably derived from the mileage charts which often appear at the back of map books showing the distance between two locations.

This approach was developed by Alan Brown, a management services officer with TAP, the Portuguese national airline, which was in need of restructuring (Brown, 1976). The following case study consists of extracts (reproduced with permission) from the approach used. A management services group is used to illustrate the case.

CASE STUDY

Organisational relationship charts deal with the factors which determine the need for organisational proximity and use a methodology to indicate relationships. Four factors have been chosen as important – objectives, job skills, job interdependence and communications. All have been given equal weight, and all are scored between zero and three. To do otherwise would, it is felt, imply an accuracy which the method does not possess and which the purpose of the chart generally does not demand.

The following scoring and conventions are used:

A: *Objectives*

Many common objectives	3
Some common objectives	2
Few common objectives	1
Objectives not related	0

B: *Job skills*

Common training and skills	3
Similar training and skills	2
Little in common	1
Different training and skills	0

C: *Job interdependency*

Jobs interdependent	3
Jobs related	2
Some common points	1
No common points	0

D: *Communications*

Very frequent	3
Regular	2

Few communications	1
None	0

A convenient method of entering the scores on the grid is:

As with travel charts, a complete matrix is used and each pair of functions therefore has two entries, as shown in the section given in Figure 2.2. Scoring should preferably be done by the supervisors or managers of the functions being studied, each scoring his relationships with every other.

Of By	Function A	Function B	F
Function A		2 2 9 3 2	2 3
Function B	2 2 8 2 2		2 3
Function	2 2	2 2	

Figure 2.2 Extract from organisational relationship chart matrix

Both entries for any pair of functions should be similar, but there are legitimate reasons for differences other than those arising from different individual interpretations. Where the functions are disparate in size or in the scope of their objectives and work, the smaller unit often views its relationships with the larger as being much more important than the larger sees them.

The example in Figure 2.3 shows the entries made for the functions in a management services department. It must be emphasised that these relate to one department only and are not necessarily applicable to others. Detailed specifications of the responsibilities and scope of work of each function would be required prior to making any comparisons.

For greater clarity, the figures have been transferred to a chart (Figure 2.4) showing only one total relationship score between each pair of functions. The chart shows the scores of closeness of relationships between all functions in the organisation. The scores range from 20, for Computer Scheduling with Computer Operations indicating a necessity for organisational proximity, to a score of 1, for Data Preparation with Work Study which indicates that the two units have little in common and could be in entirely different organisations.

Each cell in this relationship chart contains two pairs of numbers in the corners (upper-left, upper-right, lower-left, lower-right) surrounding a central large value.

	Project management	Systems analysis	Programming	Computer scheduling	Computer operations	Data preparation	Statistics	Operational research	Organisation and methods	Work study	Sum by
Project management		2 9 2 / 2 3	1 8 / 2 3	2 5 / 2 1	1 4 / 1 1	1 2 / 1 0	1 3 / 0 2	2 8 / 2 2	2 8 / 2 2	2 8 / 2 2	55
Systems analysis	2 10 2 / 3 3		2 10 / 3 3	1 6 / 2 2	1 6 / 2 1	1 3 / 1 1	2 4 / 1 2	3 9 / 2 2	2 9 / 2 2	2 8 / 2 2	65
Programming	1 7 2 / 2 2	2 9 2 / 2 3		2 8 / 2 2	1 7 / 2 3	1 6 / 2 1	1 4 / 1 1	1 6 / 2 2	2 5 / 1 1	1 4 / 1 1	56
Computer scheduling	2 6 1 / 1 1	1 5 2 / 2 2	1 6 / 2 2		2 10 / 3 3	2 10 / 3 3	1 5 / 1 1	2 3 / 0 0	1 3 / 1 0	1 2 / 0 0	50
Computer operations	1 4 1 / 1 1	1 5 2 / 2 2	2 8 / 2 2	3 10 / 2 3		2 8 / 2 3	1 4 / 1 1	1 4 / 1 1	1 4 / 1 1	0 2 / 1 0	49
Data preparation	1 3 1 / 1 1	0 3 1 / 1 1	2 5 / 1 1	1 8 / 3 3	2 9 / 3 3		1 3 / 1 0	0 1 / 0 1	0 2 / 1 0	0 0 / 0 0	34
Statistics	1 4 1 / 1 1	1 4 1 / 1 1	0 3 / 1 0	0 2 / 1 0	1 5 / 1 2	1 3 / 0 1		2 7 / 2 2	1 4 / 1 1	1 4 / 1 1	36
Operational research	3 9 2 / 2 2	2 5 1 / 1 2	0 5 / 2 2	0 2 / 0 1	0 4 / 2 2	0 2 / 1 0	1 6 1 / 2 2		2 7 / 2 2	1 7 / 2 2	47
Organisation and methods	2 8 2 / 2 3	2 9 2 / 2 2	2 6 / 1 1	1 4 / 1 1	1 4 / 1 1	1 2 / 0 1	1 5 1 / 2 2	1 6 1 / 2 2		3 10 / 2 2	54
Work study	2 9 2 / 2 2	3 8 2 / 2 2	1 3 / 0 0	1 2 / 0 1	1 3 / 0 0	1 1 / 0 1	0 4 1 / 1 2	1 8 2 / 2 2	2 7 / 1 2		45
Sum of	60	57	54	47	52	37	38	52	49	45	491

Figure 2.3 Detailed organisational relationship chart

The data is now in a form similar to a conventional relationship chart and can be used to design an organisation in a manner analogous to that used to design a layout.

Relationship comparisons

It is essential that the differences between the scores *of* the manager of one function and *by* the manager of the other function, if different, are examined closely. Some discussion should then be undertaken to resolve these differences in perception, in order that these do not become problems in the resulting organisational structure.

Simplified relationship charts

In order to make the collected information easier to use in developing alternative organisation structures, it is convenient to simplify the scoring and express it in terms of a zero to three coding, similar to that used for physical layout relationship charts (Table 2.1).

A simplified relationship chart can be developed easily from any of the previous

	Systems analysis	Programming	Computer scheduling	Computer operations	Data preparation	Statistics	Operational research	Organisation and methods	Work study
Project management	19	15	11	8	5	7	17	16	17
Systems analysis		19	11	11	6	8	14	18	17
Programming			14	15	11	7	11	11	7
Computer scheduling				20	19	7	5	7	4
Computer operations					17	9	8	8	7
Data preparation						6	3	4	1
Statistics							13	9	8
Operational research								13	15
Organisation and methods									17

Figure 2.4 Summarised organisational relationship chart

Table 2.1 Simplified scoring.

Total Score	*Code*	*Significance*
24–18	3	Must be organisationally adjacent. Same immediate superior.
17–12	2	Should be in the same organisational unit. One intermediate superior.
11–6	1	Should be in the same general grouping. 2–3 intermediate superiors.
6–0	0	Need not be in the same general grouping. 3+ intermediate superiors.

forms. Using corrected figures, the simplified chart for our example is as detailed in Figure 2.5 and led to the possible solution given in Figure 2.6.

Modifying possible organisation

In order to adapt the organisation to the needs, constraints and capabilities existing within, or available to, the enterprise, it is necessary to consider other factors.

	Systems analysis	Programming	Computer scheduling	Computer operations	Data preparation	Statistics	Operational research	Organisation and methods	Work study	Number of personnel
Project management	3	2	1	1	0	1	2	2	2	5
Systems analysis		3	1	1	1	1	2	3	2	8
Programming			2	2	1	1	1	1	1	20
Computer scheduling				2	3	1	0	1	0	6
Computer operations					2	1	1	1	1	12
Data preparation						1	0	0	0	28
Statistics							2	1	1	10
Operational research								2	2	5
Organisation and methods									3	8
Work study										9

Figure 2.5 Simplified organisational relationship chart

1. The degree of access and communications which each function requires to have with the senior manager of the group function being considered, for example on matters concerning policy, major expenditures, change implementation, etc.
2. The degree of access and communications required with functions outside the group. This will normally be high for functions providing centralised staff services.
3. The degree of technical difference between the functions. This will influence the 'span' which can reasonably be controlled by individual managers.
4. The number of personnel and their supervisory and seniority structure in each function. Again this will influence the span of control.
5. Company policy concerning management and supervisory levels, responsibilities and delegation, cost control and results accountability, promotion and recruitment.
6. Predicted volume and technological growth, or change, in line areas and the likely effect on requirements for staff support.
7. The ability and availability of individual managers and potential managers.

On reviewing the management personnel available within the example organisation, it was concluded that there was no one who could satisfactorily manage all the

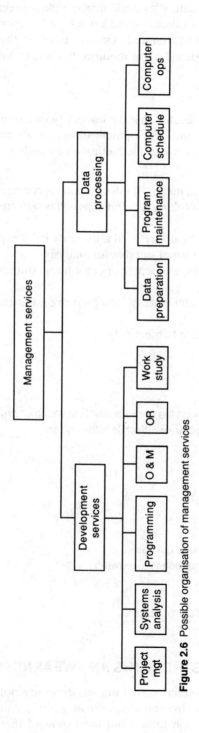

Figure 2.6 Possible organisation of management services

development services functions. There was a competent manager, with broad experience in systems development, who could manage the project management, systems analysis and programming functions and a work study supervisor, with good O&M experience who could be promoted. On the basis of these considerations, the organisation shown in Figure 2.6 was modified to that shown in Figure 2.7.

Conclusion

Experience to date has indicated that the use of organisational relationship charting is valuable in the review and development of organisational structures. The main advantages arising from the use of the methodology outlined above can be summarised as:

1. It provides a formalised means of information recording.
2. The personnel whose working relationships will be affected by the change participate in the analysis.
3. The methodology can be understood after fairly brief explanation.
4. Data is displayed in a format suitable for analysis.
5. It improves the objective element in organisational studies and reduces emotional arguments.
6. It incorporates some elements of accepted organisational theory and complements others.
7. Alternatives can be tested objectively.

ACTIVITY

Consider the effects of applying the above analysis to your own organisation. The factors that make for organisational logic are worthwhile reflecting on:

1. Objectives
2. Job skills
3. Job interdependency
4. Communications

plus:

1. Access to management and outside
2. Technical differences and technical growth
3. Numbers of staff
4. Levels
5. Ability and availability of current staff

ORGANISATIONAL STRENGTHS AND WEAKNESSES

It was hinted in the introduction that organisations are not always rated highly by those who work for them. In some cases a manager of a unit or department within a large organisation may wish to find out the extent of that feeling, and also what aspects of the organisation are considered good by its employees. In order to 'take

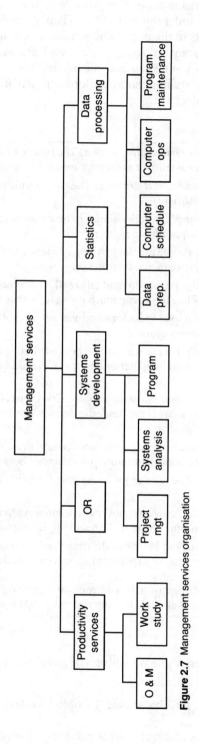

Figure 2.7 Management services organisation

the temperature of the organisation' it is possible to use a questionnaire designed originally by Woodcock and Francis (1979). Their questionnaire comprises 120 statements which members of the organisation indicate are applicable or not. These statements cover 12 different 'blockage' areas and are listed in Table 2.2. The remainder of the Woodcock and Francis text explains these blockages in more detail and suggests a number of training and development activities that can be used to assist in overcoming the blockage.

Table 2.2 Organisational blockages.

Blockage 1	*Inadequate recruitment and selection.* The people being hired lack the knowledge, personality or skills appropriate to the organisation's needs.
Blockage 2	*Confused organisational structure.* The way in which people are organised is wasteful or inefficient.
Blockage 3	*Inadequate control.* Poor decisions are made because of faulty information in the hands of inappropriate people.
Blockage 4	*Poor training.* People are not learning efficiently to do things that would materially improve their performance.
Blockage 5	*Low motivation.* People do not feel greatly concerned about the organisation and are not willing to expend much effort to further common goals.
Blockage 6	*Low creativity.* Good ideas for improvement are not being properly put to use, so stagnation occurs.
Blockage 7	*Poor teamwork.* People who should be contributing to common tasks either do not wish to work together or find that there are too many obstacles to do so.
Blockage 8	*Inappropriate management philosophy.* Conscious and unconscious management principles that underlie decisions and create the atmosphere are unrealistic or inhumane.
Blockage 9	*Lack of succession planning and management development.* Sufficient preparation for important future job vacancies is not being undertaken.
Blockage 10	*Unclear aims.* The reasons for doing things are either muddy or badly explained.
Blockage 11	*Unfair rewards.* People are not rewarded in ways that satisfy them, or the reward system works against the health of the organisation.
Blockage 12	*Personal stagnation.* People in the organisation do not display the attitudes and stances conducive to personal effectiveness and growth.

Your organisation may have more trouble with some of these blockages than others. The aim is to determine which blockages are hurting you most and to proceed to clear them.

Source: Woodcock and Francis (1979).

This analysis can be used where possible on development programmes for organisations since it:

1. Helps to get rid of the possible stance 'I would be effective if it were not for the organisation.'
2. Helps to identify areas of development needed and hopefully helps to elicit the support of senior management in pursuing them.

Table 2.3 Sample statements from organisational blockages questionnaire.

- As many dullards as efficient people are recruited.
- Skills are available but may be of the wrong kind.
- Good suggestions are not taken seriously.
- Unconventional ideas never get a hearing.

Source: Woodcock and Francis (1979).

Examples of some of the statements in the questionnaire are shown in Table 2.3.

One of the major criticisms of the questionnaire is that all the statements are negative and therefore could lead to resistance by management in its use, since the results are bound to reflect badly. To overcome this my colleague John Bothams and I have modified the questionnaire so that half of the questions relating to each blockage are positive, for example:

- Mostly efficient people are recruited.
- Good suggestions are taken seriously.

This has led us to be able to show the strengths as well as the weaknesses, in the hope that the organisation will be motivated to develop strength in all areas. This modification has been tested and validated with a number of service organisations and, recognising that the purpose is to identify 'blockages', still clearly does this, whilst ensuring that the whole exercise is acceptable to the organisation.

Also, with the use of a word processor, it has been possible to 'customise' the questionnaire to fit a specific organisation. Examples of this, using the different levels of a local government organisation, are:

For an LEA:

The LEA often needs to recruit senior staff from outside.

For a social services department:

The senior managers do not know what is expected of them.

For a residential home:

The officer in charge and assistant officers in charge take training seriously.

For a polytechnic

The polytechnic and each department act independently of each other.

For a specific library where the head of department is known by his first name:

Jake and the librarians believe that tighter supervision produces improved results.

So these two variations make the instrument more easily understood and provide for a balanced view. For example, Jake in the last instance will not feel too threatened – and may be quite pleased at some of the features that come out well.

CASE STUDY

In conducting a training programme for officers in charge and assistant officers in charge for a county council residential home, the organisational blockages questionnaire was administered to approximately 60 staff (20 officers in charge and 40 assistant officers in charge). An extract from the report will illustrate the data that emerges.

Residential Homes
REPORT ON STAFF PERCEPTIONS ABOUT THE ORGANISATION

Comments on the results

The pattern of response for all three groups is very consistent with no major variations in negative and positive areas. The OIC group, because of their greater exposure to the organisation, do differ from the AOIC group in the areas of control, teamwork and creativity in which they are more negatively skewed, but with regard to rewards their response is more positive – perhaps because they are less likely to pick up information on pay inequalities than their deputies, or they view payment and financial rewards quite differently from their deputies.

Positive areas

Those areas which can give some cause for satisfaction within SS, in which policies seem to be working effectively:

1. Management philosophy
2. Management development and succession
3. Personal growth

Recruitment and selection and training also show considerable strengths but there are also some problems within these – a typical 'curate's egg' situation.

Negative or problem areas

1. Organisation structure
2. Motivation
3. Creativity

The other areas are neither positive or negative and could, unless carefully monitored, develop into problem areas.

Observations on negative results

Organisation structure

It is understood that this has already been recognised by the department and that an exercise is underway to review this. Details of the specific statements that caused concern would be of value to this working party in order to inform their eventual recommendations.

Motivation

A problem appears to be that a limited amount of praise is given when things are done well. The management of the department should consider how they can say sincerely 'well done and thanks' more often.

Creativity

People in administration appear not to understand the implications of their decisions – which give the impression of being rigid and inflexible in an environment where considerable flexibility is desirable.

Aims

Although this does not have a negative value, discussions in all groups have centred on 'aims' and the difficulty in understanding what they are. Activities within the groups have made material available which needs additional inputs from management to give greater clarity and thus help the organisation to gain greater commitment and understanding.

Conclusions

Despite the many satisfactory areas of the organisation, the use of this instrument has clearly identified a number of areas which require some attention. The use of similar questionnaires in other settings has validated its use and the numbers who have responded, allied to the homogeneous pattern of responses will ensure that the results are significant. The fact that the people participating are not only in a 'caring profession' but do care very much for their homes, clients, staff and the organisation would indicate a need to consider seriously the comments made in this short report.

ACTIVITY

If you are in charge of a unit – or have influence with the unit manager – obtain a copy of Woodcock and Francis and use the organisational blockage questionnaire to see what emerges.

INFLUENCING YOUR ORGANISATION TO BECOME MORE EFFECTIVE

Tse (1985) indicated some of the reasons for the commercial success of Marks & Spencer and its reputation for providing quality service, being an excellent employer, etc. The feature that emerged most strongly is that somehow Marks & Spencer's management have created a *corporate culture*. This is defined more specifically in Hickman and Silva (1986) as:

> The act of developing ... especially by education, expert care and training ... enlightenment and excellence of taste. ... The total pattern of human behaviour ... embodied in thought, speech, action and artifacts and dependent upon man's capacity for *learning* and transmitting knowledge to succeeding generations.

It is getting the organisation to become a *learning community* which is at the root of excellence. Even though one or two with entrepreneurial flair are responsible for the initial ideas, there is a need to develop effective *teamwork*, and through this an effective organisation. It is through selecting, motivating, rewarding, rating and unifying good employees that such a culture is developed and continues long after the founders of the firm have retired.

As you can deduce this is not going to be developed overnight and some people, looking round their organisation, may suggest that it is an impossible goal. That is not so, since any organisation can develop and grow, but the path has to be clearly identified, and a number of people within the firm need to be not only involved, but committed.

The route to use for change is via a whole series of development activities which will include some of the ideas that have been included wholly or in part in this chapter. Table 2.4 presents an extract from a presentation made to the top management of a transport company and gives a flavour of the type of organisational development actively envisaged. This transport company, which had a stated objective of becoming the 'Marks & Spencer of the bus industry', indicated that the breadth of vision and full commitment by top management needs to be of a very high order.

Table 2.4 Specific proposals for a transport company.

1. Tackle the fleet manager development:
   (a) Initial one-day courses to diagnose skills requirements.
   (b) A linked job-centred and person-centred programme, probably of 10 days in length.

2. Match the first line commercial development with similar programmes for engineers and administration.

3. Develop cross functional communication and empathy with a project-based programme for senior managers which tackles a number of company-wide issues that are needed and identified with by participants.

4. Conduct an organisation-wide survey into management attitudes, which will highlight company strengths and weaknesses. Also indicate more clearly that which needs to be tackled.

5. Top team planning: address issues such as style, leadership, teamwork and how the team can address culture.

You will note the use of the organisational questionnaire in point 4. With many organisations some initial work on top team planning needs to be done initially in order to convince that group that gradual development and change is worthwhile.

This route is the one that most people are likely to experience when it comes to organisational change. Some programme of development should be undertaken when change is imminent so that the resulting development is the optimum.

ACTIVITY

Reflect on your perception of change in organisation and on the influence you can bring to bear on senior management. Read all or any of the following to give you some inspiration:

1. Heirs and Pehrson (1982)

2. Hickman and Silva (1986)
3. Lessem (1985)
4. Tse (1985)

References and suggested reading

Brown, A. (July 1986) Organisational relationship charts. *Management Services*, **20** (7), pp. 4–8.

Brown, A. (August 1986) Organisational relationship charts. *Management Services*, **20** (8), pp. 8–13.

Heirs, B. and Pehrson, G. (1982) *The Mind of the Organisation*. London: Harper & Row.

Hickman, C. R. and Silva, M. A. (1986) *Creating Excellence – Managing Corporate Culture, Strategy and Change in the New Age*. London: Unwin.

Lessem, R. (1985) *The Roots of Excellence*. London: Fontana.

O'Shaughnessy, J. (1966) *Business Organisation*. London: Allen & Unwin.

Ross, J. E. and Hurdick, R. G. (September–October 1973) People, productivity and organisational structure. *Personnel*, **50**, pp. 8–18.

Tse, K. K. (1985) *Marks & Spencer – Anatomy of Britain's Most Efficiently Managed Company*. Oxford: Pergamon.

Woodcock, M. and Francis, D. (1979) *Unblocking Your Organisation*. La Jolla, CA: University Associates.

3

THE OPERATIONS MANAGER AND CORPORATE STRATEGY

INTRODUCTION

Operations managers are those in an organisation whose responsibility it is to convert plans into action. Some may therefore find themselves remote from the development of corporate plans. It must be recognised that corporate plans can only be developed by bringing together expertise from the whole organisation. This means that the operations manager has a vital role to play in informing the corporate planner of the effect changes can have on the capability of the unit to deliver effectively. This is particularly true when corporate decisions can result in expansion or contraction of operational activities.

The corporate planners or strategy team should be aware of the aspirations of operations managers and their staff in terms of their views on potential developments or changes in balance in the services provided currently. Corporate planning is a systematic approach to clarifying corporate objectives, making strategic decisions and checking progress towards those objectives. Corporate objectives are the objectives for the organisation as a whole, not for parts of it. Strategic decisions are decisions which affect, or are intended to affect, the organisation as a whole over long periods of time.

The *corporate plan* is a set of instructions to the managers of an organisation describing what role each constituent part is to play or is expected to play in the achievement of the organisation's corporate objectives.

A restaurant may wish to obtain a greater share of the market, or merely exploit the market that is as yet untapped, which will in turn increase profitability. This is a *strategy*. The tactics to achieve this will include marketing (advertising, promotion, etc.), personnel (employing and training people), operations (capacity, investment in new machines methods, etc.) and finance (capital investment, evaluation of effects in financial terms).

In considering strategy in this chapter, a very simple but effective model that can be used as a framework is shown at Figure 3.1. You will note that the four parts are shown as a *continuous* cycle, since the organisation may not always be able to achieve its 'wishes' and the strategy may need to be revised as a result. This process is not static either – there is no need to wait for all the plans to be implemented. The effective plans will be broken down into identifiable stages each of which can be evaluated on a short-term as well as a long-term basis.

A further aspect which affects any planning by an organisation is the environment. Some might argue that since all organisations are beset by many potential threats and opportunities from the environment planning is of little value. However, the reverse is the case. Considering the question 'Where are we now' inevitably leads to an

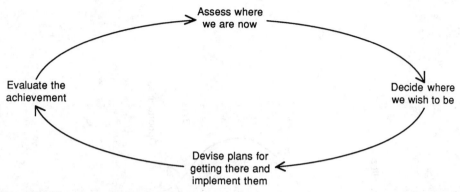

Figure 3.1 The corporate strategy process

evaluation of strengths and weaknesses, and this enables a more proactive approach to the environment to be pursued.

Figure 3.2 shows how the organisation is affected by the environment. The organisation is also determined by the four elements shown inside the bubble – the organisation's aims and objectives, the available people, talent and skills, the structures and the available technology and tasks.

Organisations, then, should assess their strengths and weaknesses, and decide quite clearly which path they are to follow – this usually entails being very good at providing a specific service. Organisational development of all kinds is then related to this. However, unless the organisation is aware of environmental changes it could become very outdated or overtaken by other organisations. In the public sector, the future of many departments is not necessarily dependent upon their performance (however assessed) but often upon political influences which can increase or diminish their importance in a very short period of time.

The first part of the corporate planning exercise, therefore, is simply to conduct a SWOT analysis – *Strengths, Weaknesses, Opportunities, Threats*. Putting this together with Figure 3.1, Figure 3.3 emerges. This is often referred to as *gap analysis*.

PLANS, POLICIES, PROCEDURES AND PROJECTS

Before we look at how the operations manager is likely to be affected by the four parts of the strategic planning cycle given in Figure 3.1, it is of value to define some terms, since there is a possibility of confusion. All of the terms we have used in the heading above (plus some other important ones) are shown in Figure 3.4. This shows how corporate plans are translated into operational plans of two kinds – *single use* and *multiple use*.

Let us now define these terms in more detail.

Corporate and strategic planning

These are both concerned with the long-term aspirations of an organisation. It is important to note that whilst British management writers talk of corporate

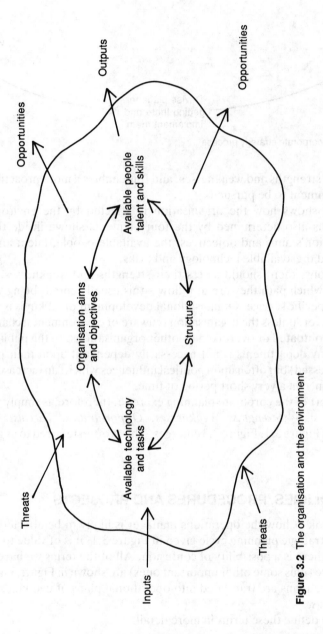

Figure 3.2 The organisation and the environment

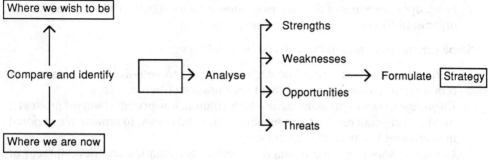

Figure 3.3 Gap analysis

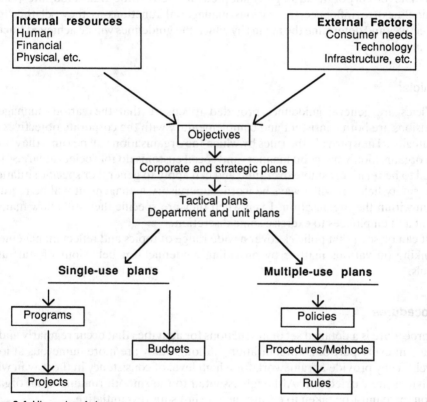

Figure 3.4 Hierarchy of plans

objectives, corporate strategy and corporate planning, their American counterparts consider strategic objectives and strategic planning only.

1. *Corporate objectives* – the long-term aims of the organisation.
2. *Corporate strategy* – the conceptual means by which the organisation intends to achieve its corporate objectives.
3. *Corporate planning* – the overall planning procedure by which the various managerial functions such as personnel, marketing, finance, production, etc. are co-ordinated towards the corporate objectives and corporate strategy. The plan is

based upon forecasts of the various economic factors (both inside and outside the organisation) likely to affect these long-term aims.

Some general examples of these would be as follows:

1. *Corporate objectives* – to go public in ten years; to be a market leader in fruit retailing; to reduce the management organisation structure, etc.
2. *Corporate strategy* – to manufacture high volume, low priced, standard products; to take over small retail outlets in major cities and towns; to remove the regional management tier from the organisation.
3. *Corporate planning* – the detailed process of consultation and development of alternative models; relating these to the chosen timescale.

Whatever corporate strategy is adopted, it needs to be translated into policies (guidelines) to influence the various managerial functions as they set their own objectives and determine the means by which the guidelines will be achieved (tactical planning).

Policies

Policies are general guidelines provided to ensure that the various managerial decisions are both consistent and complementary with the corporate objectives and strategies. They provide the rules by which the organisation will be run – they do for the organisation what good manners and social customs do for society at large. They need to be relatively stable over time and can apply to general or specific situations, e.g. safety helmets will always be worn, supervisory management will be recruited from within the organisation. Even when they are specific they still allow management and employees to exercise some discretion.

It can be seen that policies cover a wide range of topics and reflect management's thinking on various matters by providing guidelines for behaviour of staff at all levels.

Procedures

A procedure is a detailed set of instructions for activities that occur regularly and are found in every part of an organisation, although they are more numerous at lower levels. They provide a framework for a high level of consistency in the way in which activities are carried out. Although essential to the smooth running of an organisation, care must be taken to ensure they do not suppress initiative.

Procedures can cut across departmental boundaries. For example, the procedure for handling purchases can involve several departments.

Some typical procedures are:

1. *Pay procedures* – instructions on how wages will be calculated and paid to employees.
2. *Safety procedures* – can be general, e.g. procedures to be followed in the event of an accident, or can be specific, e.g. the procedure to be followed when filling lead oxide.

Procedures are complementary to policies. For example, a company may have a policy of requiring payment within one month and procedures will be established to check that this is achieved.

Rules

Rules are usually the simplest type of plan. They are statements that a specific action must or must not be taken in a given situation.

Rules can be regarded as an aid to decision-making – the only choice is whether or not to apply it for a particular set of circumstances. For example, a school may have a rule that students will not leave the school until 4.00 p.m., but the headmaster may suspend the rule and send the children home early if it is snowing heavily. Alternatively, a company may have a rule that three estimates must be obtained for all contracts above £5,000, but obviously the rule cannot apply if only one contractor can do the work.

Although many rules stand alone, others may form part of a procedure. For example, a wage payment procedure may incorporate a rule that employees must sign a receipt.

Rules can often be confused with policies and procedures. The major differences are:

1. Policies guide decisions.
2. Procedures guide actions.

Programmes/projects

These are for one-off activities such as the installation of a computer or the revision of the layout of a working area. Whilst they have a distinct beginning and a recognisable end point, it is possible to use planning techniques which link together all the different staff involved, usually from different departments and possibly including outside expert help.

A sample programme could lay down what is to be done against a timescale, whilst a project would be more complex and would need to use a *project network* to illustrate the dependencies of jobs.

Budgets

These are plans expressed in financial terms. Once the whole planning process is completed then an estimate of both costs and profits arising from the activity will be required. The expenditure pattern will be monitored regularly as a means of control.

WHERE ARE WE NOW?

The first step is to identify where the organisation is. If you are trying to find out where you are geographically you can use a map or describe your position relative to other places. So it is with organisations – they can only assess the 'now' position relative to something else. As with map reading, we need at least two other co-ordinates to identify our position, since we cannot rely solely on just comparing ourselves, say, to other organisations. There is a need also to consider:

1. Objectives
2. External comparisons
3. Internal comparisons

Objectives

We looked briefly at these in Chapter 1. We saw that most organisations will have multiple objectives and that time and effort needs to be spent in determining what they are. Writers on objectives vary in their approach to what are critical objectives for an organisation. Argenti (1968) makes out the case for *profit* being paramount since through that comes *survival*. For some service organisations even to break even is not totally critical to survival, since the deficiency can be written off or otherwise accepted. But this cannot be taken for granted and so it is essential that the objectives are quite clear – for it is against these that the 'position now' can be judged.

It is essential that an operations manager has a very clear indication as to what the organisation's objectives are and what role he or she has to play in contributing towards them. Often this understanding of role is essential to ensure that the department in question gets its share of resources, for without these the objectives cannot be achieved.

Thus some form of 'management by objectives' might be considered to be an effective way for the operations manager to ensure that the organisation is prepared to spell out objectives and agree with their contribution towards them. Again, it is easier for manufacturing industry to create objectives, e.g. cost per unit, failure or reject rate, capacity and units per unit of time, but for the service sector this needs careful consideration so that we do not provide biased data.

'Management by objectives' is a variation of performance appraisal. The essentials of MBO are given below.

Management by objectives – a definition

> The system of MBO can be described as a process whereby the superior and subordinate managers of an organisation jointly identify its goals, define each individual's major areas of responsibility in terms of the results expected and use these measures as guides for operating the unit, and for assessing the contribution of each of its members.
>
> *(Odiorne, 1970)*

The fundamental principles of MBO are:
1. A common objective ensures a unification of management action.
2. Focusing on results against a time scale increases the likelihood of achievement.
3. The greater the participation in the setting of work targets the greater the motivation for completion.
4. Progress can only be measured against a recognisable goal.
5. So if we don't know where we are going, it is unlikely that we will get there.

What we have said so far is but an indication of the process. The focal point is the discussion between managers and subordinates right down the organisational hierarchy. This facilitates the discussion of objectives, of the individual's specific contribution towards their achievement, and most importantly of the development needs associated with them.

We must also accept that objectives are not imposed from above, but are derived from a discussion with all managers. So the process of a yearly or twice-yearly performance appraisal discussion is not just to explain and evaluate, but also to ensure that the manager in question can contribute towards the objectives.

Some jobs can be much more easily measured than others. A production manager or foreman in manufacturing can be judged, for example, on throughput per time period, number of rejects per day, stoppages per week, etc. An office worker, on the other hand, can be given 'quantity in time' goals based on clerical work measurement. It may not be so easy to provide such goals for a social worker, but as long as they are *agreed jointly* rather than imposed the concept of key result areas or targets is certainly worthwhile for achieving a better understanding of the job.

Many service objectives are concerned with customer or client satisfaction and one of the ways of judging the effectiveness of a unit is linked to the behaviour of the staff. All of us have experienced the unhelpful shop assistant, the bullying manager, the uncommunicative receptionist, and so on. The way in which people exhibit behaviour in their jobs is critical to effective performance. A lecturer who always faces the blackboard, is late, fails to mark assignments and so on, is displaying unacceptable behaviour. However, he could be thought highly of by his superiors because of his excellent research work.

In order to get a balanced view of a job, then a list of all the behavioural measures associated with a job should be created and agreed. This can be done by considering either the 'ideal' behaviour or the worst behaviour. Each behavioural measure will result in a scale. Consider, for example, the case of a manager who is to be rated as follows:

Staff can go to him with problems at all times:

    Almost never   0   1   2   3   4   Almost always

Delegates work that he should do:

    Almost never   0   1   2   3   4   Almost always

Recognises and acknowledges the other person's viewpoint:

    Almost never   0   1   2   3   4   Almost always

The MBO approach and the behaviour criteria approach are complementary. They have been included to indicate that, in terms of evaluating performance against objectives, it is the development of an effective and balanced system that is vital.

Finally with regard to objectives let us quote from Reddin (1971):

The management task as seen by an individual manager:

1. Tell me what you expect of me.
2. Give me an opportunity to perform.
3. Let me know how I am getting on.

4. Give me guidance when I need it.
5. Reward me according to my contribution.

The need to ensure that the manager knows the objectives is critical to success.

External comparisons

In a local authority a study was commissioned to look at the organisation of information services, asking perhaps the obvious question: Are we getting value for money? As a preliminary to this survey, which would in turn provide information for strategic decisions regarding investments in computers and so on, it was important to find out what was being done in other authorities. For this some figures were provided – number of staff in information services compared to other staff, cost of information services per head of population, etc.

Obviously it is very difficult to get exact comparisons, since all local authorities can claim substantial differences in size, population, location and so on. However, a single department like housing can be compared more easily since differences in size and so on can more easily be accounted for.

We can very easily find comparisons for other aspects of service activity: for example, profit per square metre for a retail outlet, cost per student per annum for a college. You may be fortunate in that your organisation (or that part of it that you work for) has got well developed comparative data. However, we must not get too complacent, otherwise certain aspects can be overlooked. A college could achieve a low cost per student through having a limited number of support staff so that buildings were not maintained, clerical work was poor, and so on. So the comparisons drawn must be total and we must not just look at the 'cost' elements in isolation.

This need for comparison with external 'others' leads many organisations actively to seek to get together to swap information. This starts with groups of professionals such as librarians, town planners, management service, R & D, and so on, and then later representatives of whole organisations.

ACTIVITY

Identify:

1. A group that your organisation does/could/should get together with for comparison purposes.
2. A group that your unit does/could/should get together with for comparison purposes.

Internal comparisons

This is the area to which the operations manager will have a lot to contribute. The questions that need to be asked are those concerning effectiveness of the unit. This means that some form of audit needs to be performed which concerns itself with standards of performance.

Following on from our discussion of MBO earlier in this section, a great deal can be done to ensure *effectiveness* when discussing individual objectives with managers, who should focus on obtaining results rather than discharging duties. The objectives should be concerned with effective utilisation of resources and the use of creativity.

They should encourage managers to differentiate between the conventional 'efficiency' approach of doing things right and that of 'effectiveness' which concerns itself with doing right things.

In addition to the above often the only way the manager can understand the internal situation is to carry out some forms of diagnostic study of the unit. Since time for this is not always available to the manager, internal consultants can be used. Some organisations have a management services unit, whilst others use internal auditing. The approach should be a joint one with the manager and members of the team. Many of the techniques/approaches described in later chapters of this book also provide a guide to this approach, the philosophy of which is 'prevention is better than cure'.

As a result of the three areas of investigation outlined above the organisation and unit should now know the answer to the questions:

> 'Where are we compared to others?'
> 'How well are we doing?'

The next phase then is to answer the question.

> 'Where do we wish to be?'

WHERE DO WE WISH TO BE?

Part of the answer to this question will be revealed as a result of re-examining and clarifying objectives and looking at external and internal comparisons. This will enable the organisation to produce part of a strategy for improvement.

Most organisations cannot rely purely upon comparisons with others, and so innovative ideas need to be developed that will help the organisation to provide a better service, or in some cases a different service. Analysis may indicate seasonal, weekly or daily areas of low activity which may be used effectively to provide another service (arts centres, for example, are most likely to be more fully used in the afternoons/evenings and with more activity in the winter months).

Inevitably, the answer to this question must consist in part of a consideration of marketing.

Services marketing

The role of operations managers in marketing will vary between organisations, but with the concept of the service activity involving the customer/client (i.e. simultaneous production and consumption), then the operations manager in the service type organisation is likely to be more involved than the manager in manufacturing. Therefore, so that an effective strategy can be developed, some ideas on services marketing are relevant.

In the 1970s, discussions of service marketing focused on questions such as 'What is a service?' and 'Is the marketing of services different from the marketing of goods?' Definitions such as 'a service is a deed, a performance, an effort' and 'a service is a bundle of want satisfying attributes' (Crompton and Lamb, 1986) were generally accepted, and experts agreed that the marketing of services was significantly different. However, attempts were often made to transfer the methods and concepts used in consumer goods marketing to discussions of problems in service marketing.

The problems relating to marketing government and social services were discussed to some extent within the framework of the traditional marketing mix, looking at adjusting product, distribution, pricing or promotion decisions in order to deliver a better service. Whilst there is much to discover about the marketing of services within this framework, over concentration on it may lead to inappropriate techniques being used and new and much more appropriate approaches remaining undeveloped.

Insights into the problems faced by service marketeers are obtained by investigating the characteristics of services which are not possessed by goods. These distinguishing characteristics are:

1. Relative intangibility (i.e. compared to a tangible 'product')
2. Simultaneous production and consumption
3. Less standardisation.

The following approaches to these characteristics may be useful.

Managing the intangibles

The effects of intangibility on the marketing of services are discussed at length in an article by Rushton and Carson (1983). First, customers have difficulty in evaluating an intangible product (usually a service) before purchase (and sometimes after purchase as well). The person marketing the service needs to be able to clarify what is being offered in order to facilitate evaluation.

There are problems, too, for managers in 'getting to know their product'. A consideration of the product in terms of the classification matrices suggested by Lovelock (1983) may help to alleviate these problems (see Table 3.1).

Where the product is intangible, customers and marketeers tend to concentrate on its tangible features, for example the design of the physical environment, the appearance of staff. Attention should also be given to the tangible and intangible benefits which derive from a service.

There are of course other models which can classify the organisation and its service, but an attempt to get to 'understand the service' is an important step in both marketing and strategy formulation. Classification schemes contribute to management practice in two ways:

1. By looking at these five aspects, marketing managers gain a better understanding of their product and its characteristics, and hence the problems and opportunities which arise in the marketing task.
2. By recognising characteristics their own service has in common with other services (often in unrelated organisations) managers will be able to look beyond their immediate competitors for new ideas on solving marketing problems.

Rushton and Carson (1983) indicated that one of the difficulties of intangibility is that managers fail to differentiate between service features (i.e. what is the actual process that the people/goods go through) and benefits (i.e. what is the eventual, hoped for outcome). So the question as to whether one uses the inputs of a training programme (i.e. specific use of video, course manual, certain topics) or the outputs

Table 3.1 Methods of classification of aspects of service.

1. The service act	The nature of the service activity, i.e. tangible or intangible (e.g. transport, education)	*Relating to*	People or things as direct recipient or service.
2. Relationship with customers	Nature of delivery, i.e. continuous or discrete (e.g. banking/single transaction)	*Relating to*	Relationship to organisation 'members' or not.
3. Customisation and judgement in service delivery	The extent to which 'customer contact personnel' exercise judgement in meeting individual customer needs	*Relating to*	Extent to which services are customised.
4. Nature of demand for service relative to supply	Supply constraints, i.e. can peaks be met easily as in public utilities or not as when a theatre is fully booked	*Relating to*	Extent of demand fluctuation over time.
5. Method of service delivery	Nature of interaction between customer and service organisation	*Relating to*	Availability of service outlets.

Based on Lovelock (1983).

(more effective teamwork, able to cope with stress, etc.) is not properly distinguished unless one has a clear view of the product/service.

Synchronising supply and demand

As production and consumption of services are to a large extent simultaneous, as in a theatre performance for example, measures will be required to cope with peaks in demand; some means of lessening the effects of potentially low demand periods will also be required. One way of achieving a better balance between supply and demand may be for the service unit to target different market segments at different times (e.g. Boston Symphony Orchestra/Boston Pops).

This need to attempt to alter demand and influence capacity is dealt with by Sasser (1976) in which he describes various strategies that can be employed by service organisations to cope with this ever present problem. Like other problems it cannot be dealt with until some model of demand and supply is developed. Some of the options proposed for altering demand include:

1. Differential pricing, e.g. happy hours in pubs
2. Developing non-peak demand, e.g. weekend bargain breaks at city centre hotels
3. Developing complementary services, e.g. a bar area to wait in whilst waiting for a meal.

For controlling supply:

1. Using part-time employees
2. Maximising efficiency
3. Increase customer participation (e.g. self-service petrol)
4. Sharing capacity with other business/service outlets
5. Expand, whilst keeping central services the same (e.g. coping with an increase in the size of a university hall of residence by having two settings at mealtimes and some self-catering facilities).

Internal marketing

This is important in all areas where employees have a high level of contact with customers. As Grönroos (1983) puts it, the objective must be 'to develop motivated and customer-conscious employees'.

Many organisations are using staff development programmes for their customer contact staff which enables the idea of customer satisfaction to be properly exploited. This in itself could form a major part of strategy. In a paper by the service management group at Ashridge, Beddowes (1986) identified four issues that must dominate management's thinking:

1. Taking a *total* view.
2. Balancing customers' and staff expectations – thus if you advertise a 'caring service', you must ensure staff will deliver this.
3. The relevance and effectiveness of the delivery system.
4. Rate of organisational response to major change.

The second and third of these issues affect internal marketing. In the future team-work, commitment to quality of service, sensitivity and creativity culminating in a dedication to quality in its widest sense are seen to be the keys to success.

A more *integrated* view of the problems encountered in marketing services is given in Blois (1983) and Grönroos (1983). Blois points to the interdependence of manu-facturing and marketing activities (which is still true when provision or production of services is substituted for manufacturing). He stresses that this interdependence must be taken into account in formulating a general managerial policy, and also when considering changes to the organisational structure.

Grönroos takes this argument further. He believes that the marketing activities of service organisations cannot be separated from the other major functions of manage-ment – production and operations, administration, personnel, the development of technology – because all affect the customer's perception of service and hence future consumption. When decisions are being made about, for example, production, very often marketing decisions are being made as well. Marketing activities take place in all areas of the organisation.

Rushton and Carson (1983) quote the example of a marketing manager of a chain of restaurants who commented that he had no say in the recruitment of front-line staff. This reduced the direct control he had over marketing and meant he had to work through others to achieve his marketing aims. In other words, he had to educate/train others to recognise the importance of people-handling skills.

Thus an acceptable approach to marketing involves the training of all staff who deal with customer relations in order to give them an appreciation of the importance of a 'marketing' orientation. An example of an organisation not adequately defining 'service' is cited by Matteis (1979) in which he describes a bank:

> A bank's services rated poorly when compared with other banks'. In response, management ordered an overhaul of the services area and brought in managers with experience in manufacturing environments to make the services more efficient. That program succeeded in ensuring new processing efficiency and management control; yet it did not go far enough in terms of personalised customer service. Rather, the program tended to treat a service as if it were a manufacturing product, thus deemphasising its great strength, its uniqueness. So the bank moved in a new direction, this time redesigning for those who would appreciate the strength of services: the individual market and customer areas themselves. One change led to another: with this decentralising program came decentralised technology as well as new jobs and a new work environment.

This section should have given the organisation a number of ideas on where it wants to be. Obviously these need thrashing out with the management team so that they may be developed to a point at which they can be formulated into tangible *plans*.

IMPLEMENTING PLANS TO GET THERE

Our strategy, as a result of the analysis so far conducted, will provide for two major alternatives (or a combination of both):

Become more effective ←——————————————→ Become more market-orientated

It is more likely that the eventual strategy will require an organisation to embrace both of these to a certain degree, but it must be quite clear that they are two distinct parts and therefore need planning separately.

Plans to become more effective will follow from the approaches in the remainder of this book. We have also probably said enough to clarify the opportunities presented by an investigation of the marketing of services, whether this results in changes to the pricing structure or the development of complementary services and so on.

Planning can be defined as the process by which an individual or an organisation advances some course of action to achieve some particular objectives. If we accept that planning is a process, we imply that it is a sequence beginning when we see an opportunity or wish to satisfy a need, and ending when a decision is made on how either can be fulfilled. This is illustrated in Figure 3.5.

However, the 'preparation of plans' may not be as easy as it may at first appear. Table 3.2 gives some guidelines to help the potential planner, though it must be remembered that every planning situation is different.

The strategy project

We will assume that the strategy has been agreed and that this has led directly to the planning of projects. Having eliminated those projects which do not meet the

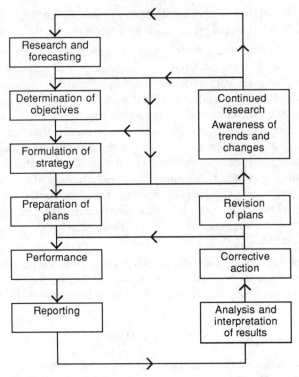

Figure 3.5 The planning/control feedback cycle

organisation's requirements on appropriateness to a substantial extent, the next test will be to ensure that the project is in fact possible.

The questions in this section stem from the headings used in relation to resources:

1. *Money*: Does the organisation have the necessary finance to fund the project, or if not, can it be obtained?
2. *Manpower*: Are the necessary human skills available within the organisation, or can they be recruited?
3. *Materials*: Will the material needed be readily available?
4. *Methods*: Does the firm have the necessary technology?
5. *Machines*: Are the necessary physical resources *in situ*, or if not, can they be obtained in time?
6. *Marketing*: Can the organisation cope with the resulting demands of customers, potential competition, etc.?

While these questions may appear obvious, they are also vital. Many projects which meet the first group of criteria – contributing towards the organisation's objectives, making the maximum use of strengths and opportunities, and minimising the effects of weaknesses and risks – will still be ruled out, for example for lack of the necessary resources.

Having satisfied ourselves on the above (and the operations manager will be quite clearly involved in answering the above questions), we next have to produce some form of tangible plan. A method suitable for this is *project network techniques* (PNT), defined as: 'A group of techniques for the description, analysis, planning and

Table 3.2 Planning considerations.

1. Planning takes time and busy managers often have difficulty in allocating sufficient time.
2. Unit strategies are not defined, thus making it difficult for managers to provide complementary plans.
3. Managers are uncertain of their specific objectives, or when they are certain of them, how their achievement contributes in a meaningful way to the corporate plan.
4. Many managers have had no formal training in planning and may rely upon their experience.
5. Every situation will have some events that influence the end result more than others. Management should limit their planning to these critical few rather than get bogged down with the trivial many.
6. Successful planning can only be achieved when the whole organisation is involved. If some managers see objectives whilst others do not, or if forecasting is carried out by marketing but not in operations, fragmented planning will result.
7. Plans prepared by specialists can often be difficult to understand by operations managers. It may be better to provide a number of simple plans for specific tasks by specific individuals which are simple to understand and easy to use.
8. As all plans relate to the future we can expect some degree of error during their implementation. It is therefore essential that plans of any reasonable importance identify those areas more likely to go wrong and have ready alternative plans which can be introduced should the circumstances require them.
9. Plans can sometimes become barriers to people's creative ability by being too rigidly applied. On the other hand, we know that when people work together freedom of action can only exist within a domain of control. To provide the right environment plans should be broad enough to allow freedom of choice and decision in keeping with an individual's authority and responsibility.

control of projects which consider the logical interrelationships of all project activities . . . It includes techniques concerned with time, resources, costs and uncertainty.'

In order to develop a PNT diagram it is first necessary to identify those activities which need to be carried out. These then need to be formed into a logical diagram. Figure 3.6 shows an example for a one-off activity of organising a conference. In studying this you will see that it has been prepared in such a way as to show the correct and logical succession and precedence of activities. Adding time data to the activities will indicate which path through the network is critical and where, if necessary, more resources need to be placed.

The diagram in Figure 3.6 is basically a very simple one and for corporate plans a much more detailed project network diagram would be used. With the use of a computer program, a considerable amount of information can be made available to all participants.

It is quite likely that a broad organisation-wide network could be the 'master plan' and smaller but more detailed diagrams could be used for the departments'/units' contributions. The whole plan can also be presented as a bar-chart against a timescale and progress can be monitored.

This technique is a very powerful method of communication which when used for strategy implementation focuses on that goal. It ensures all units contribute and enables progress towards implementation to be in balance.

The types of project which would come under the heading corporate strategy would include the following:

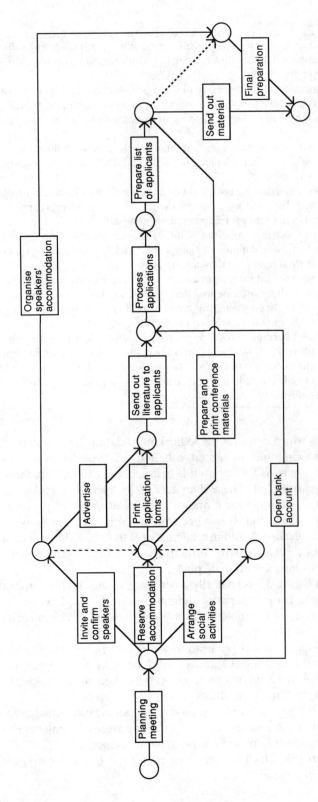

Figure 3.6 Project network diagram: organising a conference

1. Improving internal effectiveness by reorganisation.
2. Introducing the concept of caring in customer contact.
3. Introducing a range of new services to absorb extra capacity.
4. 'Adding on' new services to the existing range.
5. Computerisation/automation of some facilities.
6. Getting more involvement from this customer/client in the delivery of the service.
7. Extending the geographical area covered.

EVALUATE THE ACHIEVEMENT

This can be a continuous activity seen at different levels. If a plan is devised which identifies certain tasks to be done – changes in layout, location, advertising copy and so on – and these are linked to costs and time, then the obvious first stage in evaluation is to ask the question: 'Have we achieved the targets?'

But the real achievement is not in being efficient in discharging the *plan*, but whether the new system, additional services and so on have the desired effect and meet the objectives laid down at the beginning. These objectives must include quantifiable measures that can be clearly used:

1. Unit costs
2. Increased revenue/usage of facilities
3. Lower staff to customer ratio
4. Level of satisfaction with service.

Some means of evaluation must be established in order to monitor this effort of change. In some cases where the end result is not *just* financial or quantitative but is concerned with people's perception of an image or their satisfaction with the level/ standard of service, then various questionnaires can be used to get some idea of the effect of the change.

The final phase of performance appraisal will be used at the level of the individual unit/department. This is the follow-up discussion after objectives have been agreed and set, i.e. to evaluate performance in whatever way is considered suitable. The opportunity is also then taken to revise targets for the next period on the basis of what has been done.

CONCLUSIONS

This chapter has covered a lot of ground and has introduced you to a number of strategic issues which impinge upon operations management. It also shows how certain techniques (PNT, MBO) fit into the overall pattern.

To summarise there follows a list of things for an operations manager to do concerning corporate strategy in his or her own organisation.

Where are we now?

1. Ensure some form of MBO/performance appraisal is used so that:
   (a) You are contributing towards the development objectives for the organisation.
   (b) You are quite clear as to what they are and what your role is in achieving them.
   (c) You know how to evaluate your own performance relative to objectives.
   (d) These performance measures relate to results.
2. Find out how your organisation and your unit within the organisation compares with others of a similar type.
3. Conduct an internal diagnosis of the unit to identify how effective the unit is and develop plans for improvement.

Where do we wish to be?

1. Ensure you know your product (services) and that it can be suitably categorised.
2. Ensure that you can recognise both tangible and intangible features and that you can distinguish features from benefits of service.
3. Consider the problems of service activities in terms of synchronisation of supply and demand and consider ways of altering demand and controlling supply.
4. Consider staff attitudes towards customers in terms of total image, expectations and delivery of service.
5. Ensure that operations managers do have an input to marketing and hence strategic decisions.
6. Synthesise from the above 'where we wish to be'.

Implementing plans to get there

1. Ensure you (and others) understand fully the planning cycle and effective planning.
2. Check that resources do or can eventually match aspirations.
3. Ensure that specific plans are laid down in a way all can understand.
4. Link plans to costs/time/resources and set up controls.

Evaluate the achievement

1. Use controls to check on achievement of implementation targets.
2. Ensure measures are used to evaluate overall effect of the strategy.
3. Ensure that individual contributions are monitored by performance appraisal, as appropriate.

References and suggested reading
Corporate strategy – general

Ansoff, H. I. (1968) *Corporate Strategy*. Harmondsworth, Middx: Pelican.
Argenti, J. (1968) *Corporate Planning – A Practical Guide*. London: Allen & Unwin.
Boyce, R. O. and Elsen, H. (1972) *Management Diagnosis – A Practical Guide*. London: Longman.

Halford, D. R. L. (1968) *Business Planning*. London: Pan.

Hodgetts, R. (1985) *Management*. London: Academic Press.

Lockyer, K. G. (1964) *An Introduction to Critical Path Analysis*. London: Pitman.

Normann, R. (1984) *Service Management – Strategy and Leadership in Service Businesses*. Chichester: Wiley.

Purdie, W. K. and Taylor, B. (eds) (1976) *Business Strategies for Survival – Planning for Social and Political Change*. London: Heinemann.

Tate, C. E. and Taylor, H. L. (1983) *Business Policy – Administrative, Strategic and Contingency Issues*. Dallas, TX: Business Publications.

Thomas, D. R. E. (July–August 1978) Strategy is different in service businesses. *Harvard Business Review*, pp. 158–165.

Thorelli. H. B. (1977) *Strategy and Structure = Performance*. Ontario: Indiana University Press.

Performance appraisal

Bennett, R. (1981) *Managing Personnel and Performance*. London: Business Books.

Latham, G. P. and Wexley, K. N. (1981) *Increasing Productivity through Performance Appraisal*. Reading, MA: Addison-Wesley.

Mager, R. F. and Pipe, P. (1970) *Analysing Performance Problems or 'You Really Oughta Wanna'*. Belmont, CA: Pearman.

Odiorne, G. S. (1970) *Management by Objectives*. New York: Pitman.

Olson, R. F. (1981) *Performance Appraisal – A Guide to Greater Productivity*. New York: John Wiley.

Reddin, W. (1971) *Effective Management by Objectives*. London: MGT Publications for the British Institute of Management.

Sloma, R. S. (1980) *How to Measure Managerial Performance*. New York: Macmillan.

Watson, C. E. (1981) *Results Orientated Managing*. Reading, MA: Addison-Wesley.

Marketing services

Beddowes, P. E., Galliford, S., Knight, M. and Saunders, I. (1986) *Service Success: Who Is Getting There*? Unpublished paper, Ashridge Services Management Group.

Blois, K. J. (1983) The structure of marketing firms and their marketing policies. *Strategic Management Journal*, **4**, pp. 251–261.

Cowell, D. (1984) *The Marketing of Services*. London: Heinemann.

Crompton, J. and Lamb, C. (1986) *Marketing Government and Social Services*. New York: John Wiley.

Grönroos, C. (1983) *Strategic Management and Marketing in the Service Sector*. Bromley: Chartwell-Bratt.

Lovelock, C. (Summer 1983) Classifying services to gain specific strategic marketing insights. *Journal of Marketing*, **47**, pp. 9–20.

Lovelock, C. (1984) *Services Marketing*. Englewood Cliffs, NJ: Prentice-Hall.

McDonald, M. H. B. (1986) *How to Sell a Service*. London: Heinemann.

Matteis, R. (March–April 1979) The new back office focusses on customer service. *Harvard Business Review*. pp. 52–65.

Mokwa, M., Dawson, W. and Prieve, E. A. (1980) *Marketing the Arts*. New York: Praeger.

Morris, B. and Johnston, R. (1986) *Dealing with Inherent Variability – The Difference Between Manufacturing and Service*. Unpublished paper, University of Warwick.

Rushton, A. and Carson, D. (1983) The marketing of services: managing the intangibles. *European Journal of Marketing*, **19** (3), pp. 19–40.

Sasser, W. E. (November–December 1976) Match supply and demand in service industries. *Harvard Business Review*, pp. 133–141.

Willsmer, R. L. (1976) *The Basic Arts of Marketing*. London: Business Books.

4
METHODS OF WORKING

INTRODUCTION

The title of this chapter reveals that we shall be giving a very broad consideration to how work is done. We will here be concerned with *systems design* and *redesign*. Systems design refers to the planning which is required to set up any facility, whereas systems redesign reflects the need to continually reassess how the facility is performing from the point of view of both resource productivity and customer satisfaction.

The planning phase for any facility must include aspects such as premises, staffing and training. Decisions on how work is done, on the other hand, depend upon the type of service provided and the way in which it is delivered. In many service facilities there has been a greater tendency to include the customer within the design of the facilities – self-service shops, cash dispensers, vending machines, self-drive hire, self-catering holidays. Such examples have required a complete rethink of the way in which the service is provided with a conscious decision to redesign around the new provision. In many cases the reasons for the change is cost, but often it is also convenient from the customer's viewpoint – many of us must be delighted to obtain cash outside banking hours and with no queuing. (For a detailed discussion of these ideas see Collier (1985).)

A good illustration of the setting up of a facility is that of someone starting up his or her own business – say as a computer consultant. The aspects which need to be considered are as follows:

1. Results of market research conducted
2. Types of service provided and need for them
3. Likely share of market
4. Development of new markets
5. Advertising and promotion
6. Investigation into premises
7. Problems of reliance on one person
8. Computer equipment available
9. Time available.

And so on. The answers to the above – some constrained, for example, by limited funds – will dictate the type of service offered initially. As the business becomes successful the type of work done and type of customer aimed at may change, in which case methods of working will need to be reviewed.

One of the initial problems faced by our computer consultant will be the type of work he or she would wish to do and the work that is actually obtained. In many service operations there are conflicts between customer needs and the manner in which that service can be delivered. For example, in schools and colleges class sizes may well be larger than the pupils/students and parents/employers would wish, while as customers we have no doubt fumed at the time spent waiting for, say, a meal in a hotel or to be serviced in the post office. However, we also recognise the impossibility of staffing up to peak demand and the pressures that are sometimes brought by staff absences.

Resource productivity – which was introduced in Chapter 1 – is concerned with how effectively all the resources are being used. It would be concerned with identifying means whereby, say, floor space could be more effectively used, how more customers could be dealt with by a given group of staff, how vehicles could have less waiting time and more useful travelling time, and so on. Productivity is concerned with the ratio of input to output. It can be improved either by reduction of *imanpower, materials, equipment) or by an increase in output* (number of customers serviced to satisfactory quality), or both.

ACTIVITY

1. Consider your own organisation and list the conflicts in systems design which polarise customer satisfaction and resource productivity.

2. What do you think should be done to overcome the problems you have identified?

RESOURCE PRODUCTIVITY

In Figure 4.1, which provides examples of problems arising from methods of working or operation, resource productivity is measured by *work content*. This means that anything which is less than effective will add to the time taken to complete a task, and thus reduce the productivity of those resources. There are a number of specific management techniques designed to solve some of the problems listed, but it is not our intention to provide a catalogue of techniques which could be confusing. Rather we shall provide you with an approach to work methods which will help clarify the real problems and indicate realistic solutions.

Many solutions to work methods problems often involve the use of more sophisticated technology. Again, it would be of limited value to indicate this as an 'answer' since in some cases the application of technology can be described as 'a solution looking for a problem'. If the problem identification and solving approach is done correctly the value of more sophisticated technology will become obvious; conversely, where it is totally inappropriate can also be clearly identified. This will then help operations managers to be confident in specifying the correct method of working rather than having 'the latest gimmick' foisted on them by other enthusiastic salespeople or advisors.

PROBLEM-SOLVING

Before a problem can exist it is necessary to recognise it against some *defined aim*. If we have established objectives which are not being adequately achieved, this identifies the *effect* of the problem. This then has to be traced back to the *cause*. For

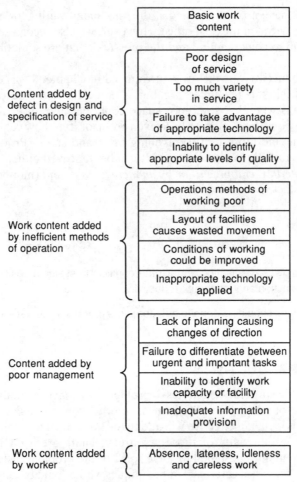

Figure 4.1 Examples of work content additions
Based on Figures 2, 3 and 4, ILO (1974)

example, if an office manager recognised that there was a backlog of filing that was getting greater each week he or she would have noted the effect of a problem. The cause could be one of several issues, for example:

1. Poorly motivated staff
2. Increase in work load
3. Other work being given priority.

Thus tracing this effect back to its cause would enable this relatively simple problem to be clearly identified.

However, even identifying the problem in this way does not provide an instant solution. Effective problem-solving would perhaps question the need for filing at all, and ask whether some documents need to be filed or whether a better and more easily accessible system is required, and so on. On the other hand, it could well be that the reason for the backlog is, say, poorly motivated staff who are fed up with the sheer physical difficulty of conducting the filing. This again gets further to the real cause of the problem.

Putting one's finger on the source of the trouble is perfectly simple when the whole matter has arisen as the result of a crisis, such as a breakdown, a bottleneck or an accident. But sometimes we have to study and improve a working procedure which has apparently nothing specifically wrong with it: we simply suspect that it is too expensive, too laborious, too unproductive, or in some other way uneconomic as a whole. Two primary questions have to be answered:

1. How can we isolate the activities which ought to be examined?
2. How wide should we cast our net?

It should be noted that even in a crisis situation the apparently crucial operation may not be the only one worth examining, or even the most important. If, for example, we are faced with a breakdown at one point, it may be due to faults elsewhere, perhaps in planning or in manning the whole chain of operations. To be on the safe side we clearly ought to examine as much of the work as possible, although we will always fear that the wider the field the more complex the net of operations – and hence the more difficult to distinguish the real problem from the irrelevancies.

Raybold (1966) identified three types of problems calling for working methods improvement:

1. The Sherlock Holmes type – as typified by the cause–effect route indicated above.
2. The creative type problem – in this type nothing has gone wrong but you are concerned to meet an increase in the specification of what you are doing. Here you need to look for creative ways to cope. An example of this in education is the development of open learning systems to cater for a hitherto untapped market.
3. The optimisation problem – nothing has gone wrong and you have not got to come up with a new system; all you have to do is to make the best use of the information you have, and replan your resources. (Much of this problem is dealt with in Chapter 5.)

Many problems have elements of all three types of category. Thus our problem-solving approach will follow these stages:

1. Define aim/objectives.
2. Identify the causes of problems.
3. Collect facts.
4. Identify alternatives, predict outcomes of each and choose the most appropriate and practical alternative solution.
5. Develop new system.
6. Install new system.
7. Ensure new system is properly maintained.

It is this basic approach which is at the root of *all* management techniques. The major difference in the approaches is based on the ability to classify the problem into one primarily concerned with, say:

1. Layout of facilities
2. Information handling

3. Capacity of work unit
4. Methods of physical work
5. Motivation of staff
6. Utilisation of facilities
7. Quality of service.

Many operations problems contain elements of all the above, but one usually predominates. In this chapter we will be concentrating on:

1. Redesign of physical work systems, and
2. Redesign of information systems.

Later chapters will deal with some of the other specific techniques concerned with layout (Chapter 6), capacity (Chapter 5), motivation (Chapter 13), utilisation (Chapter 9) and quality (Chapter 8).

TECHNIQUES FOR REDESIGNING SYSTEMS

Many 'management techniques' have been badly applied over the years, which has caused many people to blame the techniques for difficulties rather than the manner of their application. This has led to a variety of different names being used by organisations to identify the same technique, although purists might argue that there are discernible differences.

Before we move on to the next section it is worthwhile clarifying some of these terms. The official definitions are given in an appendix to this chapter. All these techniques are popularly known as 'management services' techniques as classified in the appendix. Some techniques will be referred to in more detail later in the book.

For the practising manager the essential feature is that for physical work systems the term *method study* is used, which itself is a subdivision of work study which also embraces work measurement. (This is discussed in detail in Chapter 5.)

Closely linked to method study are such approaches as *work simplification* and *work improvement*. Both are initially aimed at getting supervisors and staff to adopt a positive attitude to improving the work for which they have responsibility in the continuing quest to maximise resource productivity.

Many of the ideas incorporated in all of these approaches are concerned with getting people to be more creative in their thought processes as they approach problems. For example, it may often involve group brainstorming sessions. (Some of these ideas will be developed in Chapter 11.)

The work improvement approach has been developed by Lehrer (1965) into an 'improvement function' in which the ideas should permeate the whole organisation. The philosophy of improvement here is concerned not just with methods of working, but with means of planning, communications, organisational design, etc., thereby stressing the systems nature of the approach.

This can be illustrated neatly by considering a possible request by a warehouse manager for £25,000 to automate the loading dock, expenditure which could pay for itself within a year thus assuring a high rate of return. However, the work design group could suggest another distribution method which might completely eliminate the need for the warehouse, and which therefore provides a better solution overall.

Whilst these approaches are primarily concerned with physical work systems, as the systems develop they would come to include information systems and office procedures generally. A number of complementary techniques have been developed:

1. *Organisation and methods* (O&M), which may be described as method study in the office, and of course with the increasing use of computer based systems,
2. *Systems analysis*, which has as its main objective that of identifying the real needs of any system of information.

To summarise the approach to redesign of working methods:

1. Use a systems approach.
2. Don't be constrained by existing practices.
3. Question the real needs of any activity.
4. Above all don't be too tied down to the techniques which can sometimes limit the thinking process.

With this advice in mind the examples which follow indicate how methods of working can be improved.

In approaching the redesign of working methods we shall use the problem-solving framework given on page 61 and illustrative material from the service sector covering both physical work systems and information systems. We have already adequately discussed stages 1 and 2 concerning the definition of aims and the identification of the causes of problems in considering the broader systems approach. We can therefore commence our description from the third stage of collecting facts.

Brief overview of stages 3 – 5: Collecting facts, identifying alternatives and developing new systems

Whilst the majority of factual information will be about the present method of operating, data will need to be obtained from many sources so that the correct answers will be obtained. This is particularly the case if the answer will be one which is significantly different from the present system (as in the warehouse and automation example above). This data will include various analyses, the questioning approach, checklists, information from brochures, pamphlets and so on, even significant papers from conferences.

To illustrate this and overview the three stages we are concerned with here, Figure 4.2 shows the inductive jump necessary in the development of an improved method. This diagram illustrates well how we should always bear in mind previous work carried out by ourselves and others in the field of study, and at all times discuss every stage of the investigation with all concerned.

The inductive jump refers to the need to bring all the data and questioning together, seeing the right connection between them, observing the constraints within which one must be working, and thus finally producing an acceptable improved method. This contrasts with the 'common sense approach' which attempts to solve the problem in one quick bright idea. Consider the example of a laundry where a fact-gathering exercise revealed difficulties experienced by the staff in lifting wet laundry from trolleys into a spin dryer. The 'bright idea' solution put forward by a senior colleague (who should have known better) was to use a scoop-bottomed trolley.

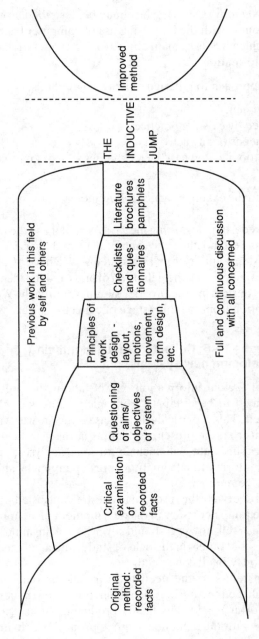

Figure 4.2 The inductive jump in developing an improved method
Courtesy R. D. Cruickshank

However, after consultation with suppliers, staff and the finance department an overhead monorail system was the method selected, even though some degree of imagination was required to fit it into the existing work area. Often when solving problems creativity such as this is helped by previous experience – even in some cases transferred from one's 'leisure pursuits'.

COLLECTING FACTS – RECORDING WORK METHODS

In order to study work with a view to improvement there is a need to develop some form of *model* of the work system. For work that is physical, e.g. operating a machine, serving petrol in a garage, collecting refuse, cooking and serving meals, then direct observation and recording is required.

Alongside the physical work system in any organisation is the information system – still mostly paperwork, but tending now towards computer and electronic systems. To understand how the information flow system operates, the recording relies on collecting data from all those using the system: what information is received, what is done with it and to whom it is forwarded. Data and information may be gathered by examination and analysis of work and procedure manuals, records, correspondence, reports, observation, interviewing, and so on.

Some examples follow to illustrate this making use of charts which are used in *method study* and O & M.

Recording Physical Work

Process charts

These may be defined as follows:

> Charts in which a sequence of events is portrayed diagrammatically by means of a set of process chart symbols to help a person to visualise a process as a means of examining and proving it (BS 32002).

The main value of the process chart is its ability to record a process, or procedure, in a compact manner thus ensuring that a complete picture is built up with nothing missing in such a way that the sequence of related events is clearly shown.

The following extracts from the description of a process together with the process chart and room plan given in Figure 4.3 illustrate the principles involved.

Background data

In a hospital pharmacy, bottles of saline solution are prepared each day for intravenous injections. The work is in two parts – (1) preparation of solution and bottling, and (2) sterilising and inspecting. The following description relates to the first part and is conducted daily by an apprentice pharmacist. It is done in a special room designed for the purpose to avoid contact with dust, etc.

65

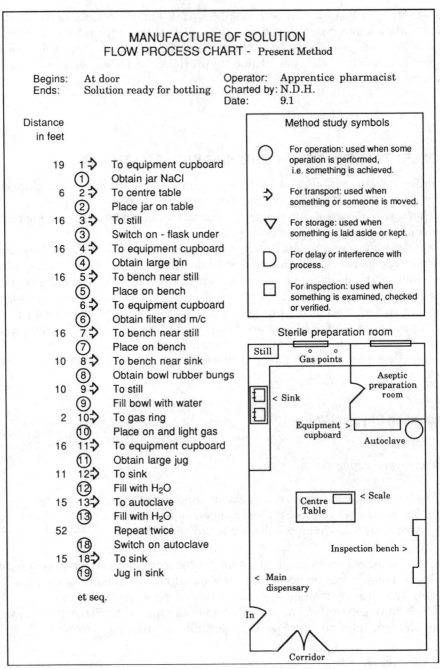

MANUFACTURE OF SOLUTION
FLOW PROCESS CHART - Present Method

Begins: At door   Operator: Apprentice pharmacist
Ends: Solution ready for bottling   Charted by: N.D.H.
                                           Date: 9.1

Distance   Method study symbols
in feet

                                          ◯   For operation: used when some
   19   1 ⇾   To equipment cupboard   operation is performed,
        ①   Obtain jar NaCl   i.e. something is achieved.
    6   2 ⇾   To centre table
        ②   Place jar on table   ⇾   For transport: used when
   16   3 ⇾   To still   something or someone is moved.
        ③   Switch on - flask under
   16   4 ⇾   To equipment cupboard   ▽   For storage: used when
        ④   Obtain large bin   something is laid aside or kept.
   16   5 ⇾   To bench near still
        ⑤   Place on bench   D   For delay or interference with
        6 ⇾   To equipment cupboard   process.
        ⑥   Obtain filter and m/c
   16   7 ⇾   To bench near still   ☐   For inspection: used when
        ⑦   Place on bench   something is examined, checked
   10   8 ⇾   To bench near sink   or verified.
        ⑧   Obtain bowl rubber bungs
   10   9 ⇾   To still   Sterile preparation room
        ⑨   Fill bowl with water
    2 10 ⇾   To gas ring
        ⑩   Place on and light gas
   16 11 ⇾   To equipment cupboard
        ⑪   Obtain large jug
   11 12 ⇾   To sink
        ⑫   Fill with H_2O
   15 13 ⇾   To autoclave
        ⑬   Fill with H_2O
   52   Repeat twice
        ⑱   Switch on autoclave
   15 18 ⇾   To sink
        ⑲   Jug in sink

        et seq.

Figure 4.3 Process chart and room plan for the preparation of saline solution
Copyright N. D. Harris

Present description of work

On entering the room the apprentice pharmacist obtains a jar of sodium chloride
from the equipment cupboard and places it on the centre table. The still is switched
on and a flask is put underneath. There are a number of flasks of distilled water on the

bench which have been made on the previous day. A large bin is obtained from the equipment cupboard and placed on the bench near the still. Also a filtering and bottle filling machine is taken from the cupboard to the bench near the still. A bowl of rubber bungs is obtained from the bench near the sink, filled with distilled water and placed on the gas ring which is lit at a low pressure. A large jug is obtained from the cupboard and used to fill the autoclave with water (3 jugs of water required), the jug being replaced in the sink after the autoclave is switched on . . . .

The bin is swilled out with distilled water from one of the flasks and placed on the centre table, together with the remaining distilled water in the flask. Sodium chloride is taken from the jar on the centre table, 2 oz is weighed out and the lumps are broken up with a knife. This is then added to the flask and shaken up. A glass rod is obtained from the equipment cupboard, swilled under the tap and used to stir the mixture.

Two flasks of distilled water are fetched from the still, each containing 4 litres when full, and distilled water is added to the mixture to make up 4 litres. This is then poured into the bin and the quantity noted. A second quantity of 4 litres is measured, added and noted.

Two further flasks of distilled water are fetched and a further 4 litres added and noted. A 1 litre measuring beaker is obtained from the equipment cupboard and swilled under the tap and then with distilled water. 2 litres is added to the bin and the total 14 litres is stirred with a glass rod and carried to the still.

The filtering and bottling machine is connected to the bin by a tube and a small amount of solution run through to swill the machine. Bottles in crates are obtained from the sink and the bottling and bunging process is ready to commence.

String diagrams

This is a useful technique which can be used to:

1. show the movement between work stations;
2. compare the values of different layouts or routes.

From recorded observation over the duration of a process the sequence of movement to and from working points is noted. On a scale plan of the working area each work point is represented by a pin. A thread/string is then wound around the pins in the sequence which was recorded.

An illustration of the pharmacy preparation of saline solution discussed above before and after this type of method study is shown in Figure 4.4. (How the results in Figure 4.4 are achieved is discussed later.)

These two techniques show the value of providing some form of model to help us understand the problem more clearly and to highlight the inefficiences of the present system.

Recording information flow

By far the largest part of office work is concerned with systems and procedures. The recording of these is complicated by the following:

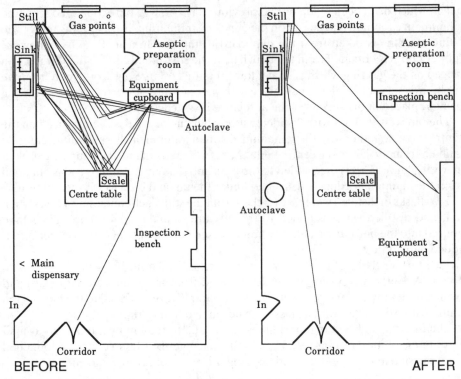

Figure 4.4 String diagrams for the preparation of saline solution, before and after analysis

1. A procedure is not easily visible and therefore not readily observable.
2. The movement of forms tends to be in batches and consequently spasmodic.
3. A procedure may not be confined to any one person, section or department.
4. The movement and flow of documents needs to be shown in addition to the operations carried out.
5. A procedure may involve different documents with additional copies.

Procedure charts

These are a useful means of recording in detail all the complicated data which normally constitutes a procedure. This type of chart cannot be built up from direct observation alone. It is also based upon the information obtained from people.

Some conventions for building a procedure chart are as follows:

1. The format is a series of vertical columns.
2. Each distinct department, section or person (dependent upon the detail charted) involved in the procedure is allocated a column.
3. The first department is usually allocated the left-hand column and so forth.
4. Process chart symbols are used to denote action.

A very simple example for planning an order is shown in Figure 4.5. A more complex version of this type of chart is shown in Figure 4.6 for the total procedure from the receipt of an enquiry until the invoice is despatched in a small wire works office.

Systems analysis

Considerable recording of information flow is carried out as a prerequisite to developing a computerised system. In the 'systems analysis' stage it is essential that the work currently being done is not merely recorded but is carefully questioned as to its necessity. Commonality of data in systems can be used to advantage to avoid duplication and to provide a more comprehensive management information system.

In central government, the procedures used are often very complex and the routes that apply to different categories of (say) applicants for state benefit will vary. This causes difficulties for those administering such schemes as well as great confusion for the public. To overcome them a number of approaches have been developed based upon the logic required to programme computers so that every question must be phrased to get a *yes* or *no* response which will then lead the computer to the appropriate part of the programme.

However complex the system it is possible to provide a record which can be critically evaluated to enable the most effective system to be designed. As computers become cheaper, software becomes more 'user friendly', and many organisations are now welcoming the chance to get their records on computer as this can provide splendid opportunities for data analysis thus giving greater control over the operations.

IDENTIFY ALTERNATIVES AND CHOOSE MOST PRACTICAL SOLUTION

The importance of alternatives

Perhaps the most important part of any problem-solving/decision-making activity is that of identifying what choices of action (or inaction) are available. The need to devote time to exploring and identifying the various courses of action that are open to the manager is a vital part of the process of problem-solving or decision-making.

The methods employed do not have to be complex – in fact a simple list with some indication of the advantages and disadvantages of each is often satisfactory. In more complex cases a number of systematic approaches have been developed which have proved their value.

Critical examination

We have covered how physical work and information can be recorded so that we can get a clearer picture of what occurs now. This record must then be subjected to a detailed critical examination so that all aspects can be considered for improvement.

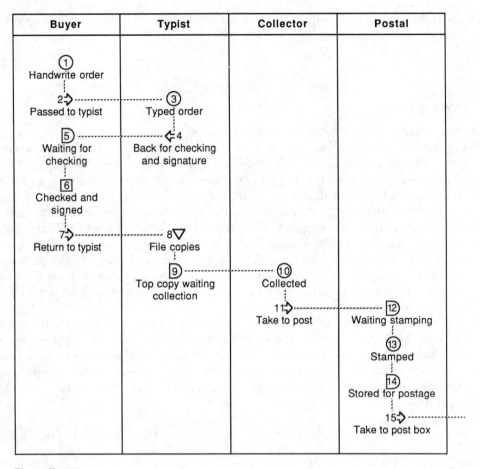

Flow diagram

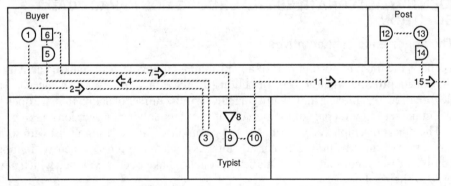

Figure 4.5 Procedure chart for placing an order

The aim of any person conducting a critical examination is to expose all the alternatives, allowing the selection process to be evaluated afterwards. To help in the exposure of alternatives a *critical examination sheet* is used (see Figure 4.7), which indicates the type of questions to be asked.

Acquiring the skill to use a critical examination sheet is not automatic. It requires a lot of patience to apply the system correctly since it is often apparently easier to use 'hunches' or 'bright ideas'. These have to be deliberately shelved until the process is completed since we are first concerned with exposing *all* possible alternatives rather than proving that one is correct.

To summarise the approach, some useful guidelines are given below.

Examination procedure

This is through the questioning technique, which is defined by the BSI as:

> The means by which the critical examination is conducted, each activity being subjected in turn to a systematic and progressive series of questions.

The questions are set out on a critical examination sheet (see Figure 4.7) with space for answers, and fall into two groups:

1. *Primary questions*. These form the first stage of the questioning technique and query the fundamental need for the performance, place, sequence, person and means of every activity recorded. A reason must be given for each reply.
2. *Secondary questions*. These form the second stage of the questioning technique whereby the answers to the primary questions are subjected to further query to determine whether possible alternatives of place, sequence, persons and/or means are practical and preferable as a means of improvement over the existing method.

Reasons for use

The recorded present method is subjected to ruthless, penetrating and systematic examination with the intention of developing a new and improved method. The critical examination is intended:

1. To determine the true reasons underlying each event.
2. To draw up a systematic list of possible improvements.
3. To show how possible improvements can be developed into a better method.

Requirements

1. A systematic approach.
2. Collaboration with all people concerned (supervisors, advisors, staff).
3. Collaboration with all people who might be able to advise, i.e. those in other departments, those outside the organisation.
4. Full technical knowledge of the activity under examination.

Method of approach

When examining the recorded facts of a process it is important to keep to a set plan and focus in turn on individual aspects of the activities recorded. However, if each

71

Customer	Manager	Clerk/Outer office	Foreman	Worker

Customer enquiry received

Job details written down

Copy job details and job cost into "quotation book"

Enter labour cost

Complete cost computed - o/heads, measuring, fixing and profit

Quotation prepared

3 copies of quotation typed

1 2 3

Filed alphabetically by customer name

Despatched to customer

Acceptance or firm offer received (phone or letter)

Details of customer - date required and order details copied or entered in order book 2 copies

1 2

Cross reference index at rear of order book

1 copy of job sheet typed

Order no becomes job no - date - description

Tally with job no prepared and attached

Order book aside

Job sheet checked

Plans or sketch appended

If a similar job has been done piece price entered

Placed aside for wages

Jobs given to workers

Put in box awaiting worker (numerically and type of job)

With W/M acting as instructions

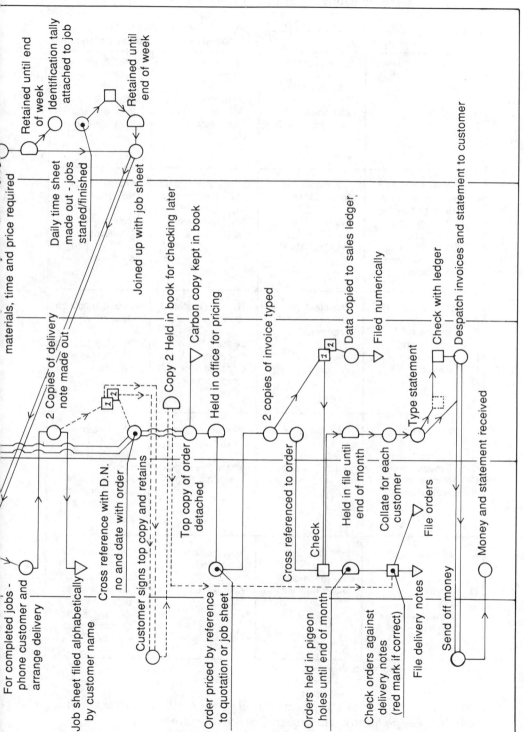

Figure 4.6 Procedure chart from receipt of enquiry to despatch of invoice

METHOD STUDY - CRITICAL EXAMINATION SHEET

	Primary questions		Secondary questions	
			Alternatives	Selected alternatives
P **U** **R** **P** **O** **S** **E**	*What* is achieved? *not* How or why is it done? Expose true reason	Is it necessary? State true reason: Specific or technical details:	*What* else could be done? Eliminate Modify Substitute	*What* should be done? Consideration of long- and short- term alternative.
P **L** **A** **C** **E**	*Where* is it done? Geographical po- sition in building Distances from activities Before and after Original reasons for location	*Why* there? Advantages: Justify: Disadvantages:	*Where* else could it be done? Combine work areas. Reduce distances.	*Where* should it be done? Consider limitations of buildings and environment.
S **E** **Q** **U** **E** **N** **C** **E**	*When* is it done? Significant reviews and subsequent activities Frequency:	*Why* then? Reason for position in method and frequency	*When* else could it be done? Earlier or later in method. Combine with step before or after.	*When* should it be done? Generally as soon as possible in method.
P **E** **R** **S** **O** **N**	*Who* does it? Person Grade of skill Number of staff Rate of pay	*Why* that person? Reason - under each heading	*Who* else could do it? Alternative under each heading	*Who* should do it? Select best alter- native. Consider training, education, staff development.
M **E** **A** **N** **S**	*How* is it done? Material Tools Equipment Operators Method	*Why* that way? Reason under each heading	*How* else could it be done? Alternatives	*How* should it be done? Select/consider: Safety quality Working method Customer satis- faction

Figure 4.7 Critical examination sheet

activity is considered in this way, a great deal of work will be involved, and so, to assist in this, *key points* from the sequence of activities are selected.

The objective of critical examination is to eliminate, combine or simplify the activity under consideration.

Rules of approach

1. Facts should be examined as they are, and not as they appear to be, should be or are said to be.
2. There should be no preconceived ideas.
3. All aspects should be approached with challenge and scepticism. No answer is accepted until proved correct.
4. Hasty judgements must be avoided.
5. Detail must have persistent and close attention.
6. 'Hunches' which occur during recording and which will have been noted should be reserved for the appropriate place in the procedure.
7. New methods should not even be considered until all the undesirable features of the existing method have been exposed by systematic examination.

Selection of appropriate or practical solution

After completing the critical examination sheet (or whatever other means of solving our problems we have chosen) the alternatives we select may not be based on 'ideal' conditions since they may not be cost effective, or we might recognise that resources are limited. So we may select a method which is better in the medium term, although we may be able to improve upon it in the long term when resources are available or when the new method is proven and investment in new equipment (say) is shown to be beneficial. Thus, for example, jumping from manually controlled activities directly to computerised or automated machines may not be feasible immediately.

DEVELOP NEW SYSTEM

We have spent a considerable amount of time and effort in identifying as many alternatives as possible. We must now try to evaluate them.

Using critical examination

The critical examination sheet (see Figure 4.6) provides a column in which you can indicate your selected alternatives. For this to be done effectively it is necessary to look at the process as a 'whole', as an integrated system. It is of little use satisfying the 'Place' aspect if this gives problems for the 'Methods' of working. There is of course also the approach which may require a 'short-term' solution with minimal cost and upheaval, followed by a 'long-term' solution dependent upon new equipment or re-arrangement of facilities which could take considerable time.

In the example given earlier of the pharmacist, a considerable number of ideas were in fact considered but they can be summarised with an extract from the report as follows.

Extract from consultant's report on pharmacy procedure

Movement

In order to reduce the need for the considerable movement, a double-tier trolley could be provided on which all the equipment can be placed, including the sodium chloride. All this can be moved to the corner by the still and the solution prepared by using the top of the trolley as a work-bench.

To avoid the need to fill the autoclave by jug and journey, it can be resited near to the sink, where it can be filled either by using the present taps and a short length of hose or by arranging for independent plumbing.

Measuring

Although the present form of sodium chloride is undoubtedly the cheapest, the possibility of using either tablets which dissolve easily or prepacked and weighed packets should be investigated. A slight increase in the cost of this material which is used in very small quantities may save a skilled person's valuable time.

The present method involves the preparation of distilled water on the previous day which is then run into flasks. These have the advantage that they allow very little dust to get in (narrow neck) and can be tightly sealed.

Instead of putting this in 4-litre flasks it would be preferable to have it already in the bin. This would require a bin with clear graduations and a close fitting lid which would allow water in and keep dust out. For ease of operation it is suggested that after 13 litres of distilled water have been collected in the bin, a 4-litre flask be used, so that this excess can be used for accurate mixing and swilling implements, etc.

Layout

Integrating the recommendations above, the proposed layout of the sterile pre-paration room is included. Here, it will be noted that the original flow production layout has been discarded with the result that the area required for doing this job is considerably reduced enabling the remainder of the space to be used for other purposes.

This is a practical demonstration of the way in which the evaluation of alternatives can be done on a relatively simple methods problem where the costs involved are not major and the main result is improvement in the use of staff time.

Developing new systems for offices, on the other hand, is concerned with directing attention at the information requirements of the system. In part it will involve the redesign of forms for the transmission of data, whether associated with a computer or not. In this case the question that must be asked frequently is: What would happen if we did not have this data/information? If the answer is 'nothing' or the effect is little then the answer is obvious.

The reverse of this is of course to provide much better information than before. However, the specification of 'what?' and 'with what frequency?' is critical to avoid a situation in which people are bombarded with information. As an example, a group of supervisors in a multinational organisation were asked to bring along all the information that they dealt with and comment on what value it had. Many complained about receiving superb computer printouts of past activities which were accurate but three weeks old. Their real information was in their notebooks! Remember also the words of Robert Townsend (1970) on 'memorandum – the last':

> ... There is no way to reply to [a memo] in real time, or engage it in
> dialogue. Murder by memo is unacceptable crime in large organisations,

and a zealous user of the xerox machine gun can copy down dozens of otherwise productive people . . . .

One of the worst examples of methods improvement in the public sector is enhancing work methods for one group such as administration in a hospital and ignoring the effect that this could have on other groups such as medical and nursing staff. By way of further example, in a technical college a group of consultants suggested such things as:

Absentee Records
The students' absentee reports to employers represent a considerable volume of work on the part of the junior clerk: registers need to be searched and cards need to be made out. The simplest way to transmit the information to employers with least drain on admin and teaching time is for each lecturer to write the name of each absentee student, the firm and date on card when calling the register.

Since the lecturing staff were not part of this enquiry you can imagine that such a proposal did not get very far!

Sometimes ideas for methods improvement can go too far. On a not too serious level consider the proposals in Table 4.1.

ACTIVITY

Consider 'correspondence costs' within your own organisation. Most organisations deal with a number of letters each day, and although there is not a great deal anyone can do to prevent people writing in with poor information, too many words, etc., thus wasting time, we can influence the costs of producing letters within the organisation itself. Think about the many ways in which total costs could be reduced: consider the manager designing the letter and the secretarial function, including capturing the ideas, typing or word processing, filing, delivery, etc.

The ideas you produce could include:

Reducing planning time	– Use standard or guide letters
Reducing reading time	– Plain letters
Reducing writing time	– Informal replies, avoid hand-drafting, train dictators, use telephone
Reduce reviewing time	– Identify routine and prestige letters and deal with them appropriately
Reduce typing time	– Train typists, use window envelopes, use word processing to ease corrections
Reduce delivery and reply time	– Attention slips, clear addressing, catching post
Reduce filing time	– Limit copies, use informal replies, question circulation lists, throw away routine actioned correspondence.

There are a number of well developed ideas for reducing correspondence costs that have not been adequately explored by organisations because 'we have always done it this way'. For example, 'informal replies' include the reply memo which asks for

Table 4.1 The triumph of improvements in work methods.

Procedural improvements in operations are now reasonably well accepted activities. The application of creative imagination in this direction has produced the following report by a work study officer who took time off recently to visit a symphony concert at the Royal Festival Hall in London . . . .

1. For considerable periods the four oboe players had nothing to do. The number should be reduced and the work spread more evenly over the whole of the concert, thus eliminating peaks of activity.

2. All twelve violins were playing identical notes; this seems unnecessary duplication. The staff of this section should be drastically cut. If a larger volume of sound is required, it could be obtained by means of electronic apparatus.

3. Much effort was absorbed in the playing of demi-semi-quavers; this seems to be an unnecessary complication. It is recommended that all notes should be rounded up to the nearest semi-quaver. If this were done, it would be possible to use trainees and lower-grade operatives more extensively.

4. There seems to be too much repetition of some musical passages. Scores should be drastically pruned. No useful purpose is served by repeating on the horns a passage which has already been handled by the strings. It is estimated that if all redundant passages were eliminated the whole concert time of two hours could be reduced to twenty minutes. Moreover, there would be no need for an interval half way through the concert.

5. It is felt that further review might yield additional benefits. For example, there seems to be still wide scope for application of the 'questioning attitude' to many of the methods of operation, as they are in many cases traditional and have not been changed for several centuries. In the circumstances, it is remarkable that work study principles have been adhered to as well as they have. For example, it was noted that the pianist was not only carrying out most of his work by two-handed operation, but was also using both feet for pedal operation. Nevertheless, there were excessive reaches for some notes on the piano and it is probable that redesign of the keyboard to bring all notes within the normal working area would be of advantage to this operator. In many cases the operators were using one hand for holding the instrument, whereas the use of a fixture would have rendered the idle hand available for other work.

6. It was noted that excessive effort was being used occasionally by the players of wind instruments, whereas one air compressor could supply adequate air for all instruments under more accurately controlled conditions.

7. Obsolescence of equipment is another matter into which it is suggested further investigations could be made, as it was reputed in the programme that the leading violinist's instrument was already several hundred years old. If normal depreciation schedules had been applied, the value of this instrument should have been reduced to zero, and it is probable that purchase of more modern equipment could have been considered.

routine information on the left-hand side of a sheet allowing the respondent to put the answers on the right-hand side. These can be used for internal memos as well as routine letters asking about prices, delivery, times, etc. Two NCR copies can be sent to the recipient who will write or type the reply and keep one copy for reference, sending the other back to the enquirer. Both parties now have full details, in less words and there is only one piece of paper in the files instead of two. The cost of filing space halved would be of benefit to all organisations. Many replies can also be written on the original letter and the whole photocopied and returned so that, again, only one copy of the correspondence is kept.

Such ideas are always applauded by people as recognisably better methods of working, but very few organisations have the courage to implement them!

INSTALL NEW SYSTEM

If the development stage has been done in conjunction with the people within the system – which if the operations manager has been involved is most likely the case – then the day when the revised system commences will provide very few difficulties. In many cases the new system will require new equipment, new technology, etc., which will need careful planning as regards its installation and the training of staff. A very simple plan using a bar chart (see Figure 4.8) was provided for an oil blending firm in which the 'production element' was linked with sales, transport and office activities to form a composite plan. More complex changes are covered in Chapter 12, and the section on project network techniques in Chapter 3, page 53, will also be of value. Part of the installation procedure will be to specify exactly what work individuals involved in the new system will undertake. This can best be done by producing a *work specification*. This is defined in BS 3138 (1979) as:

> A document setting out the details of an operation or 'job', how it is to be performed, the layout of the workplace, particulars of machines, tools and appliances to be used, and the duties and responsibilities of the worker.

The purpose of work specification is:

1. To enable those concerned to control operations and to ensure approved methods are actually used.
2. To present work details in clear, concise written form to those concerned who perform it or are affected by it, so that questions may be settled without difficulty.
3. To link the methods with time standards (if such need to be issued) (see Chapter 5).

This is absolutely essential to ensure that managers are aware of any changes in methods which will inevitably affect the time scale of operations and thus have an effect on planning.

ENSURE NEW SYSTEM IS PROPERLY MAINTAINED

Written into the work specification should be details on the frequency of checking the method after it has been installed. The method of checking will depend on the importance of the job.

The need for maintenance of a standard method is based on the concept of *drift*. Whenever any method is introduced its fine detail will depend on all the associated circumstances. If any of the circumstances change – and in practice they almost

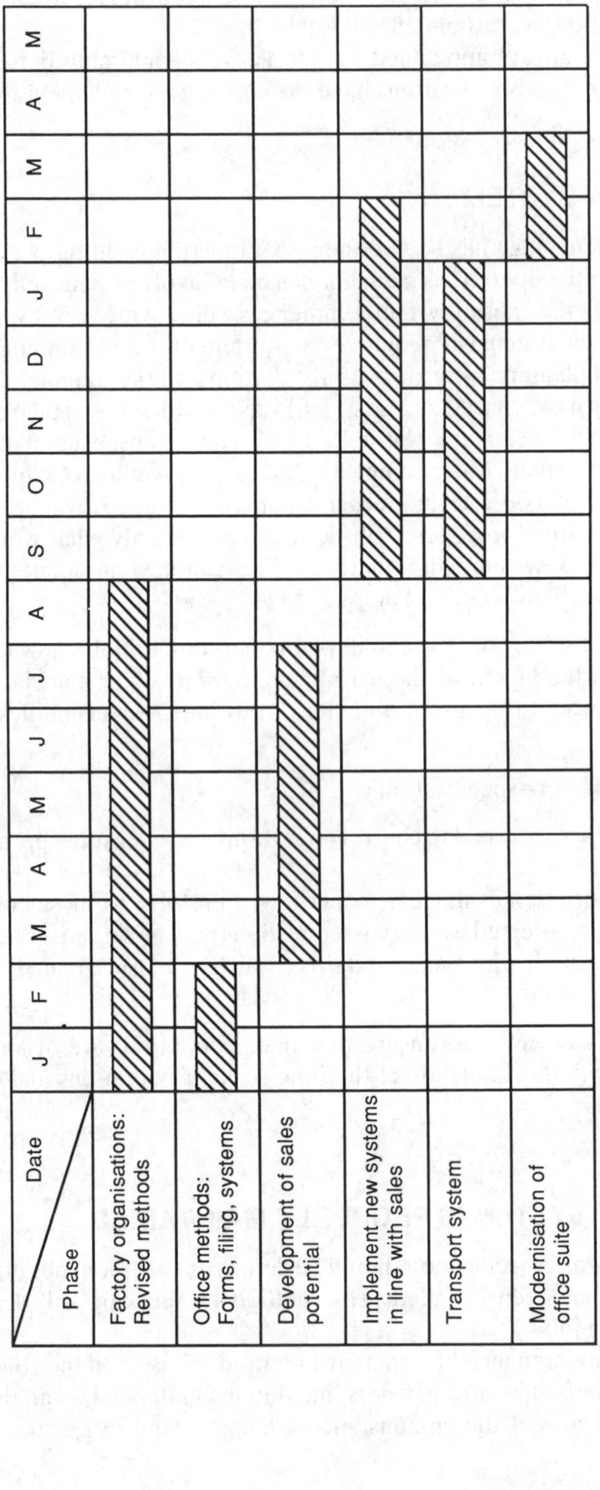

Date / Phase	J	F	M	A	M	J	J	A	S	O	N	D	J	F	M	A	M
Factory organisations: Revised methods		▨	▨	▨	▨	▨	▨	▨									
Office methods: Forms, filing, systems		▨	▨														
Development of sales potential					▨	▨	▨										
Implement new systems in line with sales									▨	▨	▨	▨	▨	▨			
Transport system									▨	▨	▨	▨	▨				
Modernisation of office suite														▨	▨		

Figure 4.8 Simple plan for introducing a new system into an oil blending firm

invariably do – then the details of the method will gradually drift away from that laid down in the specification. These changes may be introduced consciously or unconsciously by the operatives concerned.

When the check is carried out the manager can classify his findings in one of three ways:

1. No changes have occurred.
2. Changes of an advantageous nature have occurred.
3. Changes of a deleterious nature have occurred.

In the first case no action is required unless a further method improvement is desirable. In the second case the advantageous alternatives should be built into the standard method. In the third case there are two possible courses of action which may be followed. The standard method may be reintroduced, or a new study may be carried out. If the latter is accepted then particular reference should be paid to the reasons for the occurrence of the changes.

SPECIAL FEATURES OF SERVICE ORGANISATIONS

We have used the term work system design, but have narrowly defined it in terms of resource productivity and customer satisfaction. The application of these ideas has tended to create repetitive de-skilled jobs within factory and some service operations and so the attention of readers is drawn to *job design* (or *redesign*).

Job design may be defined as 'the alteration of the contents, the methods and the relationships of jobs to satisfy the requirements of the technology and organisation as well as the social and personal requirements of job holders' (Davies, 1966). A manager actively involved in redesigning jobs in one of the country's major nationalised industries summarised his beliefs in the following way:

> By work structuring, I mean the creation of a work environment in which there is an opportunity for participants to develop to their full potential as human beings and produce efficiently and competitively.

Therefore, the opportunities for full work redesign may well be applied when there is a need for working methods to be developed.

There are particular dangers for the service sector when considering ways of introducing a production-type approach. These involve thinking of 'service' as 'servitude' (Levitt, 1972). In a later article Levitt (1976) considers the industrialisation process further to grasp opportunities for service improvement.

Lovelock and Young (1979) explore the ways in which consumers can increase productivity. These are really marketing strategies, but because of the link between operations and marketing, they can equally be considered as systems improvement. They include a checklist for identifying opportunities for improving productivity consisting of questions such as:

1. Do your customers have waiting time and could this be used to improve the service delay?
2. Are employees doing mechanical repetitive work that could be done by customers?

3. Could the face-to-face meeting of customer and service personnel be avoided?

The last of these questions was developed by Chase (1978) in which he put forward the view that the less direct contact the customer has with the service system, the greater the potential of the system to operate at peak efficiency. He then goes on to classify systems by degree of contact (high or low) and also provides a number of useful questions which are concerned with the methods of service delay.

Normann (1984) considers 'the client as market and co-producer' and includes a useful checklist which is reproduced with permission in Table 4.2.

Table 4.2 Examples of some questions in 'client management'.

1. Can the timing of demand be influenced?
2. Does the customer have spare time while he is waiting?
3. Do clients and contact personnel meet unnecessarily face to face?
4. Are such contacts used to maximum effect?
5. Are contact personnel doing repetitive work which the customer could do himself, for example with customer-operated machines?
6. Do the clients sometimes try to 'get past' the contact personnel and do things themselves? Could that interest and knowledge be better utilised?
7. Do the customers show interest in and knowledge about the tasks of the contact personnel?
8. Is there a minority of customers which disturbs the service delivery system and its effectiveness?
9. Do the customers ask for information which is available elsewhere?
10. Can the customers do more work for each other, or use the resources of third parties?
11. Can part of the service delivery process be relocated to decrease, for example, the cost of premises?
12. Can the customer be given an opportunity to choose between service levels?

Source: Normann, R., Service Management: Strategy and Leadership in Service Businesses, Copyright 1984 R. Normann. Reprinted by permission of John Wiley & Sons, Ltd.

All the research and ideas discussed in this chapter should be considered in the approach shown in Figure 4.2 as 'previous work in this field by self and others'.

References and suggested reading

Briscoe, G. (June 1976) Management correspondence. *Management Services*, **20** (6), pp. 10–14.

Chase, R. B. (1978) Where does the customer fit in a service operation? *Harvard Business Review*, pp. 13–18.

Close, G. (1960) *Work Improvement*. New York: John Wiley.

Collier, D. A. (1985) *Service Management – The Automation of Services*. Reston, VA: Reston Publishing Co.

Davies, L. E. and Taylor, J. C. (1966) *The Design of Jobs*. Harmondsworth, Middx: Penguin Modern Management Readings.

Hayes, C. (November 1968) Job redesign. *Management Services*, **12** (11), pp. 4–7.

ILO (1974) *Introduction to Work Study*. Geneva: International Labour Office.

Kodak Ltd (1965) *How To Answer Business Letters Without Really Trying*. London: Kodak.

Laidhams, D. E. (1964) Looking for trouble. *Work Study and Management*, **8**.

Lehrer, R. N. (1957) *Work Simplification*. Englewood Cliffs, NJ: Prentice-Hall.

Lehrer, R. N. (1965) *The Management of Improvement*. New York: Reinhold.

Levitt, T. (September/October 1972) Production line approach to service. *Harvard Business Review*.

Levitt, T. (September/October 1976) The industrialization of service. *Harvard Business Review*.

Lewis, B. N., Horabin, I. S. and Gawe, C. P. (1967) *Flow Charts, Logical Trees and Algorithms*. Casocc Paper No. 2. London: HMSO.

Lovelock, C. and Young, R. F. (May/June 1979) Look to consumers to increase productivity. *Harvard Business Review*, pp. 168–178.

Milward, J. G. (1969) *Municipal Work Study*. London: BIM.

Nadler, G. (1967) *Work Design – The Ideals Concept*. Homewood, IL: Irwin.

Nadler, G. (1970) *Work Design – The Systems Concept*. Homewood, IL: Irwin.

Normann, R. (1984) *Service Management*. Chichester: John Wiley.

Raybould, E. B. (1966) The role of creativity in problem-solving. *Work Study and Management*, **10** (12), pp. 634–640.

Townsend, R. (1970) *Up the Organisation*. London: Coronet.

APPENDIX: MANAGEMENT SERVICES SPECIALISMS

Management services

A management function containing those specialist skills appropriate for an organisation at a specific time, which provide a problem-solving advisory service to management at all levels. Such advice is aimed at assisting the management more effectively to achieve the objectives of the organisation, in particular profitability, cost effectiveness and productivity.

(Harris, 1978)

Work study and Organisation and methods (O&M)

The systematic examination of activities in order to improve the effective use of human and other material resources.

Work study

A management service based on those techniques, particularly method study and work measurement, which are used in the examination of human work in all its contexts, and which lead to the systematic investigation of all the resources and factors which affect the efficiency and economy of the situation being reviewed, in order to effect improvement.

O&M

A management service the object of which is to increase the administrative efficiency of an organisation by improving procedures, methods and systems, communications and controls, and organisation structure.

Method study

The systematic recording and critical examination of ways of doing things in order to make improvements.

Work measurement

The application of techniques designed to establish the time for a qualified worker to carry out a task at a defined rate of working.

Work performance control

The application of work measurement techniques with other information to the appraisal of results and payment for work.

Value analysis

A systematic interdisciplinary examination of factors affecting the cost of a product or service, in order to devise means of achieving the specified purpose most economically at the required standard of quality and reliability.

Project network techniques (PNT)

A group of techniques for the description, analysis, planning and control of projects which consider the logical interrelationships of all project activities. The group includes techniques concerned with time, resources, costs and other influencing factors, e.g. uncertainty.

Note: The terms 'program evaluation and review technique' (PERT), 'critical path analysis' (CPA) and 'critical path method' (CPM) refer to particular techniques and should not be used as synonyms for PNT.

Ergonomics

The study of the relationship between man and his occupation, equipment and environment, and particularly the application of anatomical, physiological and psychological knowledge to the problems arising therefrom.

Operational research

The application of the methods of science to complex problems arising in the direction and management of large systems of men, machines, materials and money in industry, business, government and defence.

Note: The distinctive approach is to develop a model of the system, incorporating measurements of factors such as chance and risk, with which to predict and compare the outcomes of alternative decisions, strategies or controls. The purpose is to help management determine its policy and action scientifically.

Systems analysis

Activity, process or study of critically examining the ways of performing frequently occurring tasks that depend on the movement, recording or processing of information (i.e. data processing) by a number of people within an organisation.

(French and Saward, 1977)

Computers

A device which can automatically perform data processing tasks according to instructions (programs) that are stored and can be altered within the device.

(French and Saward, 1977)

Work simplification

A systematic analysis of all factors affecting work being done, or all factors that will affect work to be done, in order to save effort, time or money.

(Lehrer, 1957)

Sources

Unless specified otherwise the above are from:

BS 3138 *Glossary of Terms Used in Work Study and Organisation and Methods* (1969 and 1979). London: British Standards Institution.

Other sources are as follows:

French, D. and Saward, H. (1977) *Dictionary of Management*. London: Pan.
Harris, N. D. (August 1978) Management services – a definition. *Management Services*, **22** (8), pp. 4–9.
Lehrer, R. N. (1957) *Work Simplification*. Englewood Cliffs, NJ: Prentice-Hall.

5
CAPACITY

INTRODUCTION

Any operations manager will wish to know how much work the unit can cope with. This is a function of time, resources, scheduling and cost. The questions that need to be answered are:

1. How much work can we deal with using existing resources?
2. What effect would be produced by a change in resources (e.g. more or less people, better equipment, new technology)?
3. How do we cope with peaks and troughs in demand?
4. What effect would be produced by a change in methods of working (see Chapter 4)?
5. When do we need to change the number of resources to cope with increases in demand or a reduction in demand?

Many of the above questions are vital to the effectiveness of any operational unit. It is fair to say, however, that in manufacturing industry it is easier to see the link between output and resources, so that if we are able to get market information on a given product, resources can be precisely engineered to meet a given demand. Any changes in demand for a product can be accommodated by the use (amongst other strategies) of stocks of finished products as a buffer between an uncertain demand and a steady rate of production.

In the service sector, on the other hand, many activities are customer driven and there is a tendency for more frequent peaks and troughs. In some cases the customer may be prepared to wait ('customers in stock'), e.g. library book discharging, bus and taxi queues, hairdressers, out-patients. Such problems can sometimes be reduced by appointment systems, but even these require some estimate of the time content of work.

In some clerical work the increase/decrease in demand is less obviously noticed. A gradual increase over a number of months could result in:

1. an obvious backlog,
2. less high quality work,
3. overtime or stress for all concerned.

There could also be a cost element involved here in that if you allow unrestricted overtime the cost of the unit is increased.

Where work is being done in any capacity there is a need for the operations manager to have a clear idea as to the time scale of operations so that suitable strategies can be adopted to cope with demand changes. For example, a real capacity problem can be posed for local newsagents during school half-terms when most of the paper delivery staff may go on holiday with their parents. Often by using members of their own families the job can be done, albeit not in the usual timescale.

ACTIVITY

Define capacity in terms of an organisation with which you are familiar. Consider for example:

1. a college
2. a funeral director
3. a dentist
4. a painter and decorator

This chapter comprises two major sections. The first considers *time/work measurement techniques*, and gives a brief explanation of the various ways in which work can be measured. Included within this are less precise measurement techniques which can be of particular use to the service sector. We then go on to consider the *uses of work measurement standards and data* to show how the operations manager can use the above information to obtain better resource productivity. It is quite likely that the detailed derivation of standards will be carried out by a *work measurement practitioner*, but nevertheless it is important that the operations manager knows how such standards are derived, so that questions as to their validity can be properly formulated.

TIME/WORK MEASUREMENT

Work measurement provides management with a means of measuring the time taken to perform a task. It therefore provides a yardstick for human effort. (It can also be used for measuring work that is 'machine controlled', but since this is much easier the more difficult measurement of 'people controlled' work will be the focal point of our discussion.) It has two aims: to identify and eliminate any ineffective time, and to set sound time standards.

Work measurement is defined in BS 3138 (1979) (10003) as:

> The application of techniques designed to establish the time for a quali-
> fied worker to carry out a specified task at a defined level of performance.

Method study's function is to improve working methods by eliminating unnecessary operations and waste of all kinds. As defined, therefore, work measurement includes those aspects of work study which are outside the province of method study. Nevertheless it must not be thought of as a watertight compartment of work study. It is obviously futile to measure the work content of a job unless the method by which the work is being carried out is satisfactory. It follows therefore that good method study should precede work measurement unless time is a major factor in analysing the method, in which case the appropriate measurement technique will be used as part of the method investigation.

The qualified worker referred to in the definition above is defined (34002) as:

One who:

(a) is accepted as having the necessary physical attributes,

(b) possesses the required intelligence and education,
(c) has acquired the necessary skill and knowledge,

to carry out the work in hand to satisfactory standards of safety, quality and quantity.

To define a level of performance, reference can be made to standard performance (34001):

> The rate of output qualified workers will naturally achieve, without over-exertion, as an average over the working day or shift, provided they know and adhere to the specified method, and are motivated to apply themselves to their work.

Deriving a standard time

The second function of work measurement, setting sound time standards, is probably more important than that of revealing ineffective time, though the two are linked. Once set, the standards are effective for the life of the job, and their application will show up any ineffective time or addition to the work content.
   Standard time is defined (BS 3138: 35010) as:

> The total time in which a job should be completed at standard performance (i.e. basic time plus relaxation allowances plus contingency allowances for delay).

In deriving a standard time it is essential to:

1. use the correct measurement technique;
2. obtain an accurate specification of the job under study;
3. record the time taken accurately;
4. have a clear concept of standard rating;
5. use an accurate means of assessing relaxation allowance;
6. use an accurate means of assessing other applicable allowances.

We comment on the above requirements in the following subsections.

Work measurement techniques

There are a number of methods of measuring work depending upon the precision required. These are given in Figure 5.1.
   Generally speaking more accuracy is required when the total cycle time is very short. This would be noticeable in service operations that move towards the repetitive nature of 'production', i.e. preparing parts of school meals in a central kitchen, chambermaid work in a hotel, cleaning offices and schools, etc. However, it is unusual for service work to be confined to the 'bench-top' and so it is not unrealistic to use time study and PMTS for prime data collection.
   However, with some public utilities such as gas and electricity, there are a number

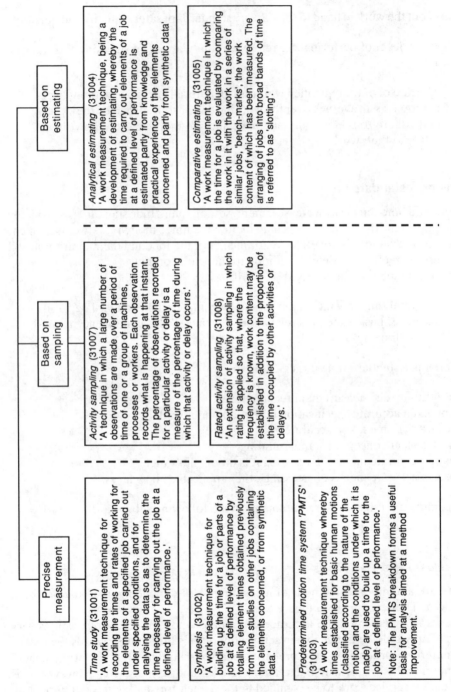

Precise measurement

Time study (31001)
'A work measurement technique for recording the times and rates of working for the elements of a specified job carried out under specified conditions, and for analysing the data so as to determine the time necessary for carrying out the job at a defined level of performance.'

Synthesis (31002)
'A work measurement technique for building up the time for a job or parts of a job at a defined level of performance by totalling element times obtained previously from time studies on other jobs containing the elements concerned, or from synthetic data.'

Predetermined motion time system 'PMTS' (31003)
'A work measurement technique whereby basic human motions times established for (classified according to the nature of the motion and the conditions under which it is made) are used to build up a time for the job at a defined level of performance.'

Note: The PMTS breakdown forms a useful basis for analysis aimed at a method improvement.

Based on sampling

Activity sampling (31007)
'A technique in which a large number of observations are made over a period of time of one or a group of machines, processes or workers. Each observation records what is happening at that instant. The percentage of observations recorded for a particular activity or delay is a measure of the percentage of time during which that activity or delay occurs.'

Rated activity sampling (31008)
'An extension of activity sampling in which rating is applied so that, where the frequency is known, work content may be established in addition to the proportion of the time occupied by other activities or delays.'

Based on estimating

Analytical estimating (31004)
'A work measurement technique, being a development of estimating, whereby the time required to carry out elements of a job at a defined level of performance is estimated partly from knowledge and practical experience of the elements concerned and partly from synthetic data'

Comparative estimating (31005)
'A work measurement technique in which the time for a job is evaluated by comparing the work in it with the work in a series of similar jobs, 'bench-marks', the work content of which has been measured. The arranging of jobs into broad bands of time is referred to as 'slotting'.'

Figure 5.1 Methods of work measurement

of repetitious activities and different regions have undertaken to develop precise standards for specific activities. These standards are then placed into a 'databank' from which data can be built up by synthesis. Similar exchange of basic data is done by local authorities. This can save a lot of effort in developing standards and time study can be used to cover those parts of the work activity which are unique to the particular organisation.

Specification of job

This is essential for any form of measurement since you need to know *what* you are measuring. Such a specification should identify quality and safety standards (see Chapter 4).

Accurate recording

This is of course fundamental. The precision is based on the type of measurement method used, but accuracy in the conduct of the measurement is essential if the resultant standards are going to be of value.

Rating

Figure 5.2 shows that the observed time in some work measurement techniques is modified by a *rating factor*. This is designed to account for variations in performance between operators and also different times of the day/week.

Rating is that process during which a time study practitioner compares the performance of the operator with the observer's trained concept of effective performance, expressed by means of numbers in accordance with a rating scale. This scale usually runs from 0 to 100 where 100 is the standard rate.

Allowances

Figure 5.2 also shows that part of the standard time includes appropriate allowances for:

1. *Relaxation*. This is based upon the demands of the job, so that a person doing work in a light, pleasant environment like an office will require less relaxation allowance than heavy manual work performed outdoors, like gardening. However, if VDU work is conducted in an office this could affect the relaxation allowance, since it may be a cause of eye strain.
2. *Other allowances*. These will vary but can include allowances for materials, delays, changeovers of machines, coping with several machines together, etc.

We can see from the above discussion that work values must be comprehensively determined. We next turn our attention to a major part of the service sector – office work.

WORK MEASUREMENT IN THE OFFICE

> *Work expands so as to fill the time available for its completion.*
>
> 'Parkinson's Law' (*Parkinson, 1958*)

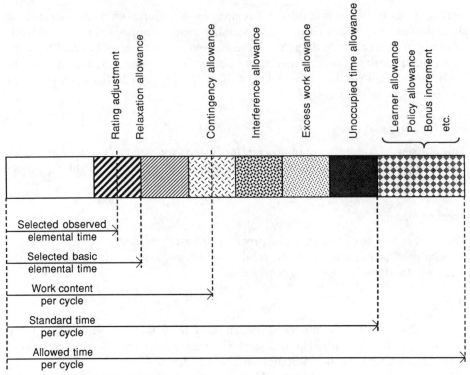

Figure 5.2 Relationship between basic, standard and allowed times
(Not drawn to scale – it is rare for allowances in total to be greater than the work content)
Notes
1. Rating may increase or reduce observed time.
2. Contingency allowance may be inside or outside work content.
3. Performance of operation in less than standard time represents a saving to the organisation; in more than standard time, a loss.
4. Note particularly the way in which various allowances are shown and that while affecting the overall time for the job they are excluded from the work content.
5. The need for such allowances is an indication that labour and/or machine capacity is not being fully utilised. Showing them in this way should constantly draw attention to this fact.

Difficulties in clerical work measurement

Although in recent years there has been a recognition that all human work can be measured, it is not sufficient that accepted work measurement techniques should be applied in offices without some consideration being given to both the psychological problems and the mechanics of application resulting from the differences between manual and office work.

Because of the nature of clerical work there are many obstacles put in the path of the investigator. However, these are not insurmountable and in many instances are no more severe than those encountered in measuring other types of service work. Nevertheless we discuss them below so that the situation is not oversimplified.

Mental work

This is involved in most clerical operations, although it is sometimes exaggerated. The type of mental activity referred to may result from lack of correct training, or no method specification, causing the operator to spend time on making decisions. A large number of clerical operations, however, are very little different from those in the factory in terms of mental work. All jobs will require skills, attention and aptitude. However, a recognition that decision-making may enter into the work studied is important, because of the care required in conducting an operation of this kind.

Qualifications of observer

It follows from the above that observations should only be carried out by people who understand the process. Otherwise, when a clerk examines a document, the observer will be unable to determine whether the operation is necessary. It may take some time for an investigator to get familiar with the process.

Ancillary work

All the work involved in a transaction may not be carried out at the same time as the basic operations. Queries involve telephone calls, letters and personal contact, and may comprise up to 20% of the mental work involved.

Expense

Because of the preceding two subsections the cost of clerical work study can be high. Another reason for high cost is the need to ensure a sufficiently adequate sample due to the inherent variability in much clerical work.

Control of quality

This is the long-standing problem involved when standards of output are set since quality standards may suffer. This can only be overcome by closely defining quality standards and implementing a method of quality control. The major difficulty here is the development of a time standard which allows for a reasonable amount of care, bearing in mind the expense of errors.

Approach to the clerical work study assignment

Although many of the difficulties mentioned above will present themselves, the correct briefing of people concerned and approach to individuals will do much to assist in alleviating these. The idea that people hate being rushed, love wasting time and resent the discipline that results from organised programmes of work measurement is not a verity. The purposeful use of time can be responsible for morale improvement.

General techniques for broad work measurement

In this group are a series of techniques which have been found to be valuable in providing work measurement data of approximate accuracy. The cost of such a study is small and may be sufficient for staffing purposes, to indicate if method changes are necessary and for labour control, where more involved and expensive studies cannot be used. (Another term is 'should-take' times. Of course these approaches are not restricted to office work and could be used for all types of service work where there is a great variety of activities.)

Use of output records

Where a job consists of relatively few simple tasks, accurately kept output records over a period of weeks will result in average times being worked out. This can be done for sections or individuals.

Simple timing

As opposed to time study which uses element breakdown and rating, this involves a series of studies of about 30–40 minutes of an operator carrying out a routine short-cycle task. Again, as a result of such studies, average times can be developed. In both this and the previous method reasons should be sought for greater varieties than ±10% in different results.

Use of personal time records

This is of particular value in an initial investigation where full details of every person's task is not known. The office personnel keep their own records of their activities over a period of several days and the data resulting from this can be used to determine average times. Since this technique is very much used, not only for measurement purposes, a detailed study step by step follows below.

1. *Step 1*. Determine a list of duties, and assign code letters to them. Units of work must also be defined to avoid miscounting.
2. *Step 2*. Design record forms – these will vary according to requirements.
3. *Step 3*. Hold meetings with personnel concerned and explain purpose of study and mechanics of record-keeping.
4. *Step 4*. Conduct spot-checks during study to ensure correct record maintenance.
5. *Step 5*. At the conclusion of the period of study use the data collected to determine average times per unit of output, or batch of units.

CASE STUDY

In a small office of an oil blending firm there were five staff:

- Senior administrator
- Two administrative assistants
- Junior assistant
- Secretary

The senior administrator had been with the firm for many years and undertook a vast amount of work, whilst the remaining group seemed to be under-utilised. This in part was due to lack of proper delegation and training, but nevertheless there was a need to establish a fair balance of work and to determine how much extra workload the team could cope with.

A personal time recording exercise was used as a basis for this. The sheet used is shown in Figure 5.3, together with the instructions for its completion.

Name				Date
Activity	Number of units	Time commenced	Time finished	Interruptions

Figure 5.3 Daily time sheet for personal recording

Objective

Time sheets are designed to keep a record of work in order that a fair and effective apportionment of duties can be developed.

Method of use

They should be filled in at the completion of one task and the start of another. Write down the task completed (i.e. typing invoices, entering customer record cards, etc.) and the number done. Show the time commenced and finished.

Since office work does suffer from a number of interruptions which are small, but nevertheless important, enter these alongside the task during which they occur. Suggested abbreviations are as follows:

    T – Telephone
    Q – Dealing with query
    O – Out of office
    I   – Miscellaneous interruptions

If possible note the number of minutes such interruptions took, i.e. T3, I5, etc.

Try to be as detailed as possible in your description of duties, and if you wish to make any comments on difficulties of tasks etc. please feel free to do so on the reverse of the sheet.

Value of data

When the data has been collected and analysed it will be possible to determine average times for certain routine tasks and also to gauge the frequency of interruptions. This will enable duties to be assigned and also assist in decisions regarding increases in staff as a result of any increased volume of work in the future.

As a result of the analysis it was possible to develop specific tasks for all of the jobs. For example

- Senior administrator:
  - Sort orders
  - Price orders
  - Record cards
  - Deal with queries
  - Supervise other staff, etc.
- Administrative assistant I:
  - Calculate orders
  - Type up working papers, etc.
- Administrative assistant II:
  - Check log sheets
  - Filing, etc.

USE OF WORK MEASUREMENT STANDARDS (AND DATA)

We have included 'and data' in brackets in the heading above to acknowledge that 'should-take' times, as suggested earlier, can be used in some aspects of office work rather than precise standards derived from more conventional measurement techniques.

Standards in any form are used by management to assist in making effective decisions regarding:

1. The design of a system (planning), and
2. The operation of a system (control).

The standard and the means of measuring it form the basis of the plan. When actual performance data is compared with the standard, any deviation is immediately seen and the best course of corrective action highlighted. Thus, when using standards, continual feedback of actual data is necessary to promote speedy remedial action if any is required.

Balancing capacity

Some form of *forecasting* will be used by many organisations to identify future demand for its services. In the public sector some organisations are also subject to budget cuts which represent limitations and again require decisions regarding what work will be done with reduced resources.

A very obvious example of the problem of balancing capacity and demand is a bus company coping with the early morning and late afternoon rush hours, with the difference in demand when the schools are closed and with a Saturday in summer when the local football team is playing at home. As you can imagine with a customer dominated demand such as this it is difficult to get a situation where all is balanced nicely. At off-peak times you will get empty buses, whilst at peak times conditions for passengers are not ideal. Some long-term planning can cope with the known factors and there is a need to have some contingency plans to cope with short-term pressures such as an overlong queue. These are often taken by the first-line managers.

There are many problems in service work of having to 'staff to peak'. In many service jobs this can be justified by staffing to peak if there is some customer led demand, and in using the remaining time on other parts of the job. For example, in a technical college, technician staff may be expected to show films, or staff video recording facilities up to a given demand. Use of a booking system limits the 'peak', but the need to provide other useful work is part of the job design.

Some peak demands which are seasonal (e.g. holiday catering) and/or have daily fluctuation (e.g. restaurants) can be dealt with by using part-time and casual staff. However, these decisions are often taken without any form of measurement and so when the information is available the decision as to how to cope with any imbalance can be more accurate.

Where capacity exceeds forecast, decisions must be made regarding the following:

1. Advertising to create demand – even within one's own organisation (e.g. a print department offering 'bargain rates' at certain times)
2. Extending the range or variety of services offered
3. Subcontracting your services to other organisations
4. Short-time working
5. Reduction of capacity

Where forecast exceeds capacity these decisions must be considered:

1. Shift working
2. Overtime working
3. Using other organisations to provide your service
4. Extending the resources – more manpower, space, machines
5. Prioritising work, so that some jobs are not done

One of the outcomes of having more capacity in service organisations is that 'work expands to fill the time available for its completion' or that less important activities are pursued. On the other hand, often when there is less capacity, a way of coping is by prioritising and it is often found that some activities were not so important at all. Thus there is a need to constantly reappraise objectives and their achievement.

Everyday use of time standards

1. *Loading and scheduling work.* This is to ensure full utilisation of resources, for example the scheduling of lorries, vans, buses, etc., in a health authority.
2. *Costing data.* Where labour content predominates and services need to be costed, whether for internal auditing or to sell services to outside clients (i.e. consultants).
3. *Dealing with the effect of unplanned interruptions to work.* When material supplies run out, machines break down or staff are absent there is a need to know how to continue to provide the service.
4. *Maintenance of plant.* If the major services have to be disrupted to allow mainten-ance then the effect of this can be planned, and work measurement data on how long the maintenance will take is also essential. Consider, for example, the effect

of the loss of vehicles to a taxi firm, or the closure of a washing machine in a laundry.

5. *Manpower planning.* As work increases or decreases in volume, so the labour force must be adjusted in order to keep the right cost balance. Other data used in this will be labour turnover, and absenteeism figures. This goes beyond merely using part-time or temporary staff but includes planning numbers of professional staff at all levels as in, say, a research and development department.

6. *Work balancing.* Closely associated with manpower planning, this is where work is carried out in teams and there is a need for a fair apportionment of work, e.g. the work of an electrical jointing team of three men. There are also examples of balancing work between men and machines, e.g. preparation, cooking and serving meals in a restaurant. The cooking part is inevitably 'machine controlled'.

7. *Alternative methods.* When different methods of work are possible the final choice may rest on the time factor, which will be linked to cost.

8. *Training standards.* When a person is being trained in certain skills, the ability must be related to the time which a task takes. Here the use of a learning theory is related to the time which the task should take when performed by a qualified operator.

9. *Payment systems.* If the organisation is going to provide some form of 'payment-by-results' system then the accuracy of standards is essential for this to operate correctly. (See also Chapter 13 for more detail on this.)

ACTIVITY

Consider work measurement in its broadest terms in an organisation of your choice. In how many ways would the data collected be used?

Work measurement brings knowledge of work. Through this knowledge factual decisions can be made and control exercised. It is essential that operations management use work measurement to its fullest.

UTILISATION OF RESOURCES

This central function of operations management is concerned with using the data so far gathered on systems design and capacity in order to plan and control operations. This will usually require developing some form of timetable or schedule. Within such a schedule it is necessary to ensure that all the resources are effectively utilised.

Whenever resources are being used it is good practice to plan for the highest possible utilisation and to ensure that some system of checking the actual use is implemented.

Scheduling

Scheduling is planning at the intermediate level. It comprises the preparation of a timetable of work for individual departments or sections, and is concerned with balancing resource requirements against resource availability. When the following information is established:

1. Time for tasks
2. Capacity of facility
3. Demand for product/service

it is possible to commence to schedule the tasks to the resources within the facility.

ACTIVITY

In what way is work scheduled in your organisation? Give an example of this.

Of course in some organisations – maybe your own – the way in which scheduling is carried out is haphazard. New jobs keep getting priority, resources fail to perform (e.g. through breakdowns, absences, lack of motivation, lack of supplies) and so planning seems to be limited. In a bus or railway company, the timing and scheduling of arrivals and departures is critical. The arrival of materials at a building site and the need for specialist skills (joiners, plasterers, etc.) dovetailing into the building work are also vital to avoid people waiting around.

Costs in service industries are crucial. One way of ensuring that unit costs are kept low is to ascertain that there is no excess work, no waiting time and that all facilities are, as far as possible, fully utilised.

Objectives

When starting to prepare a schedule it is important to determine what the objective is. This may seem obvious, but it is a point that is often overlooked. Perhaps the overriding objective is to arrange activities so that programmed completion dates are met. However, there are usually many possibilities and it is essential to ensure that the most suitable schedule is determined. It is therefore necessary to define the objectives clearly. Some of these are:

1. *To minimise costs.* The importance of taking an overall view is stressed. If minimising costs is a legitimate objective, it is possible to arrange the schedule so that this is achieved.
2. *To maximise physical resource utilisation.* If space and equipment are of prime importance, for example where it involves high capital investment and costly shut down procedures, this may be the key factor around which a schedule is constructed.
3. *To meet storage limits.* In certain cases the amount or cost of storage space may impose constraints on the scheduling process. This can apply in an activity such as running a garden centre or plant nursery where storage of plants is critical.
4. *To maximise manpower utilisation.* It may, in certain cases, be necessary to schedule work with the maximum use of operators as the major factor.
5. *To suit customers' needs.* Here the provision of transport at 'peak' times is an example.

In some cases the scheduling of facilities may be in direct conflict with quality of service. The frequency of refuse collection in a local authority is an example.

Objectives such as those listed above and others may all exist simultaneously and it is important to determine their order of priority before starting the scheduling exercise. It is stressed that overall organisation policies and objectives must be considered. Too narrow an approach leads to the construction of schedules which may be excellent from the operations point of view, but which ignore the effect on other areas such as materials, maintenance, personnel and finance.

Methods of scheduling

The key here is to link demand/forecast with available resources, having already established some work value. Many scheduling activities can be resolved by using a simple *bar chart* which shows the time across the top and the different facilities down the side. An example of this for a simple garage activity is shown at Figure 5.4. The timetable used for scheduling the work of a school or college is also a good example of a bar chart used for this purpose. (See also the implementation plan for method changes in Chapter 4.) A variety of computer software programs are also available for specific scheduling activities.

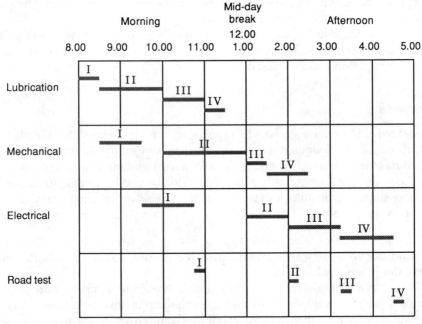

Figure 5.4 Bar chart for scheduling garage activity

CASE STUDY

The transport department of a firm is located at its headquarters which is situated three miles from the main production plant and about ten miles from the main stores, all three places being approximately on a straight line. The transport department has to move personnel between all three centres, supply the plant with materials from the store and remove finished products from the plant to the store. It also moves finished goods to the railway station, which is situated about twenty miles either from the plant or the stores. These commitments may be classified as follows:

1. Ten trucks are required on Mondays and Thursdays to transport goods to the railway station. The trucks finish unloading by lunch time.
2. Two truck loads are sent every day to move finished goods from the plant to the store.
3. Six truck loads are sent every second day to move materials from the store to the plant.
4. Transport of personnel is by means of private cars. Orders are sent at random to the transport department where all these cars are garaged.

The problems that have to be analysed are:

1. Should the transport department be centralised, with all vehicles and the maintenance garage situated at headquarters?
2. What is the best way to schedule removal of materials and finished goods?
3. Supposing that commitment 1 cannot be changed but commitments 2 and 3 can be conveniently distributed during the week (assuming a five day week), how many trucks are required if experience has shown that one truck is often marked down for repairs or maintenance?
4. Should trailers be purchased to relieve the load on trucks?
5. What procedures should be adopted to cater for passenger transportation under commitment 4?

ACTIVITY

How would you set about tackling these problems? What additional information do you require? How would you collect it, and what would you do with it when it is eventually available?

EXAMPLES OF MEASUREMENT AND SCHEDULING IN SERVICE ACTIVITIES

Work involving interaction with other people is difficult to record, analyse and measure. Much service work is customer driven, and so to illustrate how this difficulty can be overcome here are some brief examples. The first shows effective means of setting standards for:

1. Rent collectors
2. Meter readers
3. Salesmen of insurance (at regular houses)
4. Supervisors of above salesmen

These require extensive studies, first to determine what is done, and then to develop a suitable recording system. Sufficient data should be gathered to give adequate targets. For example, in a quote from Hamill (1985):

> Many useful performance targets for interactive work have been set by experience, evolution, trial and error, and on the basis of 'what I did when I was a . . .', for example the number of sales calls per day and the duration of a call. From a study of several thousand calls made by about 50 salesmen the following averages appeared for 'time at the clients' when selling one particular product:

Successful calls	20 minutes average
Unsuccessful calls	5 minutes average
Ratio of successful/unsuccessful calls	1 to 3
So total time	35 minutes per sale
Travelling time (varying with territory)	1/4 of time out selling

From the above a performance target for a 3-hour session (e.g. 2–5 p.m.), or a 4-hour session (e.g. 9 a.m. – 1 p.m.) could be set, e.g. for 4 hours:

Travelling 1/4	60 minutes average
At the client's	180 minutes average
Average number of sales (180/35)	5 sales
Average number of calls ($\times 4$)	20 calls

Above-average salesmen would set themselves higher targets (e.g. 7 sales).

Sales managers who were shown the figures might say: 'these are averages, I used to do better, but if everyone could achieve these averages, sales performance would improve by X% and they are factual. We can use them as a guide to poor salesmen.'

Another example is a hospital, an extremely complex organisational structure in which a good deal of the work performed is non-repetitive in nature. The work of all staff in wards could be identified by the conduct of a study in which random samples of activities were taken over a representative time period. The resultant data can be used to replan resources (see Torgerson (1959)).

CONCLUSION

By whatever means we are able to establish *capacity*, we are then more easily able to *control* the work, ensure *effective utilisation* of facilities and thus ensure both *resource productivity* and *customer satisfaction*.

References and suggested reading

Birn, S. A., Crossan, R. M. and Westwood, R. W. (1965) *Measurement and Control of Office Costs*. New York: McGraw-Hill.
Brearley, A. (1976) *The Control of Staff Related Overhead*. London: Macmillan.
British Standards Institution (1979) *Glossary of Terms Used in Work Study and Organisation and Methods*. BS 3138. London: BSI.

Bunker, L. (1964) *Measuring Office Work*. London: Pitman.

Currie, R. M. (1965) *The Measurement of Work*. London: BIM.

Grillo, E. V. and Berg, C. J. (1959) *Work Measurement in the Office*. New York: McGraw-Hill.

Hamill, B. J. (December 1985) Salesmen, supervisors and small offices – a case study in measurement. *Management Services*, **29** (12), pp. 8–13.

Milton, T. D. (February 1970) An activity sampling exercise. *Work Study and Management Services*, **24** (2).

Muzak (1970) *The Hidden Costs of Clerical Employment – Their Causes and Control*. London: Muzak.

Parkinson, C. N. (1958) *Parkinson's Law*. London: John Murray.

Torgerson, P. (May–June 1959) An example of work sampling in a hospital. *Journal of Industrial Engineering*.

Whitmore, D. (1970) *Measurement and Control of Indirect Work*. London: Heinemann.

6
LAYOUT AND HANDLING

INTRODUCTION

Layout and handling are part of the global 'methods of working' approach detailed in Chapter 4, and in fact the pharmacy example referred to on pages 65–76 had an element of layout and handling in its solution – the use of a string diagram. In that example the revised layout and reduction in handling was easily reached.

The reason for including a separate chapter specifically on layout and handling is that they have great potential for enhancing productivity within service facilities. There are few organisations where space is not a critical cost factor. The need to avoid excessive handling of, say, food in a kitchen or paper in an office is central to the operational effectiveness of the organisation.

Many service activities are moved physically as part of a re-organisation and frequently operations managers need to develop an optimum layout within their new location. The needs of the customer are also important, and much thought needs to be given to the design, for example, of pubs, restaurants, shops, interview rooms and the integration of waiting areas.

Layout and handling are totally interdependent and the analysis phase for the conduct of a handling/layout study in any organisation is shown in Figure 6.1. An explanation of the basic data developed for the above is shown in Table 6.1.

DEFINITION OF MATERIALS HANDLING

The process of handling materials is immediately recognisable as an activity which is costly. For many, the image of materials handling is the application of equipment ranging in complexity from a simple sack barrow to an integrated conveyor system in a flow production unit. Although the correct selection and application of equipment is often an integral part of achieving the most effective handling system, it is only one facet.

Because of the potential cost benefits to industry and the national economy as a whole accruing from effective handling methods the Department of Industry recognised materials handling as one of four industrial technologies which were to be promoted through awareness seminars, leaflets, a publications programme and considerable activity in education and training during the 1970s. As part of this campaign it provided a comprehensive definition which reads:

> Materials handling (management and technology) has three main aspects:

1. *Physical*. The movement, handling and storage of materials considered as a flow into, through and away from an enterprise.

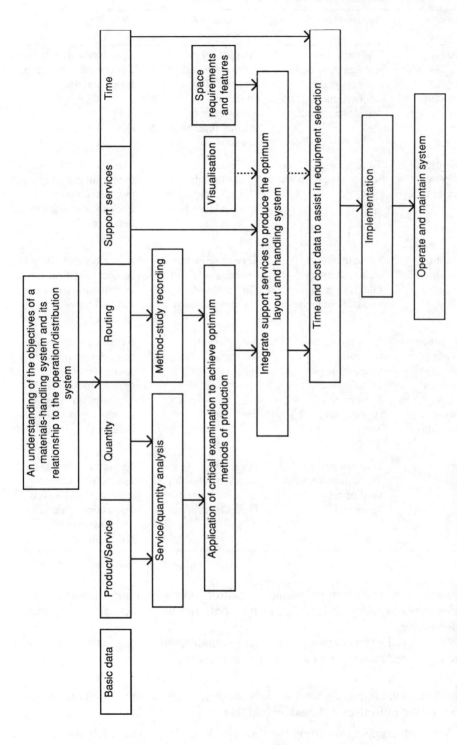

Figure 6.1 Analysis procedure for handling/layout procedures
Source: Harris and Mundy (1978). Reproduced with permission of the Controller, HMSO

Table 6.1 Guide to basic data requirements for handling analysis.

Factor	*Information needed*	*Where to find information*	*Remarks*
P Process/ service – what is to be provided and how	The variety of services provided, i.e. personal, international, transformational	Analysis of past service mix and forecast of future changes Knowledge of waiting time between customers	The more varied the mix the more complex is the analysis.
Q Quantity of process/ service types	Time for exact service type delivery	Projected volumes Peaks/troughs Daily, weekly and seasonal trends	The unit of measurement adopted must develop an effective comparison between different services.
R Routeing: sequence of service delivery	Some means of clearly showing material, customer and staff movements	Service sequence operations layout Direct observation via method study	Records should be subject to critical examination to ensure most effective sequence.
S Supporting services – what functions support process operations	Information and control Computing Distribution Personnel supervision Safety Security	Administration Transport Finance, etc.	Requirements should be reviewed frequently to cope with the dynamic nature of organisations and changes in external influences.
T Time	Forecast period Work measurement Cost of delays Schedules	Forecasts Standards developed by work study Direct measurement	The information is used to provide quantitative data on operations sequence and movement requirements.

Adapted from Harris and Mundy (1978).

2. *Management*. The effective planning, control, review and improvement of the movement, handling and storage of materials and the associated management information.
3. *Technology*. The techniques of movement, handling and storage of materials and the associated management and information systems.

This definition indicates what materials handling is and what its components are, but in terms of objectives it should be said that:

> Materials handling is getting the right goods and/or people safely to the right place at the right time at the right cost.

Materials handling is usually associated with production/manufacturing. To give an indication of its importance within service operations we will first provide a small industrial case study, then look at the office/administrative activity in detail and finally consider the importance of handling to ancillary/service operators with manufacturing.

CASE STUDY

The preparation department in a company manufacturing cotton wool had to weigh, roll and wrap cotton wool of different sizes and qualities. Difficulties in meeting increased production targets and a change in the balance of 'product mix' were causing problems. Rather than look at individual operations it was better to step back and look initially at the total system of material flow. This is the *physical* aspect. In what form and at what rate did the material arrive into the department? What delays occurred? What was the sequence of operations? What degree of back-tracking or other potential indicators of poor layout were there?

Having answered these and other questions in terms of present methods, attention was directed to the *management* of flow. Was it dependent upon considerable managerial intervention to keep production flowing? Was there a lot of documentation due to split batches? Were quality standards achieved?

Finally, attention was directed to the *technology*. Were bottlenecks formed by poor flow? Was handling between operations erratic and exhausting for the operative?

It was found to be possible to introduce better methods of handling material into the department, to regroup work activities and reduce in-process storage, to create linkages between processes (i.e. an overwrapping machine was able to feed directly to a conveyor which was used for packaging) and to provide a simple gravity chute for removal of finished cartons. Amongst the benefits were:

1. Improved plant productivity
2. Improved space utilisation
3. Lower handling costs
4. Improved labour utilisation (less interruptions to go and fetch and carry).

ADMINISTRATIVE AND OFFICE ACTIVITIES

As the volume of paperwork grows each day, many managers will be tempted to welcome any technique that can reduce the deluge and the associated costs. Techniques of organisation and methods, including systems design and form design, have made great strides in this area, but even so, a considerable amount of paperwork still remains to be produced, despatched, read, filed, transferred, written on, etc. Because paper tends to move around in discrete pieces such as reports and files, the sheer volume of movement is not always recognised, until perhaps you look at the amount of letters, memos, reports, etc. arriving at an organisation and also the amount despatched via the post office each day. Add to that the internal movement of paper and we are talking of a considerable volume and weight. Organisation and methods, as a specialism of management services, would be able to offer specialist advice on both the layout of offices, and methods of facilitating the movement and flow of paper.

This movement and flow of paper tends to be discontinuous and so aids to get paper from floor to floor in larger buildings (lifts, tilt tray elevators and pneumatic conveying between specific points) have been installed successfully in many organisations. Specialised aids for sorting, filing and storing are also available but a detailed analysis of the system will be necessary to ensure the best choice of method. Suffice it to say that the developments that have taken place in the handling of direct materials have been matched by similar developments designed for the handling and storage of paperwork.

For example, a recent installation at one of the major building societies utilised a form of stacker crane for retrieving house deeds in a large storage area devoted to this activity. Within a hospital a medical records department was running short of space and needed to extend the office, but after investigation the use of 'rol-store' type filing cabinets enabled the records to be stored and overcame the need for the extension. The 'rol-store' system enables a lot of filing cabinets to be banked together with the front rows laid on a conveyor track, allowing them to be moved to the left or right. Each row, except the back (fixed) row, will have one less cabinet than the width of the storage space, thus allowing a passage to be easily created to gain access to any of the cabinets behind. This system is particularly useful for records which need to be consulted infrequently. Similar systems are used for library storage of back numbers of journals. Such systems can also be powered if the height and weight so justify.

Some very obvious space savings can be achieved by the use of lateral filing systems or carousel filing systems in preference to normal drawer systems. Extensive use of the landscaped office has not only utilised space previously taken up by corridors, but has also assisted with workflow and communications and has improved working conditions.

The objective of any paper flow system must be to ensure that the administrative tasks can be completed as effectively as possible. George Sowerby, Managing Director of BTR, speaking at a Materials Handling Industry/Education Seminar, spoke of a total approach to materials handling, being concerned not only with the physical movement of goods, but also the paperwork. He stated that the aim should be to provide efficiency from tender to supply and that a customer should ideally receive two pieces of paper on his desk simultaneously – an invoice for the goods and a goods received note from the stores to indicate that the goods had arrived in perfect condition and on time. If this harmony between the physical handling and distribution system and the paperwork/information system can be achieved, it is likely that priority of payment will result, thus reducing the cash flow problems of the supplier.

ACTIVITY

Identify materials handling in an organisation of your choice. What is the method of movement? Is it reliant on handling technology? In what way is there any attempt to manage materials handling? Is it desirable in your opinion?

MATERIALS HANDLING AND ANCILLARY/SERVICE FUNCTIONS

In the preface we suggested that an important facet of the 'service sector' is the immediate support services within manufacturing industry. Although not much mention has been made of this group of services, the illustration of handling in this area will demonstrate how widespread the materials handling function is across the full spectrum of a manufacturing organisation.

Figure 6.2 shows the organisational areas affected by (and likely to influence) materials handling. Each of the concentric circles is numbered and the five outer circles are treated in separate sections within this chapter. The two centre circles (Groups 1 and 2) include the production/manufacturing system, immediately surrounded by 'materials in' and 'products and components out'. These together form the nucleus of the materials handling chain, i.e. are principal rather than ancillary functions. It is the other apparently less immediate areas which are to be discussed here in regard to their effects on and interactions with materials handling.

Group 3 consists of indirect materials, by-products, scrap, etc., by and large a neglected area and one in which real savings in cost can often be found.

Group 4 consists of logistic services – purchasing, packaging and transport. Purchasing determines or agrees the form, frequency and lot size in which goods arrive at the factory. Packaging prepares goods for movement, has a role in creating attractiveness and affects the mode of handling. Transport, which determines such items as frequency of departure, methods of loading, type of vehicle, etc., is clearly of vital concern to the handling system. Equally, effective materials handling is a key building block in any efficient transport or physical distribution system.

Group 5 is an advisory group – production engineering, management services and facilities management. This group is employed to provide analysis and advice for management on the effectiveness of operations. Their involvement with materials handling and their potential contribution to its cost effectiveness will be considerable. Managers will want to know how they can utilise these analytical skills to better effect in tackling handling problems. In smaller firms they may wish to utilise some of the techniques themselves in tackling their initial investigations.

Group 6 comprises the functional areas of design and research and development, and Group 7 includes the major functional areas of marketing, finance and personnel.

To illustrate the above, we will look at Group 3 and part of Group 4.

Group 3: Indirect materials, by-products and scrap waste

In the design of a production system, it is not sufficient just to be concerned with materials directly required for production. The system must also cope with indirect production materials. In engineering this implies tools, gauges, jigs, fixtures, lubricants, etc., and in other industries will include packaging materials, labels, adhesives, etc. If we are seeking to establish an optimum handling and storage system, then these items must be incorporated as an integral part, and not, as so often happens, be tacked on as an afterthought. The methods of handling the items concerned will largely be dictated by an analysis of the needs (the products, quantities, routeings, systems and timings) of the manufacturing system.

An important part of the indirect area is the 'necessary evil' of scrap or waste in its

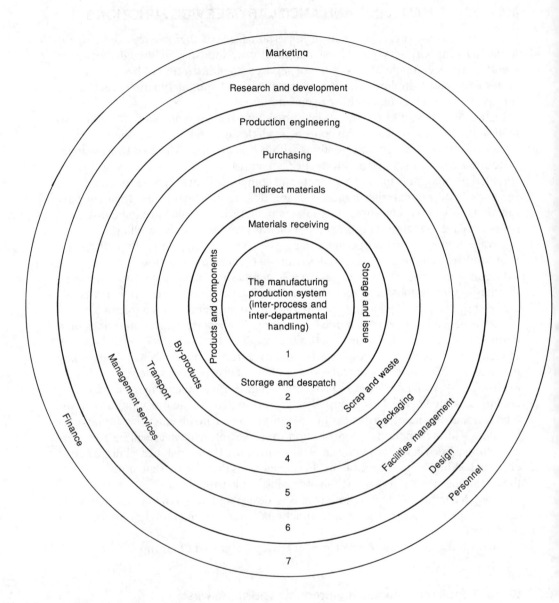

Figure 6.2 Organisation areas affected by materials handling
Source: Hesketh, Hollier and Webb (1982). Reproduced with the permission of the Controller, HMSO

many forms which has to be collected, moved, sorted and sometimes packaged before being transported away from the plant. In some cases it is obvious – a litter of swarf on the floor, for example – but in others it is less obvious, e.g. sump oil. Today the range of equipment for handling waste and aiding its eventual disposal is versatile and extensive: conveyors, pulverisers, vibrators, separators, shredders, shears, compactors, balers, incinerators, skips and skip loaders, special fork truck attachments and containers and bins, all designed to meet most needs. In terms of effective 'waste management' the objectives must be to ensure the waste itself is in a manageable and, if possible, saleable form, and to avoid the need to handle dangerous and difficult bulky material without proper aids.

This area of materials handling is worth detailed consideration since the costs and hazards of disposal can often be reduced, and the Health and Safety at Work Act will affect any particularly dangerous waste disposal. There are often opportunities to reclaim waste or to make it a more marketable by-product. One consultancy company is alleged to have advised all its young consultants to 'Dig around the scrap heap as soon as you decently can – you should find enough savings in handling, storage or disposal to pay for your assignment. With that taken care of you can start real work for the client.'

Group 4: Transport and distribution

Physical distribution management covers a broad range of activities within a company. It is concerned with the efficient movement of goods both inwards to the point of manufacture and outwards from the end of the production line to the customer. The term 'total distribution concept' indicates the wide range of aspects covered. These include transport systems, warehousing, inventory management and order processing, with packaging and materials handling being closely related.

Clearly a high degree of co-ordination is necessary to achieve the smooth operation (and co-operation) of these components. The importance of each to the overall success of the business gives some indication as to why physical distribution is becoming a key activity, and yet its practice lags far behind its theory when one hears of fragmented approaches to the process of distribution. It is an area of activity which for some companies is likely to require frequent changes in the next decade and the handling element will be a crucial component of the total system. Some of the reasons for change are the increasing importance of customer service and product availability (helped by computer control), and pressures for lower prices forcing new, more direct and more efficient channels of distribution.

On the macro-scale of distribution, management companies have reviewed the provision of warehouses and depots, revising or redesigning them to provide a more comprehensive service. One company manufacturing and selling durable consumer products nationwide consisted of many divisions each operating independently which meant that customers were getting up to three deliveries per day from the different divisions of the same group. Resolving this required organisational changes to create a corporate distribution department and a single transport network.

At a micro-level, consideration of the provision of loading bays, design and size of vehicles, materials handling methods, etc., can also produce considerable savings and improvement in quality of the distribution service. In a public utility service delivering appliances to households, the design of the vehicles was found to be entirely inappropriate to the type of goods and delivery system. Redesign and re-equipment resulted in fewer vehicles, a more efficient service and lower costs.

The more immediate concerns for the operations manager on site are likely to be in relation to the loading and unloading of vehicles. Here methods of materials handling are of special importance and need to be related to the transport economies – lorry turn round time versus payload. Even this factor is not always obvious as was demonstrated in an oil distribution firm. Rising distribution costs led to an investigation of transport methods (including whether to distribute in bulk or by barrel), which in turn led to a complete reappraisal of the range of product blends. At the same time methods of handling drums, boxes, etc., were considered: the introduction of a fork lift truck reduced turn round time for local deliveries, and provided useful cost savings.

Good materials handling is one of the basic building blocks for an efficient physical distribution system. It can only be achieved if the design of the physical distribution system takes into account its integration with handling/layout.

LAYOUT PLANNING

Having investigated what needs to be handled and how, the layout of physical facilities can be planned within reason. Many service organisations operate from buildings or rooms which were either *never* purpose-designed or, if they were, the volume of activities has outgrown the original design. As Sherman (1973) said: ' . . . many organisations go for too long "making do" even though signs of poor space management abound'. Whether you decide to move to new premises, have them custom-built, or merely decide how much you need to add on to existing premises, some detailed analysis will be required – and if movement of materials and/or paper and/or people are critical then that too must be a part of the analysis.

To illustrate the importance of analysis let us consider the layout problems of a public house. The design and layout of such a service facility is important in that it contributes to a consumer's perception of the service. A particular pub may be renowned for its 'atmosphere', and those factors that contribute towards that atmosphere must be considered, i.e. the quality of furnishings, the use of pillars and partitions, the lighting, the style and image, etc. It is clear that an atmosphere that complements the food and drink enhances the value of the total service package.

Just as good design and layout can enhance the value of a service, bad design and layout can impede service operations and hamper the achievement of organisational goals. Assuming a public house had the goals of maximising turnover, customer satisfaction and profit, then a bar designed too short or the pumps positioned in the wrong place would have the effect of constraining the numbers of customers served at a particular time. The result of this would be a negative contribution to all the organisational goals.

It is therefore not unreasonable to consider design and layout as being important to the achievement of organisational goals, this being particularly so for the public house.

The layout problem

No general overall theory or rules exist when analysing and improving a particular layout problem. The multitude of factors involved that influence layout decisions are a result of decisions made on location, basic organisation of work and design capacity. These decisions are followed by numerous less significant but important decisions related to the selection and placement of equipment, space allocations and

flow patterns. One can therefore appreciate the vast number of alternative acceptable solutions that are always available. Thus it is not surprising that people have
relied heavily on intuition, experience and improvisation. There has, however, been
some progress in a more scientific treatment of the problem.

To begin a more scientific approach to layout planning it is necessary first to state
some broad objectives of what is to be achieved.

Objectives in layout planning

Wild (1984) suggests three main objectives in planning layouts:

1. *To reduce the cost of materials handling and movement.* As with most operating
   systems, the public house involves a number of physical flows, and the extent and
   cost of these flows are affected by the layout of facilities. The movement of
   customers and staff in a public house is also influenced by the layout of facilities,
   and an improved layout will result in a reduction in the distance and time
   consumed, and hence in the cost of such movements to the organisation.
2. *To reduce congestion and delay.* Delays in providing service and queues for
   service in a pub adds nothing to the value of the service, and even less to profit.
   Poor facilities layout is often a contributing factor to a suboptimum throughput
   time in a pub. Time spent by the customer waiting in the system generates no
   turnover. The objective therefore should be 'to minimise congestion and delay
   and thus provide for the more intensive use of facilities and the more efficient use
   of capacity'.
3. *To maximise utilisation of space, facilities and labour.* Facilities layout has the
   objective of reducing the high cost of wasted space and minimising the total area
   'necessary' for the operation process, e.g. cellar, linking passages, store rooms,
   behind the bar, etc. Adequate layout also facilitates operation, maintenance,
   service and supervision, and therefore permits a better utilisation of labour.

Facilities layout problems

There are three distinguishable levels involved in layout planning:

Department:	an area containing several facilities.
Facility:	a single piece of equipment, e.g. bar.
Workplace:	the work area of one person or a work team.

1. *The layout of departments within the site.* This refers to locating, for example,
   where the lounge bar, store room, toilets, etc., will be situated within the pub.
2. *The layout of facilities within the department.* This is a small-scale version of the
   problems in (1), i.e. locating where the bar counter, the food bar, tables, etc.,
   should be within the lounge bar.
3. *The layout of individual workplaces.* This more directly involves ergonomics and
   work study applications and is concerned with a particular area such as the bar,
   e.g. location of pumps, the soft drinks, glasses, washing-up area, etc.

In the public house the principal flows the operations manager is concerned with
involve people, both customers and staff. Bar-counter staff are required to collect
together all items required for a particular customer by travelling between the

appropriate areas within the facility. Thus movement problems are of importance and minimisation of movement becomes a relevant criterion for layout planning.

An approach to layout planning

With our public house, the movement is concerned with materials (food, drink, glasses, etc.), staff and, of course, customers. We may need to create three different charts to show correct movement patterns which would then give a clue as to how the layout of departments could be improved. Two charts for materials and staff are, however, probably sufficient, recognising that the new design will be based upon considerable research on consumer behaviour and designed to provide maximum customer satisfaction.

To illustrate this one need only think of the customers in any retail activity.

CASE STUDY

Consider the layout of the display area in, say, a garden centre. The following principles may be followed:

1. Try to avoid a cluttered look and yet stock as much as possible. (This may mean reducing product lines.)
2. Ensure there is room for customers to browse and pass each other.
3. Use the 'return per square metre of floor space' as an indication of product location, i.e. prime space should not be devoted to slow moving and bulky items and quick turnover items should occupy more expensive space at the front.
4. Locate necessity items (i.e. pesticides) at the rear of the store. Customers will then move to the rear of the store passing numerous displays to acquire the desired item.
5. Plan the route through the store with care. It may be possible to create a one-way system.
6. Remember that too many obstacles frustrate customers. The challenge is one of maximising product display without antagonising shoppers.

The customer can therefore be partly programmed to respond in a certain way, within limits. Good examples are bar areas in restaurants whilst orders are taken and waiting areas in personal services, i.e. hairdressers, dentists, etc. We can conclude from examples like that of saline solution preparation in a pharmacy (see pages 65–67) and the garden centre that for some layout problems, there are a limited number of feasible solutions and that to spend vast amounts of time on detailed analysis would be of limited value. However, for our public house the answer is not so obvious since we need to have some knowledge of movement of staff, customers and materials to enable the correct placing of departments. This analysis needs to be as rigorous as any similar analysis concerned with manufacturing. Even in a firm producing a whole variety of different product groups, the analysis needs to consider all the flows through the system, such that the resultant layout will minimise costs of handling, reduce congestion and queuing and maximise use of space, facilities and labour.

SYSTEMATIC LAYOUT ANALYSIS

This can best be recalled by the letters P, Q, R, S and T (see Table 6.1):

1. Process
2. Quantity
3. Routeing
4. Supporting services
5. Time

Process/quantity and routeings

This is where we establish the movements (process) and their frequency. So, for our pub example, we consider the flows of materials (glasses, food supplies, bottles, waste, etc.) and staff and customers. Dependent upon the degree of detail necessary a separate chart for each of these three could be considered, or each type of material may need to be separately charted. To get this into perspective there are a number of charts available, as discussed below.

The string diagram

In the example shown in Chapter 4 (see Figure 4.4) there was only one person being charted. With a number of different items and using different coloured string, some indication of frequency of movement between points can be identified, providing the period over which the recording was done was representative.

The travel chart

The travel chart provides a simple tabular picture of the quantity of movements, and the string diagram complements it with a picture of the nature of these movements. The BSI definition of a travel chart is:

> A tabular record for presenting quantitative data about the movements of workers, materials or equipment between any number of places over any given period of time.

The travel chart is an extremely useful tool for plant layout and materials handling investigations. As its name indicates, its function is to record and display the quantity of material moved from one place to another, or the amount of traffic between one place and another.

One of the simplest ways of establishing the best relative locations for departments or work areas is to consider the amount of traffic between each pair of locations under consideration. The travel chart provides a simple and effective method of subjecting the interdependence of areas to a more realistic quantitative analysis as a function of density. Its main use therefore is to provide a rapid 'at a glance' picture of the volume and nature of movement from and to each department, as a basis for further analysis and investigation to reduce the extent of movement by layout rearrangement. Used to supplement flow and string diagrams with quantitative data, it reveals the dependence of one area upon another, and enables areas to be correctly located in improved layouts.

Figure 6.3 shows a travel chart for our pub example. The locations under study are identified on a plan and marked out on the axes of the chart, starting from the same origin, as shown. The areas should be logical subdivisions, i.e. homogeneous areas. Each movement as it occurs over the period of study decided on, e.g. shift, week, etc., is recorded in the appropriate box, using a '5 bar gate' or other method of counting. The 'marks' in each box at the completion of the study give a complete record of the total number of moves between any two areas.

Department to	Sub-ground cellar	Store 1	Lounge bar	Buffet bar	Kitchen	Office	Restaurant	Cold room
Sub-ground cellar								
Store 1	₩ II 70			IIII 40	III 30		IIII 40	
Lounge bar	₩ II 70	₩ II 70						
Buffet bar			₩ ₩ 100				IIII 40	
Kitchen		₩ III 80		₩ ₩ 100				
Office		III 30			₩ ₩ I 110			
Restaurant	IIII 40		IIII 40			₩ ₩ IIII 140		
Cold room					IIII 40			

Figure 6.3 Travel chart showing pub staff movements over one week

The data may be recorded in various ways. In the case of a few closely adjacent areas in clear view or, say, one operative working in a stores, that data may be obtained by direct observation and entered directly on to the chart. If more than one operative is involved, more than one observer may be required. Larger and more complex situations may be analysed from 'activity sampling' records, cine films, and so on.

To ensure a true comparison, the values in the chart representing the amount of movement taking place must be based on some common denominator. The denominator used should be the simplest possible: number of trips, number of unit loads, number of items, volumes, weight, etc. For finer comparisons, the figures may also be weighted according to distance moved, e.g. tonnes × metres = tonne metres. Where simple units, weights and so forth cannot be used, other values may prove suitable – for example, £s value of material moved where the material is expensive and fragile.

Supporting services

Whilst the movements charted above from the main activities indicate where facilities could/should be located in relation to each other, there are other features in our total activity which require effective integration. These are often mundane but important – toilets, washroom facilities, waste disposal area, entrances and exits, the manager's office, etc. Nothing is worse than to leave these until the end to be added as an afterthought. They need to be properly integrated, not just in frequency of movement, but on a mature value judgement as to how they each relate to all other departments. Obvious examples are that an office should not be next to a noisy bar, whilst the waste disposal area should be near to where most of the waste is generated (kitchen) but not too near to where smell or flies etc. may create problems.

In order that we can now get all of the above information into some sensible model, all the data generated from our PQR analysis together with identified supporting services can be put together in a *relationship chart*.

The relationship chart

A relationship chart provides a compact straightforward method of identifying, displaying and evaluating the many relationships which need to be taken into account to ensure that the various functions and services are physically located in the best possible relationship to each other. The task is not an easy one, for if there are ten departments, and each is to be related to the other nine, forty-five separate decisions will have to be taken, each of which may involve a two-way relationship.

The relationship chart reveals:

1. where relationships exist between any pair of activities;
2. the degree of importance of these relationships, denoted by a letter-rating indicating how close the two functions should be to each other, i.e. the 'closeness value';
3. the reason for the rating.

The form of the chart is self-explanatory, as can be seen from Figure 6.4 which gives the relationship chart for our pub example. The relationship rating and the grounds for the rating are shown for each pair of activities in the 'box' made by the intersection of the 'up' and 'down' lines concerned. (A number of the intersections have been completed in Figure 6.4 by way of example.)

The relationship chart procedure

1. Identify all the activities concerned in the sector under survey. List the departments, areas, etc. involved and check for omissions.
   (a) Limit any one chart to a maximum of fifty activities.
   (b) Group 'like activities' together.
2. List the activities on the relationship chart as follows:
   (a) Operating departments
   (b) Add supporting service activities
   (c) Include important site and building features (e.g. dock, rail, roads, etc.).

117

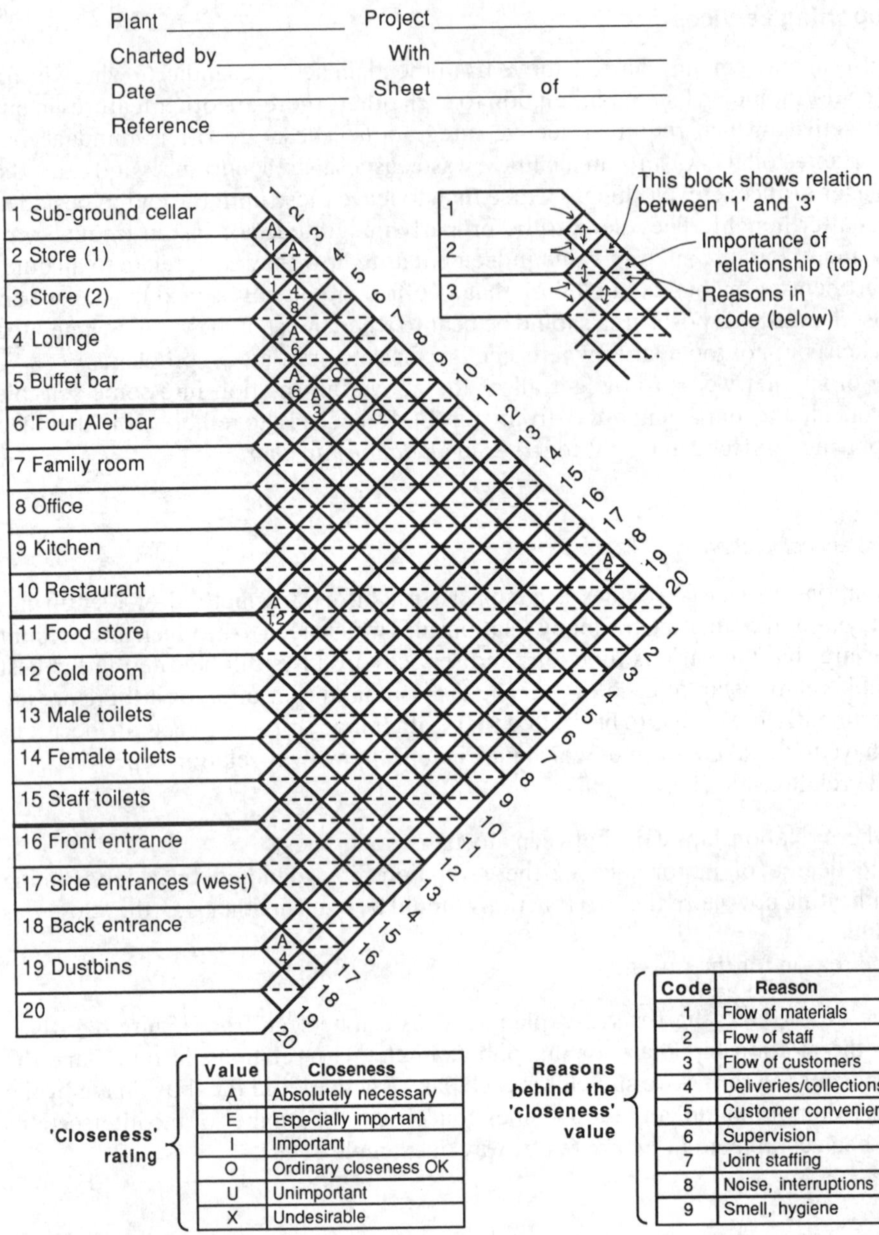

Plant _____ Project _____

Charted by_____ With _____

Date_____ Sheet _____ of_____

Reference_____

Figure 6.4 Relationship chart

3. Determine the relationship between one pair of activities and validate the reason by:
   (a) Calculation (e.g. establishing material flow from diagrams, travel charts, etc.)
   (b) Own knowledge of the activities concerned, personal visits and discussion
   (c) Issuing simple questionnaires for completion
   (d) Issuing group explanation and recording sheets

(e) Evaluating the responses
(f) Obtaining agreement.
4. Consolidate all the information derived from the above procedure into a specific set of relationships, and get this approved. The final chart will then provide:
   (a) A check sheet by which to ensure that all activities have been covered
   (b) A permanent record of decisions taken and reasons for taking them
   (c) Basic information for establishing geographic relationships in planning.

Use of the relationship chart is fully considered in Muther (1973).

Space

Before we can decide upon a layout we need to know the space requirements for each activity. There are two aspects involved: first, the actual area (in square or cubic metres), and the shape of that space, i.e. long and narrow or square. (In the case of pub lounges perhaps the shape does not matter – L-shaped, lots of alcoves, etc., may add to the pub's attractiveness.)

Calculating the space required for each of the departments concerned is not so easy as with manufacturing when there is some correlation between forecast changes in output and use of space. Decisions on the optimum size of a service activity will be based very much on market intelligence and past experience. For those in the public sector it may have to be 'make the best use of the space', and so those planning techniques are invaluable.

Time

This last of our PQRST analysis refers to the time it is going to take to get the project under way, but it must also be linked with our forecast of space required for the activities. In our pub, it may be possible to extend the size of some rooms, or even to change the balance between eating activities and drinking activities by redesigning rooms. In other areas it is not quite so easy, so some market forecasting is required.

Converting the information to an actual layout

Putting all the information together from the relationship chart, space requirements, etc., we are now in a position to propose a number of alternative layouts that:

1. Conform to the criteria laid down
2. Fit into the space available.

These will now need to be evaluated so that the most effective one can be selected.

At this stage, however, it is necessary to take a broader perspective. If only the problem of movement is considered and the alternative layouts are only evaluated in this light, it is very probable that certain quite important considerations will be neglected and we will be guilty of suboptimisation. One factor should be common to whatever considerations are adopted: *cost*. A basic objective should be to minimise the total cost involved in establishing and using the layout. This would exclude the decoration and ornament which would be an additional cost depending on the budget available.

Muther (1973) suggests that layouts should be evaluated on the basis of the following costs (adapted version):

1. *Investment*:
   (a) *Initial cost of new facilities of all kinds*:
       (i)   buildings
       (ii) construction
       (iii) machinery and equipment
   (b) *Accessory costs*:
       (i)   wiring and lighting
       (ii) bar fixtures
       (iii) furniture
   (c) *Installation costs*:
       (i)   building
       (ii) machinery and equipment
       (iii) loss of trade
   (d) *Depreciation and obsolescence costs*
2. *Operating costs*:
   (a) *Labour*:
       (i)   direct
       (ii) part-time staff
       (iii) waiting time (for custom)
       (iv) non productive – clerical, cleaning, etc.
   (b) *General*:
       (i)   floor space
       (ii) power
       (iii) fuel
       (iv) taxes
       (v)   insurance

This is a general list of the likely costs involved in evaluation. It is not comprehensive and will vary with different layouts.

Evaluation of the performance of an operating system is important as it represents a 'yardstick' by which the efficiency of the operation can be measured.

CASE STUDY

Since we have been using a public house as our layout example, it is worthwhile considering how two similar public houses can be evaluated from an operational point of view – one which is very much concerned with layout.

The Eagle

Immediately one can recognise in the layout the potential for a smooth and efficient operation. The behind-the-scenes operations are confined to one central section of the premises. The customer areas form an 'L' shape around this area. This enables the two flows (the customer flow and the bar operations flow) to operate in relative isolation. Contact between the two sides only occurs at the correct specified times, i.e. behind the bar and in the restaurant and lounges.

The Lion

In contrast with the Eagle, the Lion consists of an array of small bars, linking passages, lobbies and store rooms. It is no surprise therefore that it is a costly and difficult establishment to manage. The flow of the bar operations and the customer flow are now separated in this layout. The replenishment of bars involves a series of movements from the sub-ground cellar to store rooms and then to the bars via customer drinking areas.

DETAILED LAYOUT PLANNING

Once the block layout of a building or space is completed the detailed consideration of how the equipment, people and entrances or exits are linked within each subunit or department is the next phase. For some activities this will not be a complex task but for others it is and follows a similar pattern to the above.

The approach to layout planning detailed above has been used for all types of activities. For special consideration of two areas see Muther and Wheeler (1964) on the office and Stone (1984) on stores.

OFFICE LAYOUT

All organisations have offices and they need as much attention paid to their layout as any major customer-directed activity of the enterprise. They can employ a lot of people and with increasing use of computers have a heavy capital investment. They are often referred to as the 'nerve centre' of the organisation.

'At the dawn of information technology we have offices, which are totally unprepared for the challenge' (Moore, 1987). In his article Moore quotes a report which suggests that within ten years, one-third of all office workers could be equipped with electronic workstations. It also predicts that the average size of an individual workspace will increase by 50–100%. The demand for ancillary space for private meetings is also increasing: 'In some organisations this increase has been at a rate of 25% over two years, with the result that only 50% of net usable space in the building is occupied by work places.'

The study also goes on to say that: 'Extensive and premature renovation of existing buildings will be expensive but inevitable', that 'The cost of renovating certain types of buildings to take on information technology may be equal to the cost of constructing new buildings', and in addition: 'Most of the technology which will have the greatest impact on office design over the next ten years already exists, and is in use by most leading organisations.'

Analysis of office work activities

Although the use of conventional method study, O&M and layout planning techniques will be utilised as appropriate, the total approach is usually a little more complex and involves both work place and communication studies. A full description of the phases is shown in Figure 6.5. To give an idea of the study the communication analysis is described in more detail.

The landscaped office

The landscaped office is a sophisticated form of office planning developed in Germany during the late 1950s and early 1960s, since copied by businesses throughout the world. The German word Bürolandschaft – literally 'office landscape' – exploits the possibilities of the open-plan office (cellular offices were replaced by open-plan offices in some firms in the United States before the Second World War, but furniture in such offices tended to be arranged in a regimented fashion); the departments of a business and their furniture are arranged according to the flow of paperwork, communications and the movement of staff. The result looks casual, it seems to echo the soft lines of a landscape, an impression heightened by the use of potted plants; thick carpets, canteen units and a community atmosphere create a domestic-type environment. The advantages of Bürolandschaft are claimed to be increased business efficiency, better communications, better staff conditions and greater flexibility since the furniture can easily be rearranged and departments can easily be reorganised.

The features that inform the design of landscaped offices include the following:

1. *Privacy*. Avoid direct confrontation and the overlooking of another's work.
2. *'Subjective spaces'*. This is the name given to spaces in the office that are associated with particular persons or groups. Such spaces need careful design; no attempt must be made to form complete enclosures. Managerial positions need greater visual protection, and should be planned around this to avoid overhearing.
3. *Work stations*. These are designed with work flow and easy communication between members of a group as top priorities. The standard space per person must be respected. Groups should be easily recognised.
4. *Machines*. If machines are likely to be a nuisance because of noise, they must be segregated (remembering that sound is reflected from hard surfaces such as walls and windows).
5. *Furniture*. Individual work requirements must be carefully scrutinised to ensure that each person has as much furniture and equipment as he or she requires, but no more. There must not be a stick of superfluous furniture in the working areas, and what there is must be light and portable.
6. *Screens*. Acoustic screens, easily portable, are to be regarded as pieces of furniture. Sometimes they may be put to a subsidiary use, e.g. as a blackboard or pinboard. They must never be used in an attempt to create artificial rooms.
7. *Reception*. Plenty of space should be given to the reception area, and it is a good idea to allow a view of the 'offices' in order to acclimatise visitors.
8. *Rest areas*. No member of the staff should have to walk more than 100 feet to reach a rest area. Facilities for refreshment must be provided, and it may be possible to include a sink, a refrigerator and cupboards. Workers in surrounding areas must be protected from disturbance.
9. *Reserve area*. Space should be available to meet the need for expansion.

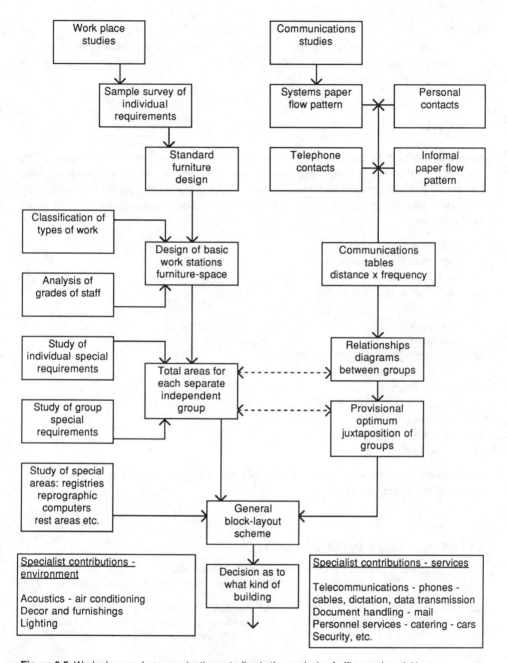

Figure 6.5 Work place and communications studies in the analysis of office work activities

The individual work station

The need to recognise that the individual's need for a 'domain' in which to work is a paramount requirement is emphasised by the three words: 'space is personal'. A desk and its surrounding area are the territory of the individual who sits there. But the boundaries may be rather diffuse, owing to a requirement to partake in a group activity as a member of a team. It is suggested that instead of people being regimented into symmetrical and uniform distribution patterns over a large area, 'small groups, self-selecting where possible, fairly close together, but with larger spaces between groups, may be more satisfactory'.

ACTIVITY

Advice is required on the layout of a headquarters office suite for an organisation. The departments/units/sections that have to be included are listed below. As a preliminary to the layout of these offices consider what else needs to be included and produce a relationship chart indicating closeness ratings *and* reasons. Use the chart to produce a suggested layout for the offices.

1. Chief executive's office
2. Chief executive's secretary
3. Conference room
4. Reception area
5. Telephonist
6. Typing pool
7. Post room
8. Central filing/records department
9. Training section office
10. Training room
11. Administrative officer
12. Finance section
13. Research and statistics section
14. Buying section

As a follow-up exercise to this relatively straightforward task consider the complexity of some organisations which you know.

References and suggested reading

BIM (1969) *Open Landscaped Offices*. Checklist No. 10. London: BIM.

Duffy, F. (1966) *Office Landscaping: A New Approach to Office Planning*. Anbar Monograph No. 9. London: Anbar.

Harris, N. D. and Mundy, J. (eds) (1978) *Materials Handling – An Introduction*. London: HMSO.

Hesketh, W., Hollier, R. and Webb, J. (1982) *Materials Handling for Senior Managers*. London: HMSO.

Institute of Personnel Management (1971) *Living in an Office Landscape*. IPM Information Report No. 8. London: IPM.

Moore, I. (May 1987) Design for working. *Management Today*, pp. 85–94.

Muther, R. (1973) *Systematic Layout Planning*, 2nd edn. Boston: Cahners Books.

Muther, R. and Wheeler, J. D. (March 1964) Order out of chaos in the office. *The Manager*, pp. 37–40.

Sherman, L. (1973) Space and facilities planning. *Management Controls*.

Stone, M. (December 1984) Store layout. *Management Services*, **28** (12), pp. 16–21.

Wild, R. (1984) *Production and Operations Management*, 3rd edn. London: Holt, Rinehart & Winston.

7
MATERIALS MANAGEMENT

For many organisations in non-manufacturing, materials management may not be a major issue or form a significant cost. Because this is so, the subject is approached here from a materials flow angle to provide a framework that can be used to analyse the importance of materials to your non-manufacturing activity.

It would be wrong to include lots of detail on such activities as:

1. Purchasing
2. Stock control
3. Storekeeping and warehousing

since these are more than likely to be the responsibility of a centralised 'materials' department (most likely called Purchasing). However, some key questions are included that the operations manager may need to ask about these functions – particularly as they affect his own department's performance.

INPUTS AND OUTPUTS OF ORGANISATIONS

All organisations, regardless of their type, can be viewed as an input–activity–output model. Whatever their purpose, even just to give advice, the minimum input would be manpower and knowledge. Moving on to actually write a report or letters, the input increases to capital equipment (typewriter) and materials (paper, ribbon, carbon, etc.). With a manufacturing organisation, the materials input, conversion and output as finished goods is more readily observable than the use of materials in, say, a hospital. The material requirements of a hospital are, nevertheless, considerable but many of them are consumed in the process of curing patients. Food, disposables, medical equipment, drugs, cleaning materials and stationery supplies (extending now to computer discs) are all essential to the effective operation of a hospital.

You only have to imagine the vast amount of material supplies used by a car firm to realise that materials is an important activity since it is a major cost source and the lack of a simple screw or washer can cause lost production time. In the hospital, any patient would be aggrieved if the hospital ran out of sutures for sewing up an incision. So control of materials is a vital element in all organisations. Those who have responsibility for dealing with the household provisioning will undoubtedly recognise the need for balance between purchasing too much, such that food gets wasted, and not having supplies available to cope with the unexpected.

ACTIVITY

1. Consider your organisation from an input–activity–output model viewpoint. Identify all the inputs and outputs. Of the inputs can you specify those which are disposable, i.e. which are thrown away, but which nevertheless are of value in the conduct of activities?

2. Find out how materials are ordered and stored in your organisation. Do you have a purchasing manager or department? Do you have a 'stores' department or section? How do people in the organisation indicate they wish to purchase materials? How can materials be obtained from stores?

So far our major concern has been with the materials *input* to the organisation. Whilst materials are *in* an organisation they need to be stored and looked after. This can range from a cupboard to a highly secure, temperature controlled warehouse. Whatever type of storage is used it costs money – in depreciation, insurance, cost of space, people and most importantly the cost of the money invested in the stock. Similarly materials have to be moved – and this requires money and means. In some offices we may only be concerned with a few boxes of paper, but in a firm where there are several hundred different stores items, the movement of these is a major logistics exercise involving management, equipment and technology. Even a hospital or local authority has need to develop methods for handling and storing a variety of materials.

ACTIVITY

Again, consider and list the *methods* used to move and store materials in your organisation.

Finally, we need to consider the distribution of the *output*. In our hospital we may send patients home in an ambulance. An ambulance service needs to be very highly planned to provide optimum service at minimum cost. In a manufacturing firm you have only to think of the masses of lorries delivering finished goods all over the country to recognise the scope of this part of the materials cycle. You may also notice that some of the big manufacturers have established a network of distribution warehouses throughout the country. The food industry, in particular the large national supermarkets, have to get their distribution system correct, since it can affect profitability considerably. Add to this the limited shelf-life of most foodstuffs and you will recognise that it is a major management activity for such firms.

ACTIVITY

How does your organisation 'deliver'? The word is used deliberately since we must not forget that many people are in 'knowledge industries' and finished products may be delivered along a cathode ray tube, via a computer, by post or possibly telephone.

Finally the importance of materials in an organisation can affect the management effort devoted to their care.

ACTIVITY

List the managers in your organisation that have something to do with the care of materials.

MATERIALS MANAGEMENT

The logic behind the development of materials management as a function in its own right follows from a consideration of the resources of an organisation. Money is dealt with by a finance function, people problems are looked after by personnel, and so a function to co-ordinate the often costly, and certainly complex, resource of materials would seem to follow. Although many firms do have a 'materials manager', this is not common, but may develop during the latter part of this century. Whether specific functional boundaries for materials management are delineated or not, in all organisations there are still those who purchase, convert, and despatch. Effective management of the function can be achieved through co-ordination between its various components. This co-ordination has been seen as being more effective in some organisations by the development of a formal 'materials' department/unit/function.

The scope and aims of materials management vary quite considerably from firm to firm and in this section only an indication of how such a function can operate can be given.

Definitions

One of the earliest and possibly the most all-embracing definitions was given by the Institute of Materials Handling in February 1965, when they produced a booklet entitled *Introduction to Materials Management* in which they state:

> ... Materials management is the name applied to that management function which co-ordinates and controls those activities in an organisation responsible for the purchasing of materials, their scheduling from supplier and from internal sources, their handling, storage and movement through the organisation, and their despatch and delivery to the customer. To assist in this, the function must also be responsible for the control of inventory, materials handling engineering, and associated work study and layout planning.

Bailey and Farmer (1982) indicate that the management of materials has to do with the following activities – production planning and control, purchasing, storage, inventory planning and control, external transport, internal transport and materials handling.

An American source, Ammer (1974), is a little less specific but states:

> Materials management is a basic part of any organisation that produces a product or service of economic value. Thus it is essential not only to manufacturing, but also to service industries, and it exists not only in profit-making enterprises, but also in the public and private not-for-profit sectors of the economy.

In mentioning the scope of materials management, Ammer concerns himself primarily with the confusion between materials management and purchasing, and suggests that purchasing is but a specialised part of materials management. In listing the parts of materials management the following five major areas emerge:

1. Production and materials control
2. Non-production stores

3. Purchasing
4. Traffic
5. Physical distribution

According to the book one is reading, different functions are included or expunged from the scope of materials management. Obviously one cannot be too precise, since the emergence of a co-ordinating manager for materials will be different depending upon the organisation. A large brewery, for example, with its own distribution company or division would exclude traffic and physical distribution. In a mass production firm where the potential cost reduction in purchasing is high, the materials management function may be separated from purchasing.

The materials cycle

Materials start with design or in some cases research and development. They end up, available for the eventual user, in the form of the manufactured product, or as part of the eventual service. One has only got to think of any product that is used frequently by people – motor cars, pens, reading lamps, TV sets, etc., to recognise the many different materials and the way in which they need to be brought together into a coherent system. In a relatively straightforward activity like a parks department, the materials include seeds, plants, labels, petrol for mowers, boxes, string, etc., all of which require co-ordinating. Even though materials management as a function can vary between enterprises, the materials cycle will illustrate the pervasive, inter-territorial nature of materials management which will affect and, in turn, be affected by other major functions in the organisation.

The manufacturing materials cycle

Design and research and development as we saw were the beginning of this cycle where know-how, styling, consideration of different materials for compatibility, wear, etc., are a vital part. In many cases liaison with suppliers can be done via design to get components or materials provided according to specification. Quality levels are determined here also.

The next stage is often referred to as the sourcing stage in which the major decision is: Do we make parts internally, or buy them ready-made or part-made from outside? Once these decisions have been made, then purchasing strategies have to be developed for all the above – material for conversion, parts for purchase, and other important ancillaries like packaging.

The next two stages are probably linked in with the above – planning of production and the ordering process.

Receiving, which is the next stage, links in again with quality standards and is concerned with ensuring that the materials meet the standards.

Once received the materials need to be stored and adequate and suitable storage facilities need to be provided. Quantity control also needs to be set up on the amount in stock to avoid as far as possible any individual item not being available when required.

After the completion of the production process, the final stages are packaging, storage and distribution of the end product. Between all these stages of the materials cycle, physical movement of the materials has to take place.

The non-manufacturing materials cycle

In all organisations some specification is developed about the 'end service'. This can be equated to the design stage and enables the management to specify the materials requirements. Whether to make parts internally is not so much of a decision for the service sector, although some hospitals do have pharmacies with considerable production output, and most food will be cooked on the premises which can also be clearly seen as a production facility. Sourcing will occur, and for some areas the purchasing function will be the 'materials' function, and because of centralised purchasing will wield considerable power both within and without the organisation.

Storage, stock control and internal distribution are also major activities within the public sector, which can be very costly in terms of space, distances travelled and frequency of journeys. Often this activity is done by special groups of employees (porters, drivers, messengers, etc.), or it may be that departmental staff (clerks, nurses, cleaners, etc.) will collect their own materials. In the latter case the costs are not easily identified.

In a large organisation there is often a need to create sub-stores near to the centre of operations which may or may not be centrally controlled. The materials are very often consumed in the provision of the service, so that packaging and storage are not predominant. In some cases sending out of information in the form of booklets, leaflets, etc. may be an activity, but the materials are most likely consumed in some form by the client (car owner, diner, patient, student).

ACTIVITY

Describe the materials cycle for your own organisation. Trace the inputs of materials in their raw state, the storage, the use, and the eventual disposal or distribution. If you work in the manufacturing sector do the same for a non-manufacturing activity you are reasonably familiar with, e.g. dentist, library, hairdresser, shop, garage, restaurant. Or you could select a non-manufacturing activity within your firm, i.e. maintenance, security, etc. If you work in non-manufacturing, try to find a manufacturing firm and follow the cycle through.

Interlinks

The interlinks between functions are an important aspect of materials management shape and size in organisations, as we have already seen. Production or operations is the central major group around which most of the materials management function will be taking place.

Many of the people involved in these activities may well be production or operations personnel. Marketing may well be involved in helping to determine design, and almost certainly will be involved in co-ordinating decisions regarding what to buy, when and how many.

Materials management organisations

Earlier it was suggested that materials management would exist in an organisation regardless of whether it was a designated function. Rises in the costs of materials during the 1970s have caused many organisations to reconsider their organisational structure to include a materials management department. However, the decision to set up a separate function and its eventual shape is dependent upon a number of trade-offs – purchasing cost v. quality, inventory costs v. manufacturing costs, inventory costs v. purchasing costs, etc.

> Organisational design is a complex undertaking . . . . personalities, skill availabilities, personnel policies and other factors are important in deciding on the best materials organisation. The main rationale for an organisation structure must be the tasks to be accomplished and the trade-offs to be made . . . .
>
> *Miller and Gilmour (1979)*

The most important factor to be stressed is that the costs associated with material purchasing, storage and handling should be understood and controlled. Whether that can be achieved best by a centralised function or a co-ordinated approach will be a matter of individual choice.

OBJECTIVES OF MATERIALS MANAGEMENT

General materials objectives

In addition to the general organisational objectives, the overall general materials objective should be to supply the organisation with the goods and services it requires:

1. at the right time,
2. with the appropriate quality,
3. at the lowest prices, and
4. at the lowest possible internal cost.

Primary materials objectives

Prices

The prices paid for materials in an organisation have a major effect on the overall cost of the product or service. Thus a major effort is required to reduce prices paid or keep prices steady in times of high inflation in order to reduce operating costs. The constraints are:

1. The problem of buying materials which are less costly but still perform the required function of the original material whilst ensuring that the technical and aesthetic aspects of the quality of the finished product/service are still maintained as well as ensuring that the effects on manufacturing are not in any way deleterious. This point is extremely important – the effect on every aspect of the business can be considerable and the total effect can be very difficult to quantify or assess.

2. The size of the problem – with thousands of different and differing items to be bought each year and with potential sources all over the world, then the problem of ensuring that the best possible materials are purchased is very difficult to ensure without a large number of buyers.

High inventory turnover

The faster that stock turns round the less capital is tied up in inventory, and the utilisation and efficiency of capital is improved. Thus the return on capital is improved and/or the organisation has to borrow less. In addition, storage and inventory carrying costs are generally lower.

The ratio of sales revenue/average inventory is frequently used as a measure of inventory turnover in industry. However, as sales revenue embraces labour and overhead costs and profit as well as material costs, a more direct measure of the efficiency of stock movement is spending on purchased materials/average inventory value. This can also apply to non-manufacturing more easily.

Continuity of supply

Disruption in the supply of raw materials to manufacturing industry is a major problem. The reason given frequently for poor stock turnround figures is lack of reliability on the part of suppliers. Indeed in a survey conducted by BIM (Report 35), poor delivery performance by suppliers is the most common reason given for poor performance by British manufacturing industry. There are several important effects of such inadequacies:

1. Excess stock costs due to the increase in stock levels caused by the lack of predictability of raw material supply.
2. Loss of customers' goodwill if failure to supply on time results in late delivery of the finished product/service.
3. A variety of excess costs associated with disruption of supply:
   (a) Alterations to production/operations schedules
   (b) Excess transportation costs
   (c) Excess chasing costs.

(2) and (3) are difficult to quantify and make the problem of assessing a supplier's worth all the more intractable.

Quality and reliability

An assessment of the quality appropriate to the 'business one is in' is the first consideration. Once manufacturers have determined the quality level and received the appropriate quality from a supplier, then it can be difficult for a new supplier to break into that supply situation, if his quality, consistency and other factors are unknown.

The results of poor quality or lack of consistency in quality can be considerable, affecting the ultimate consumer through the manner of operation of the product or receipt of service through aspects of goodwill and through increased production costs as a result of operational problems caused by indifferent quality and high scrap and rework levels. In some industries consistency of quality may not be such a problem (e.g. sand), but when the purchased products are in a relatively highly manufactured state, e.g. electronic equipment, it normally is.

Relationship with suppliers

The establishment of good, friendly, efficient relationship with one's suppliers is a natural achievement, although its worth cannot easily be quantified. Companies who have highly efficient materials organisations spend time and money in an effort to make sure that suppliers are well informed about the needs of the company. This, of course, is a mutual benefit. By receiving information on the needs of the recipient, the supplier is better able to plan his own manufacture. Thus a spirit of friendly co-operation is a major benefit; difficulties arise if another supplier comes along with a better/cheaper product – how much is the old supplier worth?

Records

The creation of records should not be seen as an end in itself. Records kept on the performance of suppliers, on stock levels and the decisions which have to be taken to ensure constant supply of good materials are of fundamental importance to the organisation. The records must be such that the information in them enables people to do a better job. Frequently records (and stock records are a notorious example of this) *prevent* a good job being done. Review of the type of records kept, their value to the organisation, the type of information which *should* be available and the appropriate accuracy is a necessity.

Computers and the vast increase in their use in recent years provide advantages in reducing clerical effort and potential for reducing arithmetical errors. However, whether manual records or electronic records are used, their relevance and faith in their accuracy are equally important.

Personnel

Any system, whether it be concerned with materials or any other aspect of a business, is only as good as the people who design and operate the system. Materials management is fairly new in concept and aspects of it have been rather ignored in the past. The development of adequate personnel in terms of education, training, status and career prospects is the only way to change an inadequate situation into a more favourable one. People, even though they may account for a relatively small proportion of total spending, are the most important asset of the company.

Secondary materials objectives

New materials and products

It is a hackneyed expression in marketing circles that 'the company which does not change goes out of business'. This is also true of materials. It is materials personnel who deal with salespeople/suppliers who have new products to sell. By themselves, materials personnel cannot commit the organisation to new materials, but they must initiate communication to the people concerned if there is anything new of interest.

Standardisation

It is the complexity arising from large numbers of different items which causes many of the difficulties in materials management. It follows, therefore, that the fewer the items, the simpler and more efficient their management will be. It is the job of materials management to ensure that as many standard items as possible are used. Non-standard items are expensive, although if a standard item is purchased which has to be considerably processed before it can be used, it may be cheaper to take the non-standard one. Standardisation is another joint exercise with operations staff, costing and suppliers. It is, however, the responsibility of materials management to ensure that the same items are not lurking in the stores in several locations under separate names/code numbers.

Forecasting

A knowledge of what the future will bring would be a marvellous asset to any organisation. With respect to materials, a knowledge of future prices would be of enormous help, and the intelligent buyer tries to buy before significant price leaps. It is an area fraught with difficulty as many have found to their cost. Similarly, a knowledge of future demand for the company's products makes buying and stock control so much easier. Thus, close co-ordination and co-operation with other management functions with regard to prices, sales campaigns, advertising, as well as a keen interest in economic trends will be of help.

Conclusions

There can be no standard set of objectives which will hold for every organisation. Those listed above are a range which apply with varying emphasis to different companies. Some place emphasis on holding down prices and attempt to buy cheaply (wool, cocoa, the 'futures' markets generally). Others clearly see other aspects of major importance, e.g. aero engineering must see reliability of product as of paramount importance. It is always a juggling act to achieve a virtually impossible balance of low prices, highest quality, perfect supply, zero stock outs, low general inventory. Materials management must be aware of these conflicting objectives and find a suitable decision model which enables the various trade-offs to be quantified as much as possible.

ACTIVITY

Consider the various primary and secondary objectives listed here and try to establish your own organisation's materials management objectives.

PURCHASING

As indicated earlier it is not intended to provide a detailed guide to purchasing practices and procedures, but to provide the operations manager with a useful checklist on purchasing effectiveness in his or her organisation. Perhaps the only time we appreciate this quality (or lack of it) is when supplies requested are not forthcoming.

Table 7.1 lists the functions of a purchasing department (excluding stores and stock control). The operations manager must ask if these functions are being performed effectively. In particular, there will be concern about the effect that shortages or delays may have on the performance of operations.

Table 7.1 Functions of purchasing department.

1. Selecting sources of supply.
2. Getting 'best' prices for required items.
3. Issuing purchase orders to selected supplier.
4. Ensuring that goods arrive at the required time and place in the required quantities and quality.
5. Ensuring that prices charged are correct.
6. Negotiations in connection with errors – wrong dates, quantities, quality, packaging, prices, discounts.
7. Carrying out purchasing research into new materials, suppliers and methods; analysing economic indicators and trends; evaluating 'make or buy decisions', cost analyses; supplier visits.
8. Material budgeting.
9. Advising on material standards and specifications.

Public sector purchasing

It may be of value to consider the rules and regulations concerning purchasing if you happen to work in the public sector. This is covered in Bailey and Farmer (1977), Chapters 4 and 5, as well as in other specific references shown in the suggested reading given at the end of the chapter.

STOCK CONTROL AND STOREKEEPING

The reason for having stocks of any kind is that they act as an uncoupling process between an input process and an output process. Thus regardless of the frequency of input and output the stock centre remains a buffer between the two (see Figure 7.1). One reason for poor inventory control is a lack of awareness of this uncoupling effect of stock. Systems installed arbitrarily without an understanding of their mechanism can lead either to excessive stocks or to violent fluctuations in stock levels.

Figure 7.1 Stock system

Lack of stock can lead to many sorts of wasteful expenditure. On the other hand, holding stock in store is a costly activity and one that deserves some scrutiny. So, a balance must be reached between these conflicting costs so that total cost is as small as possible. Thus stock control is concerned with *quantities*, *times* and *costs*.

In manufacturing, stock control can be seen as of importance at several points during the production process. The three main stocks held are:

1. *Raw materials*: the stocks of parts, subassemblies or materials that the company uses in order to manufacture its products.
2. *Work-in-progress*: the stocks of partly manufactured items that are either held in special stores or are 'in progress' on the factory floor.
3. *Finished goods*: the stocks of completed products that are ready for despatch to customers.

In addition, a manufacturing firm may have need to hold stocks, namely:

4. *Maintenance stocks*: the stocks of spare parts and other items that are or may be needed for the maintenance of the factory or machines and equipment.
5. *'Services' stocks*: these are stocks of general items necessary for the various service departments. They can vary considerably, but include such items as cleaning materials, stationery and other general articles necessary for all the support functions in the business.
6. *Inspection stocks*: stocks of materials necessary to enable the products and processes to be tested or inspected to ensure they are achieving the required quality.

In non-manufacturing, due to the 'service' element, there is little opportunity to 'store' the 'product'. You cannot store care, bus rides, school lessons, etc. Therefore the major emphasis will be in the latter three types of stock. However, there are aspects of service activity which can be directly related to the production process, and whilst effective stock management is unlikely to produce massive savings, some benefit should accrue to the organisation. For example, subunits such as catering, printing, maintenance (particularly where renovation of such items as lawnmowers occurs), the hospital pharmacy (producing large quantities of supplies such as sterile dressings) can all be treated to some extent as a 'production unit'. However, the use of materials in other areas may well be mainly concerned with movement and handling rather than large stocks of many different types of materials.

ACTIVITY

With reference to your own unit:

1. Identify stocks that are held.
2. Indicate the reasons for holding such stock.

Locations

In organisations such as county councils, health authorities and bus companies where there are a lot of different locations – schools, residential homes, job centres, depots,

135

etc. – the problem is to what extent one trades off the cost control of central bulk buying and the consequent need to distribute, with allowing individual units auto-nomy to purchase and store their own materials.

There may also be a 'political' problem in terms of releasing control over some issues. This can often only be resolved when an independent investigation is carried out either to improve the present system or to prove that one or other system is beneficial in cost terms. However, one of the features of such an investigation is the impact materials or lack of them can have on customer service.

CASE STUDY

A good example of the 'service' element of stores and one that is common to most organisations is that of maintenance.

Stock requirements

One of the most important aspects of maintenance stores management from a cost standpoint is determining stock requirements. Maintenance stores items are usually divided into three general categories:

1. standard stores items such as nuts, bolts and pipe fittings with a predetermined rate of use and approximate known requirements;
2. insurance items which do not have established turnover;
3. complete assemblies or machines which are often referred to as spare equipment and which are usually capitalised.

Proper stores item classification is necessary, both from an analysis and accounting standpoint, to provide a sound basis for management decision-making.

Parts requirements

For stores items which are low unit-value parts having high turnover, a maximum–minimum system will provide a sound approach to control. Basically, this system consists of:

1. a minimum or protective stock level which is a function of the cost of a stock-out, demand for the item and availability of replacement supplies;
2. an order point which is established by the delivery period of replacement stock;
3. an order quantity which, in conjunction with the order point, establishes the maximum stock level.

Calculation of requirements

Realistic rather than rule-of-thumb order quantities can be established by means of the *economic order principle*. Basically, this is a simple method of balancing carrying costs and restocking costs to obtain minimum total costs. The economic order quantity (EOQ) is that quantity of a specific item which results in the minimum total cost when both restocking and carrying costs are considered and included. The formula for the economic order quantity, found in standard works on the subject, minimises the sum of the ordering and stock holding costs. It can be shown mathematically that the economic order quantity (EOQ) for any item is equal to:

$$EOQ = \sqrt{\frac{200 \times \text{Annual Usage} \times \text{Cost of making one order}}{\text{Unit cost} \times \text{Holding costs per year as a \% of unit cost}}}$$

For example, suppose the unit cost of an item = 20p; annual usage = 3,000; cost of ordering/order = 80p; holding costs = 15% per annum. Then using the formula:

$$EOQ = \sqrt{\frac{200 \times 3,000 \times 80}{20 \times 15}} = \sqrt{160,000} = 400 \text{ units}$$

Control should be concentrated on items where expenditure is high but evaluation is required of all items. Emphasis must be placed on the vital few and not on the insignificant many. Through this approach the cost of frequent ordering of many low-cost items with attendant excessive clerical expense can be minimised.

Parts storage location and distribution

Even with frequent truck deliveries, central stores may be inadequate in a large plant. In this situation, low-cost, high-turnover items should be supplied to the area maintenance shops on a weekly basis, and self-service issue without a ticket saves maintenance labour time and also reduces clerical work.

When area stores supplement central stores, they should be limited to a seven to ten-day supply and be controlled by means of a simple weekly inventory and order form. By comparing consumption with the maximum stock for a several week period, it is possible to adjust the stock level to a realistic figure.

Application of ideas

The maintenance stores considered in this case study are concerned with engineering parts for machine repairs, but there are very similar types of stores and stock control problems throughout the service sector, namely:

1. Stocks of office supplies
2. Food and cleaning materials in a home
3. Drugs, dressings, etc., in a hospital or clinic

ACTIVITY

Identify an example of 'maintenance' stores in your organisation. Note that the cost of not having them when you need them is high. The cost of reordering frequently is also high, but overstocking can lead to problems of obsolescence, waste and cost of space.

References and suggested reading

Ammer, D. S. (1974) *Materials Management*. Homewood, IL: Irwin.
Ammer, D. S. (1983) *Purchasing and Materials Management for Health Care Institutions*. Lexington, MA: Lexington Books.
Bailey, P. J. H. and Farmer, D. H. (1977) *Purchasing Principles and Techniques*. London: Pitman.
Bailey, P. J. H. and Farmer, D. H, (1982) *Materials Management Handbook*. London: Gower.

Farmer, D. (1985) *Purchasing Management Handbook*. London: Gower.

Harris, N. D. and Skedd, A. (1980) *Materials Management – A Guide for Accountants*. London: Institute of Chartered Accountants.

Heinritz, S. F. and Farrell, P. V. (1981) *Purchasing Principles and Management*. Englewood Cliffs, NJ: Prentice-Hall.

Hyman, S. (1979) *Supplies Management for Health Services*. London: Croom Helm.

Institute of Materials Handling (1965) *Introduction to Materials Management*. London: Institute of Materials Handling.

Lee, L. and Dobler, D. W. (1977) *Purchasing and Materials Management*. New Delhi: McGraw-Hill.

Miller, J. G. and Gilmour, P. (July–August 1979) Materials managers – who needs them? *Harvard Business Review*, pp. 143–153.

Page, H. (1981) *Public Purchasing and Materials Management*. Lexington, MA: Lexington Books.

8
QUALITY AND RELIABILITY

INTRODUCTION

Quality and reliability are the most important aspects of all organisations since they have a direct effect on customer satisfaction. Take, for example, the servicing of a car. Some of the factors affecting customer satisfaction are:

1. Attitude of staff
2. Punctuality – amount of waiting for service
3. Standard of service received (the reliability aspect) – Do you need to return because the plug leads became loose?
4. The way in which your car is looked after during the service – upholstery, steering wheel, carpets
5. Explanation of what was done and why
6. Reasonableness of the bill
7. Availability of car at specified time

Repeat customers depend on all the above factors. All of us have experience of poor service, defective products, etc., and probably advise friends and colleagues to avoid making the same mistake.

There have been pressures by the Department of Industry in the UK to ensure that all firms have a properly documented quality assurance system, with board level responsibility. The high quality of many overseas products – particularly Japanese – has caused UK management to look seriously at the methods that should be used to avoid poor quality, rework and customer complaints of any sort.

Definitions of Quality

Different people may have their own ideas of what they mean by quality. Let us look at three.

Degree of prestige

In these terms we can distinguish between the quality of a high class hotel and a boarding house. To a large extent, prestige relates to the particular market sector. No one would expect to be able to stay at a high class hotel for the price of the boarding house. Likewise, the boarding house could not expect to be able to charge 'five star' prices. However, in our second definition of quality each of these two organisations may achieve or fail to measure up to the standards required of them.

Fitness for purpose

Of course, the specifications for the services offered by the five star hotel and the boarding house may be quite different, along with their customer expectations. Nevertheless, in their own way, they may measure up to their customer expectations or fail to do so as the case may be. The services delivered need to match the services offered, regardless of how prestigious the establishment.

Customer satisfaction

Quality ultimately is measured in terms of satisfied customers. It is not enough simply to monitor complaints and assume that quality is good enough provided that people don't complain. They might simply vote with their feet and not return.

Causes of poor quality

These include the following:

1. Lack of real concern for quality throughout the organisation.
2. Failure to bring quality into marketing and design from the beginning.
3. Lack of well-considered specifications for materials, methods and processes.
4. Haphazard methods of operation.
5. Poor supervision resulting in:
   (a) either weak or excessive discipline
   (b) poor morale among workers.
6. Badly trained operators together with poor method instruction.
7. Poor working conditions.
8. Poor job specifications.
9. Physical plant and tools in a badly maintained condition.
10. Material varying from specification.
11. An incorrectly organised and ineffective inspection/auditing system.
12. Poor top management control.
13. Lack of incentives.

THE CONCEPT OF TOTAL QUALITY

All service work consists basically of the following three stages:

$$\text{Input} \rightarrow \text{Process} \rightarrow \text{Output}$$

and so quality efforts are needed at all three stages of the work. This is, therefore, the *total quality concept* – the whole organisation and everyone in it is affected. Organisation-wide involvement is required as quality is too important to be left to a few specialists.

The service itself can usually be broken down into a series of intermediate stages:

$$\underbrace{\text{Input} - \text{Process} - \text{Output}}_{\text{1st stage}} \rightarrow \underbrace{\text{Input} - \text{Process} - \text{Output}}_{\text{2nd stage}} \rightarrow \underbrace{\text{Input} - \text{Process} - \text{Output}}_{\text{3rd stage}}$$

It is clear that the output of one stage is the input to the next. For example, in a restaurant the output of the food buyer's efforts is the chef's input. The chef's output is the input to the waiter's stage, and so on.

However, no matter how good the chef is, he or she needs good raw materials of adequate quality to be able to work to the specification requirements (menu). In turn, the chef may have produced a magnificent meal, but it needs to be served properly before we reach the ultimate goal – customer satisfaction.

Let us now consider how the total quality concept may be applied in a service organisation.

Attitudes

The quality of service is very much based on people. As total quality is organisation-wide, the attitudes and behaviour of everyone is paramount. Every single action by every single person has some bearing on the quality of the work performed, and has consequences for the organisation's image which is portrayed to the rest of the world. To give a few simple examples, consider the following:

1. The personality and manner of a telephone operator or receptionist.
2. The accuracy of paperwork – letters, invoices, etc.
3. The 'housekeeping' – the tidiness of offices and other work places.
4. The ability to keep appointments and other activities to schedule.

These all give off powerful signals about the organisation to an outsider.

One of the most important steps, therefore, is to get everyone to *care* about the quality of their work. This means getting them to be very much aware of quality and to take a personal pride in everything they do. Attitudes cannot usually be changed overnight, and so persistent encouragement towards the 'pursuit of excellence' is essential.

Involvement

Much attention has been given in recent years to the idea of getting people, at all levels, involved with quality improvement activities. At the individual level this may take place within the structure of the 'suggestion scheme'. However, more effort has been directed recently to organising small groups of 'problem-solvers' under such titles as quality circles, task forces, action teams, quality improvement groups and so on. Each of these group types has its own particular structure and methodology. For example, some teams consist of supervisors only, some of subordinates led by their immediate supervisor, some are management led groups, some are multi-discipline or multi-departmental groups, and so on. However, there is an underlying common objective of all of them: quality improvement.

There is no universal structure which can be guaranteed successful every time. Management would do well, therefore, to consider carefully what sort of structure would be appropriate within the existing organisation. After all, such activities are intended to supplement and fit in with the existing structure and should not be seen as a threat to any manager, supervisor, shop-steward, worker, etc.

Before setting up such groups, the intending participants usually attend a short training course on problem-solving methods, data gathering, creative thinking, team-building, organising meetings and presentation techniques before embarking on their selected quality improvement projects. Some of the projects may be quite small in themselves but the collective effort of many groups can be considerable. As the Japanese put it, 'It is better for a hundred people to make one step forward than one person to make a hundred steps.'

A UK water authority introduced quality circles in two of its divisions in 1983/4. Initially in each division about twenty participants were trained as outlined above. Only at the end of the training period were participants asked to decide on quality circle participation. Almost everyone volunteered and useful projects have since been tackled.

Much literature has appeared on the subject of quality circles in one or other of its guises in the last ten years, most of it being concerned with how to introduce circles or the analysis of circle failure. Perhaps these articles miss the main point that company-wide involvement is the ultimate objective. It is relatively easy to get a few groups off the ground in the early stages. In fact, most authors advocate a low-key small-scale start-up situation. However, there seems little point in all the effort involved if circles, task forces, quality improvement teams, etc., do not become company-wide. In fact if restricted to just a handful of individuals there is a danger of their being held to be an élite minority; such a result would be counterproductive. Management needs to consider how quality improvement activities can be progressively spread through the organisation.

Most of these group activities are held to be voluntary, but as it is almost impossible to get everyone to volunteer for anything, this 'voluntary' aspect tends to contradict the principle of company-wide total quality. The management style – autocratic, democratic, etc. – therefore needs to be appropriate and the programme carefully managed.

Alternatively every supervisor, section leader, etc., could be required as a regular part of his or her job to set up at least one group from their subordinates. While perhaps falling short of involving every employee, it would ensure a company-wide operation. It would also give everyone a chance to participate not only in quality matters, but also in solving other problems such as organisational and communication issues.

It is also useful for group achievements to be internally publicised on notice boards, through house magazines, etc. This keeps everyone informed about the progress being made, and there is evidence that this encourages others to form their own groups.

QUALITY RELATED COSTS

In today's competitive market there is little room for inferior service or service the quality of which is not consistent. In the future there will be even less room. Purchasers will usually go to some lengths to obtain good value, and in many products and services one has a clear idea of what one can expect to obtain.

The provider is, therefore, compelled to give to the customer all he or she can possibly afford at the price in the way of reliability, customer satisfaction and service. There is always a fine balance of operational costs against performance and quality. Failure costs money, the alternative being the 'zero defects' or 'right first time' approach with the emphasis on the *prevention* of defective work rather than *correction* afterwards.

Quality related costs can be broken down under four main headings:

1. Prevention costs
2. Appraisal costs
3. Internal failure costs
4. External failure costs
} = Total quality costs

Prevention costs

Prevention costs are the costs of actively rooting out the causes of defective work and eliminating them. The majority of firms do not yet have a systematic and formal part of their organisation devoted to such investigations, i.e. with designated people held accountable for getting prevention results. Not enough is spent on prevention while money is wasted in the other categories.

Appraisal costs

Appraisal is a vastly uneconomic way of trying to achieve quality. Apart from being expensive it is not even practicable in most of the service sector to employ an army of 'inspectors' who check up on other people's work. A bus 'inspector' only sees a small sample of the total journeys made, for instance. The quality of the work needs to be built in and controlled by those directly involved with doing it.

The use of inspection, on the other hand, is likely to produce all the wrong kinds of attitude in the general workforce: 'Oh, it doesn't matter if I make a mistake, because Inspection will pick it up and correct it.' Or alternatively, 'I will hide this mistake in case I get into trouble.' It is fundamental to the total quality concept that the responsibility for quality lies firmly with the person who does the work, not some externally imposed quality 'expert'.

Having said that, there is still room for random audits of the system. A quality audit is analogous to a financial audit, in that it is intended to demonstrate whether the system, as laid down, is being operated correctly and whether there is room for improvement. It is not the audit's purpose to 'catch people out' – if it were used in this way it would engender defensive attitudes.

Internal failure costs

These costs refer to mistakes made but discovered and corrected in-house before reaching the customer. The only redeeming feature of an internal failure is that it didn't get outside the organisation and upset a customer. The costs of internal failure include the costs of corrective actions, investigations, rework, additional paperwork, delays, extra labour and material costs, etc.

Another important aspect of internal failure costs is the effect on the morale of employees. No one enjoys having their mistakes pointed out. Hence the prevention activity must do everything possible to encourage people to do the job right first time.

All mistakes are preventable in principle. To pursue the zero defects approach requires a great deal of dedication, however, from all concerned. There must be total understanding of what is required and how it is to be achieved.

External failure costs

These costs are incurred by mistakes discovered by the customers with consequent loss of goodwill, additional work under guarantees, disruption caused by the necessary rescheduling of the work load, extra labour and material costs and so on.

Figure 8.1 shows a typical relationship of prevention, appraisal and failure costs, before and after quality improvement. Increasing the quality effort mainly in the form of greater prevention activity results in an even greater reduction of failure costs. An extra bonus is some reduction in appraisal costs. After all, if we achieve zero defects and right first time there is little need for appraisal. Figure 8.1 also shows the untruth of the claim that if you want quality, you have to pay for it. As Crosby (1979) has shown, the payoff from the right amount of prevention effort can be considerable.

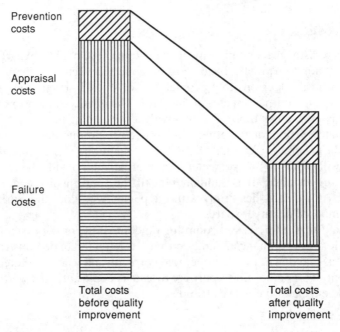

Figure 8.1 Relationship between prevention, appraisal and failure costs before and after quality improvement

Total quality costs can actually be reduced by spending more on prevention activities. If the relationships are as obvious as this, how is it that all firms don't operate at the optimum quality level? First, it is necessary to set up a quality cost measuring system – this is not normally encountered in a typical accounting system, and many firms simply don't know their quality related costs. BS 6143 gives a very detailed description of such a cost system. Secondly, prevention efforts are an investment, an act of faith. While the prevention costs will be incurred from day one, the reduction in failure costs will take time to achieve. Thus management needs to be convinced of the total quality concept and be prepared to invest in it, confident of getting a good return in due course.

144

QUALITY SYSTEMS FOR SERVICE ORGANISATIONS

The design of the quality system is management's responsibility. This means that management must devise quality objectives and policies, together with the organisation and procedures needed to achieve them. The main components of an effective quality system are listed below.

Organisation

An effective quality problem-solving organisation is required with appropriate responsibility and authority delegated to all departments which can affect quality. In the total quality concept, this must affect every employee in some way, and is a recognition that quality cannot be simply left to a specialist function.

Nevertheless, an independent quality representative should be appointed with authority and responsibility to ensure adherence to the quality system. It is not so much that this person is responsible personally for quality, more that it is his or her task to ensure that everyone else is. The person chosen for this role should be sufficiently senior to be able to get things done and a good communicator at all levels to gain the necessary co-operation.

Planning for quality

Work of adequate quality needs to be planned, it cannot be expected to happen of its own accord. There needs to be proper co-ordination at the planning stage of the various functions of the service organisation such as purchasing, operations, sales, marketing, etc.

Control of service operations

Agreed standards should be set so that service personnel understand what is acceptable and what is not. These standards should be backed up by properly documented work instructions.

Records

Unless clear records are kept, it becomes difficult to carry out any kind of quality investigation. It is impossible to solve problems without the right information, so easy retrieval is a must. A microcomputer database system may be a cost efficient way of building up such files. Increasing consumerism in the form of product liability legislation virtually demands a cast-iron record-keeping system, maintained over an appropriate length of time. For example, if a hairdresser was accused of damaging someone's hair and could produce authenticated records to show that only safe chemicals had been used on the occasion, the records may form an important part of a defence case against such a claim. Proprietors need to weigh up the cost and complexity of detailed record keeping against the risks involved if no such records are kept.

Corrective action

The zero defects concept is that no mistake is excusable. The condoning of errors merely encourages them. However, no matter how well organised the firm, eventually a mistake will occur. The causes of error or non-conformance need to be investigated so that, in the short term, effective corrective measures can be taken. Ideally, of course, a longer-term solution is to eliminate the need for any future corrective action. Records kept of corrective action will assist future investigations.

Documentation

It is important that all quality related documents are not only correct, but kept up to date, with records kept of any changes made to them. Obsolete paperwork/ procedures should be promptly removed from places of work to avoid confusion. The responsibility for this should be allocated to a designated person.

Equipment

Equipment should be regularly checked at suitable intervals and appropriate records kept of any repairs, adjustments, etc.

Purchases

The service organisation should buy materials and/or other services from reputable suppliers only. With established reliable suppliers, there should be little or no need to have to inspect materials on receipt at your own premises.

Final inspection

Where possible a final check on the completed service is desirable. To be effective, this final inspection should be able to determine that work done at all previous stages of the service has in fact been performed properly. Final inspection can, therefore, be treated as an audit of the total quality system. If work is regularly subject to inspection, it is important to identify its status at any time:

1. Work completed but not yet inspected
2. Work inspected and passed
3. Work inspected and rejected for investigation

Final audit may be carried out on a spot-check or random basis.

Random sampling

All samples can exhibit sampling error, i.e. results which are untypical due purely to chance. Such unintended bias may lead to erroneous conclusions. It is important, therefore, that the risk of such error is taken into account when carrying out random checks.

Preservation of quality

It is vitally important that service work properly carried out at one stage is not undone at any subsequent stage. The designers of the quality system should identify how this could happen and aim to prevent it. For example, a patient's temperature, pulse rate, etc., in a hospital ward could be correctly measured at the time but incorrectly recorded or interpreted. Likewise, a properly resprayed car could be inadvertently scratched when driving it out onto the garage forecourt.

A fundamental question throughout the quality system design should be: 'What are the opportunities for error?' The view should be that mistakes don't just happen, they are caused either by a poor system or by poor people. Improve the system and the opportunities for error are reduced. Improve the people and the quality should be even better.

Training

All service personnel should be adequately educated in quality matters and trained to do their job properly. This seems so obvious as to be hardly worth stating, yet lack of proper training is a major cause of quality problems. The investment in training is a prevention cost and will pay for itself in reduced customer complaints, provided the rest of the quality system supports the personnel involved.

Review of the quality system

Of course no system is perfect, and so a periodic review should help to identify weaknesses in the present system and how it can be strengthened. Regular minuted review meetings of key staff should aim to review the quality improvement progress made and plan the next projects for the forthcoming period.

CLASSIFICATION OF ERROR

It is useful to classify errors, or defective work, into three categories:

1. *Critical*. A critical error is one which totally prevents the service from fulfilling its intended purpose. Examples are:
   (a) person booked on the wrong flight;
   (b) babies mixed up in a maternity ward;
   (c) a student turns up for the wrong examination.
2. *Major*. While not a critical mistake, a major error is one which has a serious effect on the quality of service. Examples are:
   (a) name misspelt on coffin;
   (b) blurred photograph;
   (c) incorrect postcode.

3. *Minor*. A minor error is a departure from specification, but one which will not seriously affect the quality of service. Examples are:
   (a) inadequate sugar in coffee from vending machine;
   (b) inconsequential typing errors;
   (c) slight smudges left after window-cleaning.

The amount of irritation/distress generated clearly depends on the category of error. Some minor errors could probably be tolerated whereas just one critical error would not.

There is no hard and fast rule to establish to which category a particular error should belong. What may be critical for one person may merely be a minor irritation to someone else. Allocation to a category will, therefore, depend on the particular type of business and its customers.

It is also not enough, therefore, simply to monitor and investigate 'errors'. The analysis over a period of time should show the trend in each category. Clearly the action required over critical errors may be dramatically different to that required for minor ones.

RELIABILITY

The reliability of a service may be apparent in various ways:

1. *The ability to deliver*. For example, a domestic appliance service organisation's guarantee to bring a service engineer to your home within a few hours.
2. *Work carried out to a given standard remains effective*. For example, a repaired leaky roof stays sound for its expected life.

Such examples of reliability are easily demonstrated by the lack of recalls. There is nothing more frustrating to a customer than to find that the job hasn't been done properly the first time.

Statistical approach to reliability

The more links there are in the service chain, the more reliable each link must be if the service is to be adequately reliable overall. Even seemingly simple services can be broken down into several stages. For example, in a branch library a customer request for a book may consist of at least the following:

1. Record customers request
2. Raise interlibrary loan paperwork
3. Despatch paperwork to main library
4. Record receipt of book
5. Inform customer
6. Issue book to customer
7. Return book to main lending library

An error or delay at any of these 'stages' could result in a less than satisfactory service either to the customer and/or to the image of the library. Obviously such failures need to be minimised in order that the total reliability of the service can be considered adequate.

Each of these so called 'stages' would need to be broken down even further into minutely detailed actions if we were to have a full description of this service. However, we will instead look at a simpler case involving only five stages to explore the statistics of reliability. Figure 8.2 shows the five stages in cascade.

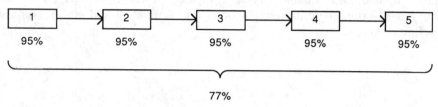

Figure 8.2 Overall reliability of a service in five stages

Q. Given that each stage is 95% reliable (i.e. it has an independent probability of 95% that the work will be done correctly) how reliable is the service?

A. The service reliability is $(0.95)^5$

$$= 0.95 \times 0.95 \times 0.95 \times 0.95 \times 0.95 = 0.77 \text{ or } 77\%$$

Therefore some error or errors can be expected to occur on 23% of occasions. You may consider that this overall reliability is less than adequate.

Q. How reliable must each stage be in order that the total service reliability is 95%?

A. This is illustrated in Figure 8.3:

$$(0.95)^{1/5} = 0.9898 \text{ or } 98.98\%$$

Notice in Figures 8.2 and 8.3 that each stage must be more reliable than the total service. There is no point, however, in any link being significantly better than the rest, as of course the overall reliability cannot be better than its weakest link.

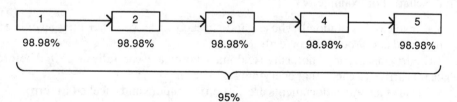

Figure 8.3 Individual reliability to achieve an overall reliability of 95%

It follows that services requiring many stages of work will demand a very high degree of reliability indeed from each stage to ensure that the total service is adequately reliable. The calibre of the staff and the systems they operate at each stage is clearly demonstrated by the total reliability of the service and vice versa.

STATISTICAL METHODS FOR DETERMINING QUALITY

Attribute Charts

A graphical record is kept of the number of errors found and compared with an appropriate limit. An example is given in Figure 8.4. The chart clearly shows that there was a serious deterioration in quality at samples 9 and 10. Action must therefore be taken.

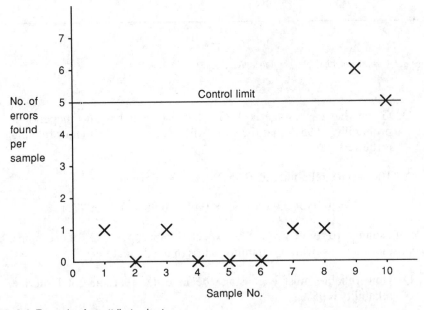

Figure 8.4 Example of an attribute chart

Applications

Attribute charts are suitable where the work done can be classified simply as error free or defective. A sample of *n* jobs is examined and the number of faults recorded on the chart. For example:

1. 500 invoices are randomly chosen and checked to see whether they have been prepared and processed correctly.
2. 10 bedrooms in a large hotel are randomly chosen and carefully inspected before clients arrive to check that everything is in order.
3. 100 sets of air travel documents are chosen at random and checked for error.

Designing an attribute sampling plan

Ideally, of course, there would be no errors but perfection may not always be attainable. Two important quality levels should be established:

1. *The acceptable quality level (AQL)*. This is the maximum tolerable level of error

expressed as a percentage. In the case of critical errors the AQL should be 0%. It may be possible to be more tolerant of minor defects.

2. *The lot tolerance percent defective (LTPD)*. This is an error rate which is quite definitely intolerable. If the work contained this error rate then the sample plan used should detect this fact reliably so that action can be triggered.

A perfect sampling plan would always accept good work and always reject error-ridden work, i.e. it would always be fair. Unfortunately, random samples may be biased purely by chance and give an unfair impression of the total picture. That is, a relatively good sample could be drawn from work which was not good (β error). Alternatively, a sample could contain more errors than would have been fair, giving an adverse impression of the work done (α error).

Such β and α risks can be minimised by a suitable choice of the sample size and control limit. Table 8.1 gives examples of sampling plans and their characteristics for various sample sizes, AQLs and LTPDs, based on probability theory. The control limit is the maximum number of errors permitted in the sample. If this limit is exceeded then it can reasonably be inferred that the work is unacceptable against the specified quality levels.

Table 8.1

Sample size	Control limit	% AQL	% LTPD	α risk	β risk
5	0	2.5	40	25	10
20	0	0.65	12	12.2	8
50	0	0.25	6	11.8	5
200	1	0.25	2.4	9.0	5
500	2	0.15	1.5	4.1	2.5

As can be seen from the table, good control can only be assured by large sample sizes. It is impossible to assure good quality to a high level of confidence by using small sample sizes. For example, Table 8.1 shows that with a sample of only 5 items, there is a 10% risk that no evidence of errors would be present in the sample even if 40% errors occurred in the work. As in most things, you get what you pay for in statistical sampling. (For further details of attribute sampling plans see British Standard specification BS 6001.)

The non-detection of problems

The risks of non-detection of problems can be assessed using probability theory. For example:

Q. If we take a random sample of 10 items of work from a total of 200 of which 195 are satisfactory and 5 are unsatisfactory, what is the probability that the sample will contain no defective items?

A. Average expected number of defectives in the sample $= 10 \times 5/200 = 0.25$

Furthermore, the probability of zero defectives in the sample $= e^{-0.25} = 0.78$ (78%) where e is the constant 2.71828 (base of natural logarithms). We can conclude therefore, that it is extremely unlikely, given that 5 pieces of defective work existed in 200, that some of the defectives would be found in a random sample of only 10. Sampling on this scale cannot be relied on to pick up evidence of trouble. A larger sample would be more effective – and more expensive.

Using the above equations it can be shown that with a sample of 100 items we would stand about a 92% chance of discovering bad work in the same circumstances. Of course, following the discovery that some work was not satisfactory it may be necessary then to examine the rest of the work to identify all the errors.

These figures reveal the fallacy of trying to 'inspect' quality into the work by sampling. A small sample may be cheap but is ineffective. To be really effective, the sample size must be extraordinarily large, perhaps even 100%, which is cumbersome and expensive. The only *real* practical answer in such a case is to concentrate on prevention and to reduce the error rate to such small proportions that no 'inspection' is necessary.

PROBLEM-SOLVING IN QUALITY IMPROVEMENT

A suitable procedure for tackling quality problems is given below:

1. Identify quality problem.
2. Gather data on the problem area.
3. Identify causes of the problem.
4. Generate alternative 'solutions' for each cause.
5. Evaluate alternatives.
6. Choose appropriate solutions.
7. Recommend solutions to management and obtain approval.
8. Implement solutions.
9. Monitor results.

Similar procedures have been followed successfully by many quality improvement teams.

The 'brainstorming' method is used to speculate on possible causes of the problem and to suggest alternative ways of solving it. Brainstorming is a group procedure to generate a large number of ideas in a short period of time. Each person in the brainstorming group is encouraged to put forward as many ideas as possible, suspending judgement, developing other group members' ideas and even encouraging wild ideas. Paradoxically, the brainstorming procedure is usually the least time-consuming part of the problem-solving process. As many as 100 ideas can be generated in half an hour from a group of six to ten people, provided they are acquainted with the technique.

The data gathering stage is usually more time-consuming, as it is necessary to obtain sufficient 'proof' that the real causes of the problem have been established.

Quality of information

No manager is better than the information he or she uses. Management decisions cannot on average be better than the information on which they are based. Even though good decisions may occasionally result from no more than inspired guess-work, this is not a sound long-term basis for management judgement.

In the early days of computers, the emphasis was to produce vast quantities of printout – what is described nowadays as 'too much data, not enough information' – a situation which is generally regarded as no longer tolerable. An up-to-date management information system (MIS) is one where the emphasis is on the *quality* of the information, not the quantity. The MIS should be designed, therefore, to supply each manager/supervisor/worker with information which is relevant, timely, accurate and in the appropriate form, to avoid the confusion and overload caused by superfluous 'data'.

Cause and effect diagrams

A useful way of analysing and depicting a quality problem is the 'fishbone' or cause and effect diagram. Figure 8.5 shows an example. Of course, each of these 'causes' may in turn have other causes. For example, 'wrong programme' may be due to a mix-up of discs in turn due to a poor system: 'careless operator' may be due to lack of motivation, too many distractions, or unsuitable person and so on. The cause and effect diagram should not be made too detailed, however, or it will defeat its purpose of clarifying the make-up of the problem.

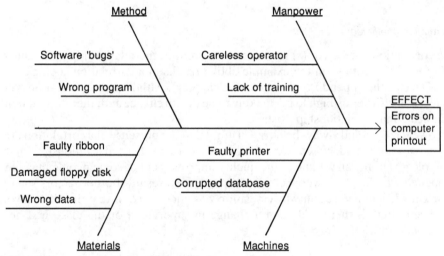

Figure 8.5 Example of a cause and effect diagram

Once it has been established which are the real rather than apparent causes then action needs to be taken on each one of them. Such actions will probably be separate and quite different. For example, the corrective action needed over 'lack of training' would be quite different from the handling of 'faulty printer'.

Although simple enough in principle, the fishbone diagram has proved itself to be an effective aid to a systematic and thorough approach to quality improvement, both during the analysis stage and as a visual aid when a team presents its results.

Causal relationships

A quality investigation requires the establishment of cause and effect relationships, for example the relationship of error rate to the amount of training given. If the extent of the nature of such a relationship was established it could be used to derive the optimum amount of training.

Methods of measuring such relationships are given below.

Scatter diagram

Relationships can be depicted as scatter diagrams, examples of which are given in Figure 8.6.

For example, suppose ten clerical assistants were given various amounts of training and the 'improvement' in their quality of work measured subsequently was as follows:

	Person No.	1	2	3	4	5	6	7	8	9	10
x	No. of days' training	5	7	10	6	11	4	15	12	8	16
y	% Quality improvement	26	25	33	18	34	25	35	29	23	29

Figure 8.7 depicts this data in scatter diagram form. It can be seen that there is some relationship but that it is not perfect, i.e. the plots do not lie on a straight line.

Correlation coefficient

The correlation coefficient (r) measures the extent of the relationship on a scale of -1 to $+1$. The data from the example above results in a correlation coefficient of $+0.6766$ (see the appendix at the end of the chapter). Although the correlation is not perfect it is sufficiently high to be unlikely to be due to chance and, therefore, it tends to indicate that a relationship exists.

However, it should always be borne in mind that the presence of a correlation does *not* prove cause and effect. Correlations need to be treated cautiously. In the example given, for all we know, the quality improvement of some people may have happened whether they were retrained or not, be a result of other factors such as their knowledge that a quality investigation was under way, or that the office layout had been altered, there had been a change in supervisor, or the place had been recently decorated.

Regression

Although the plots are scattered it is convenient to represent the relationship by a straight regression line. (For the above data, the appropriate equation is $y = 19.42 + 0.88x$. The calculation is given in the appendix at the end of the chapter.)

Despite their limitations the correlation and regression 'least squares' method can prove extremely useful.

Chi-squared test

This test can sometimes be used to show 'beyond reasonable doubt' whether differences in quality results are significant or not. For example, suppose a comparison has been made of the quality of service over four different transport 'routes' as follows:

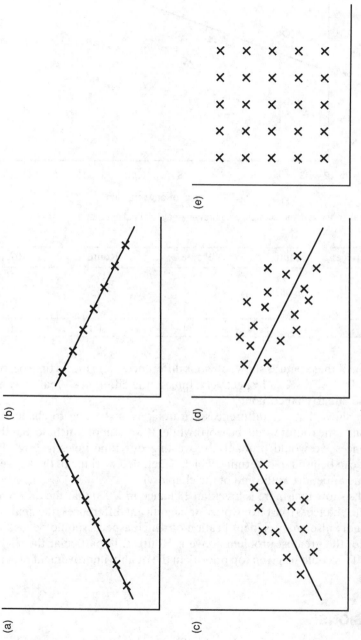

Figure 8.6 Examples of scatter diagrams: (a) perfect positive correlation; (b) perfect negative correlation; (c) positive correlation; (d) negative correlation; (e) no correlation

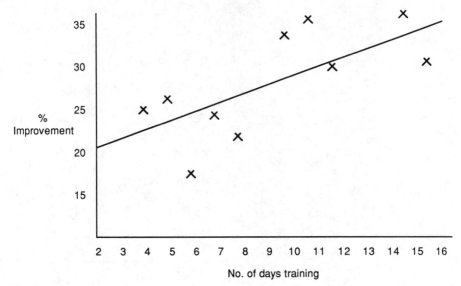

Figure 8.7 Scatter diagram for example of improvement in clerical assistants

Quality of service	Route 1	Route 2	Route 3	Route 4
On time	95	80	175	150
Slight delay	40	14	15	20
Serious delay	15	6	10	10
Total journeys	150	100	200	180

Examination of these figures shows obvious differences, e.g. the on time percentages were 63%, 80%, 87%, 83% respectively, but are the differences 'real' or could such variations be due to chance alone?

If we can show that the differences are unlikely to be due to chance then an investigation of the routes would be worthwhile. If we cannot conclude that there are real differences we would probably be wasting our time investigating. The *chi-squared test* can be used to determine which. (Detailed working of the above figures is given in the appendix at the end of the chapter.)

The results show that there is less than 1 chance in 1,000 that the differences are merely due to chance. Apart from 'proving' significant differences, the analysis given in the appendix also enables identification of which aspects should be tackled first. For example, the greatest problem above is Route 1, in particular the slight delay figure (40). This could be given top priority in the quality improvement programme.

CONCLUSIONS

The operations manager will need to identify those aspects of quality and reliability that are present with the service that is being offered. The chapter has shown the approach to apply to ensure that quality defects are prevented. It has also shown how to set up a system of monitoring so that control can be exercised. The most important concept is that of total quality – this is seen as a central feature of the service delivery and contributes directly to both resource productivity and customer satisfaction.

References and suggested reading

British Standards Institution (1981) *Quality Costs*. BS 6143. London: BSI.
British Standards Institution (1972) *Sampling Procedures and Tables for Inspections by Attributes*. BS 6001. London: BSI.
British Standards Institution (1987) *Quality Systems*. BS 5750/ISO 9000 series.
Caplen, R. H. (1988) *A Practical Approach to Quality Control*, revised edn. London: Business Books.
Crosby, P. B. (1979) *Quality is Free*. New York: McGraw-Hill.
Crosby, P. B. (1985) *Quality Without Tears*. New York: McGraw-Hill.
Hostage, G. M. (July/August 1973) Quality control in a service business. *Harvard Business Review*, pp. 98–106.
Johnston, R. (1986) *A Framework for Developing a Quality Strategy in a Consumer Processing Operation*. University of Warwick.
Juran, J. M. (1974) *Quality Control Handbook*, 3rd edn. New York: McGraw-Hill.
Moroney, N. J. (1962) *Facts From Figures*. Harmondsworth, Middx: Penguin.
Oakland, J. S. (1986) *Statistical Process Control*. London: Heinemann.
Price, F. (1984) *Right First Time*. Aldershot: Wildwood House.
Stebbins, L. (1986) *Quality Assurance*. Chichester: Ellis Horwood.
Wallis, P. N. (1961) *Quality Control in the Office*. London: Current Affairs Ltd.

APPENDIX: DETAILED CALCULATIONS

Correlation method

The *correlation coefficient* is calculated from the following formula:

$$r = \frac{n\Sigma xy - (\Sigma x)(\Sigma y)}{\sqrt{(n\Sigma x^2 - (\Sigma x)^2)(n\Sigma y^2 - (\Sigma y)^2)}}$$

Example

x	y	xy	x^2	y^2
5	26	130	25	676
7	25	175	49	625
10	33	330	100	1,089
6	18	108	36	324
11	34	374	121	1,156
4	25	100	16	625
15	35	525	225	1,225
12	29	348	144	841
8	23	184	64	529
16	29	464	256	841
94	277	2,738	1,036	7,931

$$r = \frac{(10 \times 2,738) - (94)(277)}{\sqrt{(10 \times 1,036 - 94^2)(10 \times 7,931 - 277^2)}}$$

$$= \frac{1,342}{\sqrt{(1,524)(2,581)}} = \frac{1,342}{1,983} = 0.6766$$

Regression 'least squares' method

The *regression equations* are calculated as follows:

$$y = A + Bx \qquad \text{where } B = \frac{n\Sigma xy - (\Sigma x)(\Sigma y)}{n\Sigma x^2 - (\Sigma x)^2}$$

$$A = \frac{\Sigma y - B(\Sigma x)}{n}$$

$$B = \frac{1{,}342}{1{,}524} = 0.88$$

$$A = \frac{277 - 0.88(94)}{10} = 19.42$$

$$\therefore y = 19.42 + 0.88x$$

Chi-squared method

	Observed values (O)				Row total		Expected values (E)				
	95	80	175	150	500		119	79	159	143	500
	40	14	15	20	89		21	14	28	26	89
	15	6	10	10	41		10	6	13	12	41
Column total	150	100	200	180	630		150	100	200	180	630
					Grand total						

Each expected value is derived thus:

$$\text{Expected value} = \frac{\text{Column total} \times \text{Row total}}{\text{Grand total}}$$

e.g. for Column 1, Row 1, the expected value $= \dfrac{150 \times 500}{630} = 119.$

Calculation of chi-squared

O = Observed	E = Expected	$(O - E)^2/E$	Priority ranking	
95	119	4.86	3	
80	79	0.01	11	
175	159	1.67	5	
150	143	0.36	7	Biggest misfit:
40	21	16.70	1	top priority for
14	14	0.00	12	investigation.
15	28	6.22	2	
20	26	1.16	6	
15	10	2.81	4	
6	6	0.04	10	
10	13	0.07	9	
10	12	0.25	8	
	$\Sigma((O-E)^2/E)$	= chi^2 = 34.76		

159

Tested against the critical value from tables the result is highly significant (critical value for 6 degrees of freedom = 22.46). Such a result could be expected to occur by chance alone only in 1 occasion in 1,000. We can conclude, therefore, that the differences are real.

From the above figures, it can be seen that the biggest 'misfit' is Column 1, Row 2 (O = 40, E = 21). This aspect would be worth top priority investigation.

9
CAPITAL ASSETS AND THEIR UTILISATION

INTRODUCTION

Within all spheres of service activity there is a noticeable increase in the reliance on facilities which require a major investment, i.e. buildings, machines, vehicles, specially designed equipment, computer systems, etc. Not all of these need be bought – in fact leasing is used quite extensively. (Leasing refers to 'a contract to use capital goods owned by others in return for a rental'. Usually such contracts are for a minimum specified period and include maintenance undertaken by the owners.)

Whenever assets are considered and however they are to be 'owned' a number of decisions have to be made:

1. Is it worthwhile overall? Some items may be 'nice to have' but it must be demonstrated that they are going to make a beneficial contribution to the effective operation of the unit.
2. Which model should be purchased (or specialised firm engaged in the case of customised equipment)? This is rather like the consumers' *Which?* and requires complex consideration of such features as:
   (a) Reliability
   (b) Maintainability
   (c) Capital costs versus running costs
   (d) Degree of obsolescence (this can prove a decisive reason for leasing)
3. Once equipment is installed there are decisions on:
   (a) Maintenance, repair and running costs
   (b) Utilisation
   (c) Replacement
4. An overriding feature of such decisions is the degree to which the assets are considered are 'out of date'. This has been particularly noticeable in computing systems – where a highly competitive market has created a number of lower-cost alternatives which means that for some larger organisations updating is not a major capital decision, but more of a spares replacement decision.

What has been said so far indicates that for most operations managers decisions on capital assets will not be entirely within their control. As the major user of the assets it would be wrong to allow the decision to be made without the operations manager, and equally wrong to expect that person to be the sole decision-maker. The decisions are very high risk and commit the organisation for a number of years in terms of fitness for purpose, and all capital assets carry a 'use cost' whether it be energy, repairs, or consumable items like discs, paper, etc.

Because of the many people in an organisation who need to be involved in these decisions, here is an obvious need for a systems approach. This has been variously named as:

1. Life cycle management
2. Asset management
3. Terotechnology

Here is a definition which summarises the approach:

> A combination of management, financial, engineering and other practices applied to physical assets in pursuit of economic life cycle costs.
>
> *Note:*
> Its practice is concerned with the specification and design for reliability and maintainability of plant, machinery, equipment, buildings and structures, with their installation, commissioning, maintenance, modification and replacement, and with feedback of information on design, performance and costs.
>
> (Committee for Industrial Technologies, 1974)

This means that all parts of the decision cycle related to capital assets are dependent upon other parts.

This chapter is structured on the basis of the groups of major decisions that we have mentioned:

1. Do we need the capital asset?
2. Selection of equipment
3. Maintenance
4. Utilisation
5. Replacement

DO WE NEED THE CAPITAL ASSET?

Perhaps the most fundamental decision here is to review the service objectives. Often service is synonymous with 'personal service', but more and more the customer/client is involved in the process by some self-service method. For many customers being in control and not being involved with others is seen as an advantage. In a recently government-sponsored project entitled Training Access Points, an information base which was menu-driven was put on a computer terminal so that customers/enquirers could access the information until they narrowed their requirements to the type of training opportunity, level and location, and then they could get a printout. Although such points will initially be staffed, the intention is to have unmanned points with a telephone link line for further advice and referral. This would obviously need careful siting to avoid vandalism, and simple controls to avoid misuse.

The absence of people can often enhance the service so that only the complex enquiries need to be dealt with personally. The remainder (often up to 80%) can be serviced by customer access. Many people feel inhibited using a service when they need to articulate their enquiries to another person.

In the case of computer-based activities the need for a total systems approach is vital, since the quality of the hardware has got to be complemented by the software and updating procedures.

Whilst decisions of a different kind are taken regarding 'buildings and structures', often at a 'service delivery' level the need for a basic decision on whether to mechanise, automate or computerise is based on the effect this is likely to have on the customer/client, not necessarily purely on whether it is possible. On the other hand there are likely to be some obvious benefits as a result of the investment. These are listed in Table 9.1.

Table 9.1 List of benefits of automation.

1. *Labour saving.* Intrinsic by definition. Important to realise this is not the only or often most important consideration. Training problems are eliminated.

2. *Plant utilisation saving.* Reduces waiting between operations. Pinpoints delays to those parts getting quick corrective action. Not dependent on availability of operator.

3. *Increase of maximum unit capacity.* Overtime etc. can be worked independent of labour. Not affected by tea, lunch, etc., breaks. Supervision is reduced to minimum and performance is independent of it, i.e. no variation day v. nightshift.

4. *Space saving.* No need for access and movement of operator. Reduced gangways. Minimises in-process storage and WIP, thus gives potential to use inaccessible parts of area/space.

5. *Progressive optimisation.*
   (a) Due to automatic unit performing consistently and not suffering deterioration due to operator change/illness, human fallibility.
   (b) Eases management worries in that instructions will be followed to the letter. Consistency in product quality does away with inquests (usually pointless) about quality problems and complaints.
   (c) Rigid control provided by system gives a stable background against which further improvements can be introduced.

6. *Benefits of progressiveness.* Many people/units are very keen to be associated with new equipment/methods/systems and gain more knowledge and skills.

Despite the possible obvious advantages there are also some problems that must never be overlooked. It is unlikely that workers will be totally negative but positive attitudes can only be developed by adequate attention to the management of change (see Chapter 12).

A very important issue is also ensuring that the equipment is going to work once installed and the back-up system removed. The commonest cause of dissatisfaction at work (29%) was 'recurrent technical trouble or powerlessness during breakdowns' (Clive Vamplew, *British Journal of Industrial Relations* (November 1973), cited in McBeath (1974)).

Financial justification

One very obvious factor is whether we can justify the expenditure in terms of savings or profits. This is not an easy calculation. Some of the more common accounting methods for capital expenditure evaluation are given below.

Payback period

This is a widely used method. It is simply a rule that a proposed expenditure must be recoverable in, say, three years. It is useful if there is a tight cash position, but it does not consider capital wastage, the timing of investment and payback, and the returns after the investment is repaid.

Return on capital

The method used for historical evaluation of return on capital throughout industry is profit after depreciation (before or after tax) as a percentage of initial capital. If this method is used for prior evaluation of capital projects, it has the two serious disadvantages of ignoring timing and ignoring the actual amount of capital still locked up in a project.

The net gain method

This method takes account of the timing of investments and returns. If money is invested in a bank deposit account its value after n years is increased by interest compounded annually. The value of principal (P) and interest is:

$$P \times (1 + i)$$

where i is the rate of interest paid as a decimal (e.g. $10\% = 0.1$).

Discounted cash flow (DCF)

Conversely the value now of a return of £P n years hence (the discounted value) is:

$$P \times \frac{1}{(1 + i)}$$

This formula provides a basis for placing all investments in a project and all returns on a common footing.

The complicating aspects of capital return evaluation are:

1. There may be several amounts to be invested in phases.
2. The amounts may be different.
3. The timing may be irregular.
4. The returns will be spread over several years.

The DCF formula enables all these difficulties to be overcome by converting all investments and returns to their discounted total values at a particular point (preferably the beginning of the first pay-off year).

A market rate of interest is assumed. If the difference between discounted returns and investment is positive (indicating a rate of return greater than market) the project goes ahead. However, grave disadvantages for the method lie in the difficulty of setting the rate of interest, in the fact that interest rates change and in the fact that the supply of money is limited.

The DCF method is illustrated in Table 9.2 which shows the calculations for a tilt-tray sorting machine for British Rail for which the initial outlay is £20,300. The saving over manual methods is estimated at £10,000 and the calculations take account of all taxes and allowances. The result is a net present value (NPV) cash return of £2,919 for a capital outlay of £20,300, with a return on investment of 20%. This is for 25,000 parcels per day, but with a higher rate of parcels, the profit over the manual system would be higher, resulting in a higher expected rate of return.

Table 9.2 DCF calculations.

Year:	0	1	2	3	4	5	6	7
1. Cash outlay	(20,300)	—	—	—	—	—	3,000 resale value	
2. Cash returns (profit over manual system)	—	10,000	10,000	10,000	10,000	10,000	—	
3. Running costs	—	(1,000)	(1,000)	(1,000)	(1,000)	(1,000)	—	
4. Net cash in (2) − (3)	—	9,000	9,000	9,000	9,000	9,000	—	
5. Capital allowance at 25% on reducing balance	—	5,075	3,806	2,855	2,141	1,606	(balancing allowance) 1,817	
6. Residual value of ½ capital allowances	—	15,225	11,419	8,564	6,423	4,817	Nil	
7. Taxable returns (4) − (5)	—	3,925	5,194	6,145	6,859	7,394	(1,817)	
8. Corporation tax at 35% (1 year delay)	—	—	(1,374)	(1,818)	(2,151)	(2,401)	(2,588)	636
9. After-tax cash flows (4) − (8) + (1)	(20,300)	9,000	7,626	7,182	6,849	6,599	412	636
10. 20% factor	—	0.833	0.694	0.579	0.482	0.402	0.335	0.279
11. Present value (10) × (9)	(20,300)	7,500	5,292	4,158	3,301	2,653	138	177
12. Net present value	£2,919							

Conclusion: The investment is worthwhile.

SELECTION OF EQUIPMENT

Once the decision has been taken to acquire new equipment rather than leave things as they are then a systematic approach to selection is vital. Let us use as an illustration for this the selection of office machinery – a job which could be very easy, e.g. 'We will have a word processor to replace/supplement our typewriters'. However, sometimes poor selection results.

Poor selection

It is pointless to dwell too long on why we make mistakes, but perhaps these words may serve as a warning:

1. Unfamiliarity with equipment available.
2. Believing too much in sales people.
3. 'Keeping up with the Joneses'.
4. Lack of operator training in use of equipment.

Some of the effects of poor selection are as follows:

1. Organising the job to suit the machine rather than vice-versa.
2. Being unable to cope with peak loading.
3. Having expensive equipment which is completely inflexible with a low utilisation.

You should realise that these are only three of many other possible reasons. We propose to look very carefully at the problem of poor selection and see how it can be avoided. Considerably greater care is often taken in the selection of machinery for manufacturing than in the selection of office equipment. Although the investment in office equipment is less, there is no reason why the firm should not endeavour to get a reasonable return on its investment.

Analysis of clerical methods

An analysis and critical examination of the work under review should be carried out and all the improvements possible should have been completed in respect of:

1. elimination,
2. combination, and
3. simplification.

Further, this should result in developing the 'best manual method' with which any proposed mechanised method must be compared (see Chapter 4).

When it is confirmed that there is need for machinery, a full description of the necessary requirements of the machine should be prepared. This should contain the following information:

1. Type of work (purpose)
2. Quantity of work
3. Quality requirements
4. Frequency or speed
5. Any special stationery requirements.

Such data could be labelled as the 'office machine specification'.

The type of work or purpose will indicate the general category of machine (accounting, adding, typing, etc.) but with many hybrid types of machine and a considerable range within each classification, the remaining information is required in order to select the most suitable machine or machines. Remember, despite the flexibility of many computers it is a waste (of money and potential) to have a complex machine which is only going to be used on a simple task.

Capacity and potential utilisation

In some cases it may be necessary to justify a machine on utilisation or to show other work that could be dealt with by it. To assist in this, work measurement techniques can be used. If necessary, such techniques can also determine the number of machines to be purchased.

Choice of machines

When the choice has been narrowed to about three machines the final decision will depend upon the following factors:

1. *Comparative costs*:
    (a) *Initial cost* – return on investment, amortisation period, installation costs, training costs and costs of ancilliary equipment.
    (b) *Operating costs* – a direct comparison with the best manual method, namely:

Manual costs:	*Machine costs*:
Clerical wages	Operator's wages; any remaining clerical wages
Stationery	Machine depreciation; machine maintenance
Value of office space	Stationery; value of office space

2. *Comparative speeds*. Often variations in speed are reflected in costs since it is true to say that time equals money in most enterprises. Perhaps an important factor which would be considered here is the speed at which information transmission is required.
3. *Quality of work*. Errors in calculation and transcription are usually minimised by machines, but quality may be reflected in presentation – legibility of copies, for example. Here integration with form design is an important aspect by which quality may be improved.
4. *Flexibility*. What effect will the machine have on peak loads and changes in volume of work?
5. *Ease of operation*. For example, what skills are necessary to operate machines, and how much operator training is required?
6. *The effect on labour force*. For example, redundancy and how to overcome the problems that arise.
7. *Reliability of equipment*. Data on this aspect may be available from *Which?* type reports. Breakdowns must be considered and how they will be handled without spare machine capacity. Can spare machines be made available by the manufacturer?

8. *Noise*. Special soundproofing may be required to isolate noise from other clerical operations.
9. *Power supply*. Points and wiring may be required to facilitate flexibility of layout.
10. *Supplementary equipment*. This is a 'fixed' cost – cutaway desks, special chairs, tables, boxes and files for cards, special stationery, etc.

Actual bases for selection

Although due weighting should be given to all the above factors, the only criterion used for selection is often the cost of purchase rather than comparative costs. Yet other organisations use 'ease of use' by present staff as the *only* method of selection.

Lease or buy?

The usual advantages claimed in favour of leasing are:

1. Scarce capital is freed for other uses.
2. The risk of obsolescence is borne by the lessor for short- and medium-term contracts.

Against this, one can argue that capital can probably be obtained as cheaply by the lessee as by the lessor, and that the obsolescence factor is incorporated in the rentals by way of a premium. Furthermore, the lessor will normally have no economies over the lessee in equipment purchase price, taxation, maintenance costs, obsolescence risk or cost of capital, at any rate as far as a medium or large firm is concerned.

On the other hand, particular circumstances that might favour leasing include:

1. Random peak demand.
2. Seasonal demand – provided that the season of peak demand for all users does not coincide.
3. Uncertainty – where a firm has a requirement for an asset only for a part of the asset's expected life, e.g. for three years out of ten such as when there is a risk associated with a new venture.
4. Specialisation – where a specialised firm is hired, e.g. contractors to distribute goods at peak periods.
5. Low utilisation – where the lessee requires an asset intermittently over a long period, e.g. a computer for five hours per week.

The best way to compare 'lease or buy' alternatives is by a modification of the DCF method in which the costs are the purchase price and the income the payments to the lessor, including tax payments and reliefs when paid. The 'profits' can be expressed in terms of the costs (or capital invested) and compared with other investment opportunities.

MAINTENANCE

Once equipment is installed it needs maintaining. The cost and the problems of sudden failure of equipment can influence organisations to adopting maintenance contracts with manufacturers or suppliers – this has been a particularly dominant feature of computer and photocopier installations. Similarly the 'leasing' arrangement has an inbuilt maintenance feature. The costs associated with this need to be carefully considered, but obviously for small units without the capacity to employ specialist technical staff, the leasing or contract arrangement acts as a form of insurance. With some contracts the price paid is based on speed of response – and so the effect of failure needs to be considered with great care not just by the operations manager, but also by the whole organisation.

One aspect of the 'maintenance' of floors, walls, windows, etc., is regular cleaning. Many organisations are finding this is a task that can be subcontracted to specialists at a known cost.

Of course some equipment can be purchased or rented and function for years without any faults or problems occurring – we all know of the TV and car that have had little done to them and work seemingly for ever. It is a reasonable policy – if it is thought through – to have a system that only responds when the equipment fails. It can be argued that continually fiddling with equipment by some preventive scheme can cause as many faults as it prevents. Records of failure and maintenance are important to establish a policy relating to this. Undoubtedly most people will be familiar with a maintenance policy which uses some form of planned preventive maintenance (e.g. car servicing) and this is quite widely used.

General considerations of the maintenance of equipment

It is the service manager's responsibility 'to ensure that, at minimum cost, plant and equipment are available for productive use, for the scheduled hours, operating to agreed standards with minimum waste' (Health and Safety at Work Act 1974). Maintenance is therefore conducted to:

1. improve safety;
2. maximise efficient utilisation of equipment;
3. avoid repair costs;
4. improve cost control;
5. reduce downtime;
6. boost employee morale;
7. reduce costs;
8. prolong the age of the asset.

To fulfil these functions, maintenance must be planned and based on a strict programme of inspection and servicing. The frequency of inspection generally depends on the conditions under which the equipment is operated, but in most cases the manufacturer's recommendations are sufficient. To maximise productivity, repairs and replacements should be anticipated, and it is essential therefore to keep the question of maintenance well in mind in deciding whether to buy a particular item of equipment.

The first thing to establish is what work the equipment is to do and whether or not it is fitted to do it. Information should be sought on probable maintenance costs, and, if the order is placed, the manufacturer should be asked for detailed preventive maintenance instructions. Once the equipment is on site, the instructions should be embodied in standing procedures, which should be complied with by workshop personnel as well as the equipment operators. The service manager or maintenance engineer will need to familiarise himself with the equipment warranties so that in the event of breakdown he knows where the responsibility lies.

A planned maintenance schedule should be prepared and adhered to. The service manager/maintenance engineer should, in co-operation with supervisory staff, ensure that the equipment is not exposed to risk of damage by misuse, and a record should be kept of the maintenance work performed on each machine or piece of equipment and of the maintenance costs. These records will shed light on the skills needed for maintenance, and enable adequate maintenance facilities to be built up. If a firm does not have the facilities or labour to carry out its own maintenance, it should keep a record of the cost of any maintenance contracts it has entered into with outside specialist firms.

Failure to plan adequate maintenance will lead to repairs and losses in production which almost invariably turn out to be far more expensive than the planned maintenance scheme which could have prevented them.

Types of maintenance

Maintenance is work undertaken in order to keep or restore a facility to an acceptable standard. It may be planned or unplanned. The various types of maintenance are illustrated in Figure 9.1 and described below.

1. *Planned maintenance* is the work known beforehand to be necessary to achieve the above aims, and is therefore organised and carried out with forethought, control and records. It can be either preventive or corrective.
2. *Unplanned maintenance* is work carried out without organised planning, control or records, either as a result of an emergency, or (on an *ad hoc* basis) to accommodate non-urgent jobs when spare labour becomes available.
3. *Preventive maintenance* is any work conducted to prevent failure.
4. *Corrective maintenance* is any work undertaken to restore a facility to an acceptable standard.
5. *Running maintenance* is planned preventive work carried out whilst the facility is in service.
6. *Shutdown maintenance* is planned preventive or corrective work which can be carried out only when the facility is (or is taken) out of service.
7. *Breakdown maintenance* is that planned corrective work which is carried out after a failure, but for which advance provision has been made in the form of spares, materials, labour, etc.
8. *Emergency maintenance* is any unplanned work necessitated by unforeseen breakdown or damage.

Developing a planned maintenance scheme

A good planned maintenance scheme will have three basic features:

1. An operations schedule covering inspection, lubrication, adjustment, rectification and periodic overhaul.
2. Some means of ensuring that all of these operations are carried out in accordance with the schedule.

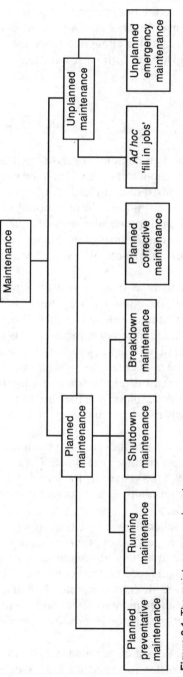

Figure 9.1 The maintenance work system

3. A method of recording the work as completed, and of assessing the results.

As is the case with any planned activity, to be effective maintenance must be controlled, and so will require the maintenance of records. Recording information must take up as little of the maintenance staff's time as possible, though the records should, of course, be comprehensive enough to make the scheme worthwhile. The information recorded should answer four basic questions:

1. What is to be maintained?
2. How is it to be maintained?
3. When is it to be maintained?
4. Is maintenance effective?

To answer the first question an equipment register will need to be kept. Its form will depend on the type and amount of equipment to be covered, but, in the case of large organisations, it may consist of a card index giving details of each mechanical, electrical and other facility requiring periodic attention. Each card should be treated virtually as the identity card for the particular piece of equipment or component, and should include technical and manufacturing information, a reference to a drawing or the manufacturer's handbook, and a note of the supplier and whether the item is still available.

Once the item is recorded in the equipment register, consideration can be given to the method of carrying out the maintenance required. Particulars can then be entered in the overall maintenance schedule which should be kept to provide a comprehensive picture of the maintenance requirements of the whole plant. The schedule should show, in detail, all the work to be done for each piece of equipment covered. Here too, it may be convenient to produce the schedule as a card index. Each card should detail the periodical operations required and specify the logical sequence of the steps involved, explain how they are to be carried out (referring to any special tools or materials required) and point to any safety precautions which need to be observed.

Note that, these days, records like these can be computerised, and even if the item is far away its maintenance record can be examined. For example British Rail's Total Operating Process System (TOPS) covering locomotives (and rolling stock) can be accessed by any point with a terminal. So a 'strange' locomotive on 'foreign' rails can be 'looked at' within seconds.

At first the maintenance schedule will be based largely on the recommendations given in service manuals, or on records of past repairs, replacements and downtime. However, manufacturers' handbooks are sometimes of only limited value (for example, they may give no guidance on the replacement life of components), and existing 'in-house' records are often incomplete. The initial schedule information may therefore have to be supplemented later, and thereafter it will need to be updated in the light of the experience gained from working the system and any feedback of data.

If the maintenance schedule is a comprehensive one (as it commonly is in large organisations) a series of master job specifications detailing the various periodic operations required by individual machines will need to be compiled from it. The degree of detail will naturally depend upon the equipment to be maintained, the experience of the maintenance personnel and the control and supervision exerted.

Some simple items may need nothing more than a small checklist, but for more complex equipment, especially if the turnover of staff is fairly high, the job specification could well be prepared in more detail, to ensure standardisation.

Feedback of information to management is essential if the maintenance scheme is to meet the actual requirements of the application. The maintenance staff should therefore be provided with a well-designed form enabling them to record and analyse the apparent cause of defects found by the supervisor, and to note any corrective action taken or still required. Management should not rely upon verbal reports, which are often forgotten or misunderstood.

The maintenance programme

Next, using the maintenance schedule, a maintenance programme should be prepared listing each item of plant and its reference number, and specifying when each should receive special attention throughout the planning period. The mechanical, electrical and lubrication maintenance required by each item, and the intervals between maintenance, should be given against each item and entered on a timescale (making allowance for holidays). Every operation will then fall within the specified time limits, and the weekly maintenance working load will be spread as evenly as possible.

The maintenance programme should be prepared in consultation with production staff, so that they are aware of future running and shutdown maintenance requirements, as well as the downtime, labour and materials entailed. In the case of shutdown maintenance, the downtime must be established in advance, and if at the end of the period agreed further work is still required, it must be booked for a later date. Only two reasons can be accepted for not handing back a machine at the agreed time: the risk of danger to personnel, and the possibility that further damage will occur from restarting (which would in effect classify the uncompleted work as emergency maintenance).

Recording and analysing results

The compilation of the equipment register, maintenance schedule, job specifications and maintenance programme will be of little value if no provision is made for recording and analysing the results achieved. To do this, a history card should be kept for every item of plant, summarising the failures suffered and the action taken to rectify them, the causes and the effects of breakdown, the man hours devoted to maintenance operations, and the machine downtime. The history card will provide a measure of the efficiency of the department and the methods used. The information should be obtained not only from the maintenance men, but also from any production staff who request assistance when a fault develops between routine inspections, for it is the unexpected failure which shows up weaknesses in the maintenance scheme, and which should therefore be given prominence in the record.

As the problems are ironed out, the need for unscheduled maintenance should decrease. If the need persists, it will mean that there are areas in which maintenance is inadequate. On the other hand, if faults are eliminated altogether the scheme should be reviewed to ensure that overmaintenance is not making it uneconomical.

Consequently, the history record has two aims: to show where maintenance is inadequate, and to indicate where it is being applied to excess.

Maintenance costs will increase with the age of the plant until eventually a stage is reached when it will be cheaper to replace than to maintain. To arrive at a decision, the costs of acquiring and installing the new equipment, and of any associated break in production during installation, will need to be weighed against the costs of the more intensive maintenance which would have prevented the breakdown, the costs of disposing of the old machinery, and any design benefits resulting from the new machinery. The history record should indicate the stage at which this evaluation should be made (see later).

Simple or complex, the maintenance scheme must, if it is to be effective, conform to the above outline. Figure 9.2 provides a diagrammatic representation of the maintenance system.

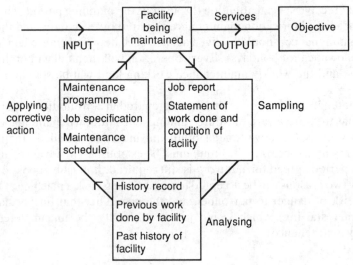

Figure 9.2 Planned maintenance control system

Maintenance cost effectiveness

Maintenance management has always been an 'after the event' activity. Decisions regarding system design and operation have been regarded as being outside the maintenance function. For many instances this is the case even with regard to technical specification.

Maintenance, therefore, in decision-making terms must rely on past history, in so far as it applies, and wait until the system has been in use for a sufficient period of time to show its *use behaviour* before an effective maintenance strategy can be formulated and applied. Maintenance managers, then, in their decision-making role are faced with a 'time-lag' of experience. It is not an uncommon situation to find that the time it takes to gain sufficient knowledge of the behaviour of an item of plant or equipment to be able to manage it effectively is too long to be of value. The damage has been done, the excess costs incurred, the profits reduced, even lost, and a new system installed.

Time costs are seldom if ever known, even with a good management accounting system.

Cost effectiveness

The need for cost effectiveness may be defined as follows:

> The development of a system or equipment that is cost effective, within the constraints specified by operational and maintenance requirements, is a prime objective. Cost effectiveness relates to the measure of a system in terms of 'System Effectiveness' and Total Life-Cycle Cost.
>
> (*Committee for Industrial Technology, 1974*)

In the last decade there has been a growing awareness of the need for measures of the effectiveness of systems in relation to their costs. Exercises in cost effectiveness have been focused both on the analysis of the system as if it were already designed, and on the costs of producing and operating it. Traditionally cost accounting is concerned with past history and fiscal accounting periods. Maintenance expenditure is not related to any fiscal period but rather to the behaviour of the system at variable points in its life cycle.

Cost effectiveness is concerned with decision-making and decisions involving the future. This in turn requires prediction and prediction is, by its nature, uncertain. For all the difficulties and problems to be found in predicting the future behaviour of plant and equipment, the ability to work within a predicted 'life plan' for the equipment, whether this be provided by the supplier or developed for existing plant by the user, is of immense value to the maintenance manager and the organisation as a whole. This has been recognised for some time in the armed services and the aerospace industry. It is only in recent times that other organisations have begun to move in this direction.

Any sophisticated calculations concerning the above would be of particular concern to capital intensive industries like engineering, chemicals, etc., though perhaps less applicable to service industries. However, with more and more sophisticated equipment in hospitals, waste disposal plants, etc., it is likely that some operations managers will wish to review the extent to which the costs over which they have control are dominated by the capital equipment.

UTILISATION

A survey of a local authority showed that individual copying machines in different departments were used on average for 2% of the available time. Because unskilled people were using them, the risk of damage and waste of materials was high and so the survey inevitably led to consideration of another policy for copying. Whilst we might expect a very high utilisation of production equipment – and even materials handling equipment – the use of some office equipment is bound to be more intermittent. However, it is a factor for which the operations manager is responsible and should be able to monitor – in particular when there is a need to present a case for replacement or additional equipment.

Whilst the high utilisation figures of manufacturing are not likely to be reached by all equipment, it may be worthwhile to establish some comparative figures. Whilst floor cleaning machines in a residential home and glass washing machines in a pub may only be available for a short time each day (i.e. cleaning staff working hours and pub opening hours), if that time is the machine availability, then the utilisation time relative to this indicates what capacity is available. Computer equipment is also likely to be very much in demand only at certain times and utilisation studies may lead to a variety of conclusions, one of which could be to extend or stagger working hours to increase machine availability.

As a guide to the manager Figure 9.3 is a useful explanation of machine utilisation.

Machine maximum time:	The maximum possible time which a machine or group of machines could work within a given period.	
Machine available time:	The portion of a time cycle during which a machine could be performing useful work.	Not worked
Working day/week		Overtime
Machine running time: The period when a machine is actually operating	Machine idle time	Machine ancillary time cleaning	Machine down time
Machine running time as standard*	Low performance	* Running time that should be incurred in producing the output if the machine is working under optimum conditions.

Figure 9.3 Explanation of machine utilisation time
Based on BS 3138 (1979)

In order to provide a suitable 'yardstick' for machine utilisation the following ratios can be of value:

Machine utilisation index[*] : $\dfrac{\text{Machine running time}}{\text{Machine available time}}$

Machine efficiency index[*] : $\dfrac{\text{Machine running time at standard}}{\text{Machine running time}}$

Machine effective utilisation index[*] : $\dfrac{\text{Machine running time at standard}}{\text{Machine available time}}$

* Although the term 'machine' has been used this can cover 'equipment', 'system' or 'process', or any other term substituted at the discretion of the user.

REPLACEMENT

At various other points in this chapter the life cycle of equipment has been mentioned, and if records are kept of costs it should be possible to identify the optimum

Table 9.3

Year	Depreciation (D)	Maintenance (M)	D + M	Cumulative D + M	Average D + M p.a.	Residual value
	£	£	£	£	£	£
1	2,500	350	2,850	2,850	2,850	7,500
2	1,875	700	2,575	5,425	2,712	5,625
3	1,406	1,050	2,456	7,881	2,627	4,219
4	1,055	1,400	2,455	10,336	2,584	3,164
5	789	1,750	2,539	12,875	2,575	2,373
6	593	2,100	2,693	15,568	2,595	1,780
7	445	2,450	2,895	18,463	2,638	1,335
8	334	2,800	3,134	21,597	2,700	1,001

point for replacement. However, this is only going to work if 'all other things are equal'. Many such replacement decisions are based on other considerations such as selling before the optimum time, prestige (i.e. having the 'latest' model) and possibly the need for a larger, smaller, faster, or more adaptable piece of equipment. In some cases we hold on to equipment well past the optimum time to sell if we cannot find a buyer or have no finance available for replacement.

However, to demonstrate the mathematical method to decide when to replace we will consider a simple model taken from Sussams (1984) for vehicle replacement which takes into account costs which are incurred at a decreasing rate with time and/ or mileage – in particular depreciation – and costs which are incurred at an increasing rate with time and/or mileage – in particular maintenance.

It can be shown that a reducing balance formula gives a good approximation to actual depreciation. It can also be shown that the increase in maintenance costs from year to year (averaged over a group of similar vehicles used on the same kinds of work) is approximately linear. The ratio of total maintenance costs to total depreciation over the full life of the vehicle varies somewhat depending on the type of vehicle, the way in which it is used and the efficiency of the organisation carrying out the maintenance. However, for the majority of vehicle fleets, this ratio lies in the range from 1/1 to 1.5/1.

Let's take as an example a vehicle costing £10,000. This depreciates at 25% per annum on a reducing balance to a residual (scrap) value of £1,000 after 8 years. During the same 8 years we assume that maintenance costs of £12,600 would be incurred, i.e. £350 in the first year, £700 in the second, £1,050 in the third, etc. Table 9.3 gives these values for each year.

In this case it can be seen that the minimum point is reached in year 5. A more accurate result could be obtained by taking shorter intervals (e.g. of a quarter or a month). However, in practice, such fine divisions have no real meaning and it can be seen that, in this example, the difference between years 4 and 5 is negligible – only £11. It can also be seen that the residual value at the end of year 5 is less than the amount which will be spent in that year if the vehicle is not sold. On the other hand, the residual value at the end of year 4 is more than the amount which will be spent that year if the vehicle is not sold. This is another way of indicating that year 4 would be too early and year 6 too late. Figure 9.4 shows these results graphically.

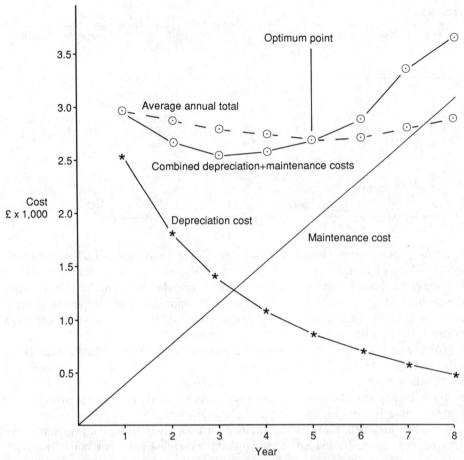

Figure 9.4 The optimum time for replacement is reached when the average of the cumulative sum of the depreciation plus maintenance costs reaches its minimum value, i.e. the end of the year
Source: Sussams (1984)

Note:
It is a convention to take the scrap value of a vehicle to be 10% of its purchase price. Barring accidents, the time taken for a vehicle to reach this 10% level will depend on the rate (miles per annum) at which it is used and on the quality and amount of repairs and maintenance performed. Each time period can be associated with a different rate of depreciation, thus:

Years to reach a residual value of 10% purchase price	*Depreciation rate (reducing balance) %*
6	33
8	25
10	20
12	16

CONCLUSIONS

This brief look at capital assets has considered those aspects that will aid the operations manager in the types of decision associated with them. We have highlighted the need-to-buy/lease decision, looked at the selection process, maintenance policies and means of establishing utilisation figures, and finally touched on the methodology for considering replacement.

References and suggested reading

British Productivity Association (1970) *Materials Handling*. London: British Productivity Association.

British Standards Institution (1979) *Glossary of Terms Used in Work Study and Organisation and Methods*.3138. London: BSI.

Clay, M. J. and Walley, B. H. (1965) *Performance and Profitability*. London: Longmans.

Committee for Industrial Technologies (1974) *Terotechnology – Concept and Practice*. London: Department of Industry.

Harris, N. D. and Mundy, J. M. (1978) *Materials Handling – An Introduction*. London: HMSO.

Health and Safety at Work Act (1974). London: HMSO.

Hill, T. (1983) *Production/Operations Management*. Englewood Cliffs, NJ: Prentice-Hall.

McBeath, I. (November 1974) Why workers won't automate. *Management Today*, pp. 109–116.

Makower, M. S. and Williamson, E. (1967) *Operational Research*. London: Teach Yourself/EUP.

Sussams, J. (November 1974) Maintenance – subcontract and save. *Works Management*, **27** (10), pp. 30–32.

Sussams, J. (March 1984) Vehicle replacement. *Management Services*, **28** (3), pp. 8–14.

10
RESOURCE PROBLEMS

RESOURCE MANAGEMENT

Many of the previous chapters have dealt with the operations manager's approach to the specific resources related to methods, capacity, layout and materials. Subsequent chapters deal with aspects of managing people.

Perhaps the common factor about these resource management problems is that they can reasonably easily be recognised and also quite clearly categorised. The modern systems approach to management demands that frequently we have to approach the task of management in not such a simplistic manner, and look at the total system as a complex series of interactions.

This may seem very off-putting, but we do not intend in this chapter to do more than to help managers to recognise the variables that would indicate that a problem needs to be pinpointed. This 'pinpointing' of the problem will often rely on the development of a *model* which enables the variables in the real world to be adequately captured, so that the model can be manipulated – often on a computer – and the answers to a series of 'what if' questions can inform management of the best decision.

Many texts on management spend a lot of time in developing skills for managers in how to solve detailed statistical and mathematical problems which relate to resource utilisation, but the approach that is advocated here is that the manager is not an expert in statistics/mathematics/computing activities, but is aware of the existence of a problem and can adequately interpret information when it has been processed. The manager has got to have confidence that the information being used in the model is valid.

OPERATIONS RESEARCH

A generic title for the development of solutions to complex problems which generally require the use of 'models' in their solution is *operations research*. Here are two definitions:

> The application of the methods of science to complex problems arising in the direction and management of large systems of men, machines, materials and money in industry, business, government and defence.

> *Note*: The distinctive approach is to develop a model of the system, incorporating measurements of factors such as chance and risk, with which to predict and compare the outcomes of alternative decisions, strategies or controls. The purpose is to help management determine its policy and action scientifically.

> (*BSI, BS 3138, 1979*)

180

The application of scientific methods, techniques and tools to problems involving the operation of a system so as to provide those in control of the system with optimum solutions to the problems.

(Churchman, Ackoff and Arnoff, 1957)

In line with operations management, operations research reflects the need for more research type data gathering. Again it must be emphasised that most managers will not apply this themselves, but, having identified a specific type of problem, open up dialogue with others (other managers, management services, consultants, statisticians, R&D, etc.) to develop a model and solve the problem.

The stages of operations research follow very closely to the problem-solving approach (see Chapter 4) as is shown below. Operations research terminology is given alongside to help in the later stages of this chapter.

Problem-solving approach	*OR approach*
1. Identify aims/objectives.	1. Identify aims/objectives.
2. Identify problem causes.	2. Identify problem variables.
3. Collect facts.	3. Collect facts and build into a scientific model.
4. Identify alternatives, predict outcomes of each and choose the most appropriate and practical alternative solution.	4. Experiment with scientific model to develop optimum alternative(s) from which the most appropriate and practical solution can be selected.
5. Develop new system.	5. Translate back to 'real life' and verify solutions.
6. Install new system.	6. Install new system.
7. Ensure new system is properly maintained.	7. Ensure new system is properly maintained.

The term 'problem variables' is used in stage 2, since only by changing variable parts of the system – say the number of checkout points in a supermarket – can there be an effect on the length of queues.

Stages 3, 4 and 5 emphasise, more than say work study or O&M models, abstraction by the use of numbers and computers. Experimentation can then take place which enables hypothetical questions to be posed. So, if you have a detailed network plan for a project concerned with setting up a new advisory facility for the public, you can judge the effect of, say, delays by suppliers of goods or adverse weather conditions, and then translate that into the 'real life' situation with that additional knowledge.

Even though an element of abstraction is involved, it is not 'pie in the sky' but is intended to enable the effects of all sorts of variables to be considered. This will therefore help the manager to organise the available resources more effectively.

MODELS

Before we consider the types of problem that can be dealt with by the techniques of operations research, it is worthwhile considering the idea of *models*.

Nature and role

Models have been with us since the toys we played with as children helped us learn more about the real world. A model is always an abstraction to some degree of the real-life thing or process, and in as much as models are used for intellectual attacks on problems, it follows that some form of forecasting or prediction is implicit. The model does not necessarily duplicate all aspects of the real-life problem but can concentrate only on the pertinent features under review.

It is a mistake to think that the building of models can be the starting point. It is very important that the model be validated to ensure it adequately represents the particular aspect of the real world in which we are interested. This may have to be done over and over again until an acceptable model is developed.

Types of model

Because of the variety of problems that exist the following categories are not exclusive but can serve to indicate the types of models most often used in management. The models listed have been put in order of ascending abstraction from the real-life situation.

Physical models

These represent physically some aspect of the general problem. A small working model or prototype is an example of an attempt to represent all aspects, whereas a three-dimensional plant layout model, a two-dimensional plant layout model or an architect's model are all physical models which concentrate on pertinent features. With the layout models mentioned here their value lies in the quick and easy communication of information, and their use in forecasting alternative arrangements can be readily seen.

Pictorial models

Sketches and cartoons are perhaps the best forms of these. A thumbnail sketch to show a new idea or a cartoon warning of the dangers of unsafe practices leading to accidents are good examples.

Graphical models

Variables are represented in a two- or sometimes three-dimensional space. These are used frequently to summarise a whole host of statistics and one can quickly call to mind the sales volume/period of time graph used to indicate sales trend. As an example of the use of graphs in decision-making one can consider the quality control chart or the break-even chart, both of which give a clear indication of the future trend and allow management to act accordingly.

Schematic models

These are used to show information where the physical relationships are less important. Examples are an organisation chart, a flow process chart or a network diagram.

Mathematical models

These are the greatest abstraction from real life where mathematical symbolism is used to depict factors in a real world situation. The symbols rather than the physical objects can then be manipulated.

Any formula or equation is a mathematical model but when a large amount of data is used formulae become complex and the use of a computer helps in manipulation.

The types of model most used in OR are mathematical and schematic. Examples of both of these are given later in the chapter.

Advantages and limitations of mathematical models

Advantages

The greatest advantage is that the mathematical model allows for experimentation, which overcomes the need for management to 'suck it and see'. Also the mathematics used takes account of the inherent randomness and variability in all operational problems. Further advantages are:

1. It is possible to describe and comprehend the facts of the situation better than any verbal description can hope to do.
2. Relations between the various aspects of the problem which are not apparent in a verbal description are uncovered.
3. The type of data required to solve the problem quantitatively is indicated.
4. Establishes measures of effectiveness.
5. Explains situations that have been left unexplained in the past by giving cause and effect relationships.
6. It is possible to deal with the problem in its entirety and allows and ensures consideration of all the major variables of the problem simultaneously.
7. A model may be enlarged step by step to a more comprehensive model to indicate all other major variables of the problem neglected in a verbal description.
8. The solution can be adequately described verbally.
9. It is often the case that the factors entering into the problem are so many and so difficult that only elaborate data processing procedures can yield significant answers.

Limitations

Although what has been said so far about models is very true, there is a danger of looking for more from mathematical models than can reasonably be expected. For the privilege of avoiding the cost of committing the real resources in experimentation we pay the price of working with limited representations of reality and thus obtaining results of limited realism.

We must also be aware of the danger of the term 'optimal solution'. This is not an incontestable solution, but simply a deductive statement made within the context of the mathematical model. Thus its optimisation is the way in which the solution to the *model* is reached, and we must remember the model does not perfectly capture reality.

Conclusions

A successful problem analysis using a model must meet three requirements:

1. The model developed must be rich enough in reality to lead to improved policy decisions, yet it must not be so complicated that deductive reasoning with it is beyond the talents of the analyst.
2. The data required must be reasonably possible to obtain. A model containing unreasonable variables is of little use.
3. Finally, the conclusion derived must be acceptable to management. No matter how reasonable the results, there is little to call success until management accepts them and begins to act upon them.

A non-management type model

A TV show about pain featured a woman who had suffered from back pain for twenty years. Having tried everything else, she was referred to a pain clinic. Their advice was to keep a 'pain diary' in which the level of pain was related to the activities undertaken, thus building up a model which could be used to predict which activities should be avoided leading to less pain.

TYPES OF PROBLEM

Let us now consider the types of problem that could concern us – and which can be solved in this way. This is not intended to be an exhaustive analysis, but should provide an adequate sample of the more commonly encountered types of problem.

There are various ways of approaching this – either as a random list of problems or by attempting to categorise the problems into like groups. Buffa and Dyer (1978) adoopt the latter approach with three categories:

1. *Evaluative models*. These are concerned with decision trees, in which the use of probability theory can help to evaluate alternative decisions.
2. *Predictive models*. In these forecasting methods are used first to consider the environment and then the system performance. In this group is waiting line theory which covers all types of queuing problems.
3. *Optimising models*. These include models that can identify the correct levels of stock/inventory, and those which optimise use of resources. Included in this group are network scheduling models used for planning and one-off projects, in which the environment is usually relatively certain. In the other models, part of the problem is concerned with the unknown features of the environment.

Buffer and Dyer (1978) spend over four hundred pages explaining the above in detail, but using this as a framework we can select some examples relevant to the service sector, indicating what the operations manager 'needs to know' about the techniques so that a meaningful dialogue with the technical experts can be conducted – and also so that the results can be interpreted realistically.

EVALUATIVE MODELS
Decision trees

Any service activity will at some stage be contemplating growth or diversification. If, for example, a bus company was contemplating investment in new vehicles to ensure an increased route coverage but was conscious that there were risks of increased competition, it might wish to evaluate this in some detail before making the investment.

In the evaluation, not only the risk of competition and its effect on revenue would need to be considered, but also other forms of increasing route coverage – e.g. purchasing second-hand, increased use of existing fleet with added maintenance costs and breakdown risks, etc. All this can be represented in the form of the branches of a tree – each decision leading to perhaps two or three alternative outcomes.

Before detailing the above let us look briefly at the structure of such a *decision tree*, taking a more familiar example using the biggest risk factor of them all – the British summer. Suppose you are contemplating organising an outdoor event – say, a charity fête – which ideally should be outdoors in the sunshine, but which you suspect will in all probability be outdoors in the rain. You have the choice of using the church hall or are prepared to have a marquee. Each of these decisions has a cost factor (it may be nil) and can lead to various 'payoffs'. This situation is shown in Figure 10.1.

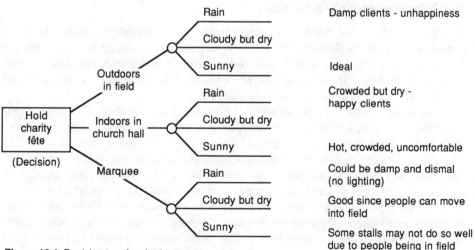

Figure 10.1 Decision tree for charity event

The last decision has a cost attached which must be taken into account. If this decision cannot be left until the morning of the event since the hall/field/marquee needs to be booked in advance, the only way of being able to reach a sensible decision is to include in the figure some 'probability factor' about the likely weather conditions. After recent summers most would say assume a 90% chance of rain, but use of past weather records allied with the latest meteorological office trends may be able to give more precise data and thus help in the decision.

If, in addition to considering the effect on people, this were translated into a likely attendance (which in turn could affect the financial outcome of the event), then you can see that this approach is useful in reaching a decision which can attempt to maximise financial rewards. Even if the only decision that creates cost is the hiring of the marquee then this can be included in the overall calculations.

Suppose that, based upon meteorological data, the following probabilities were obtained:

Rain   – 50%
Cloudy – 20%
Sunny – 30%

which can be expressed as 0.5, 0.2, 0.3 respectively. This will apply to all decisions. We could also assume that the numbers attending could be affected by the weather. Finally, based on last year's experience the amount people will spend averages at £5.00 per head.

Armed with all this we can produce a decision tree as shown in Figure 10.2. In this the probabilities are used, alongside the estimated attendance, to produce for each decision an estimated payoff so that the choice should be, despite a 50% chance of rain, to use the field.

PREDICTIVE MODELS

The Delphi forecasting technique

In service facilities the need to forecast changes is as important as the ability of commercial firms to identify the number of products to make to meet market demand. This has already been considered as part of our discussion of capacity (see Chapter 5) dealing with day-to-day or week-to-week fluctuations in service demand by using overtime, shift work, casual labour, etc.

At the other extreme the question must be asked what technological changes could affect the service we are currently providing – are we prepared to change objectives, or to be involved in a different method of service delivery when changes occur? In education, for example, there are not only technological changes (computers, video, open learning) but there are many other demands placed on the provider: changes in curriculum emphasis (education or preparation for work), government intervention (more testing), changes in control of colleges and schools, etc. Whilst many committees meet to discuss these issues, the real planning to cope with them rarely takes place, since people are unwilling to put some figures down on paper and guess what effects these figures could have, collectively and individually.

To achieve this one can use the *Delphi forecasting* technique which is designed to obtain the most reliable consensus judgement from a group of experts. It is suggested that it is very useful in generating preliminary insights into subjects in which the factors to be assessed and their influences are inadequately specified. The method brings to light the factors taken into account by the experts in reaching their

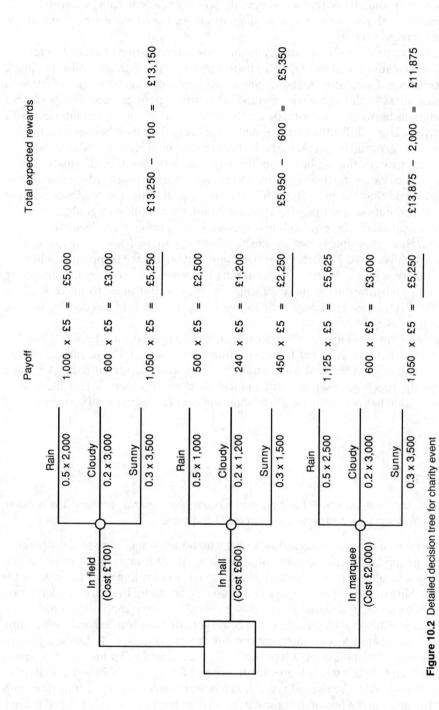

Figure 10.2 Detailed decision tree for charity event

conclusions. The research also shows that the method can produce a consensus forecast from managers that is acceptable when empirical data is unreliable or unavailable and is closer to reality than forecasts based on existing models of personnel requirements.

The Delphi technique is essentially an intensive interrogation of each of a group of experts by means of a series of questionnaires interspersed with controlled feedback of information. Committee meetings and direct confrontation between experts with opposing views both have obvious drawbacks; 'office politics', personality clashes and relations between a subordinate and a superior, for example, can interfere with objectivity. These difficulties are avoided in the Delphi method because interaction among the experts is accomplished through an intermediary who poses the questions, gathers the replies from the experts, provides the information they request, and issues further questionnaires and information. Advocates of the method argue that the procedure of successive questioning and feedback without direct confrontation encourages independent thought and allows a gradual formulation of the problem, thereby leading to a considered, consensus judgement.

The Delphi experiment was conducted with a panel of seven managers in a national retail company to determine the number of buyers the company would need 'one year from now'. A series of questionnaires were sent out to managers giving them an opportunity to request information they would need to make such an estimate. This was gradually refined by using a series of feedbacks on the questionnaires.

The final consensus figure, when arrived at, and compared with the actual number of buyers within the 'one year from now' timescale was found to be more accurate than any other conventional forecasting methods using historical data. Although such an approach seems less mathematical than many others it is a method of modelling that has proved to be worthwhile and could be used for all sorts of service forecasting.

ACTIVITY

Using the brief description of the education system given above, consider the types of changes by which your own service facility could be affected.

Between very short-term forecasting coping with hour-to-hour, day-to-day operational changes and the major changes of technology, there is much historical data that can be graphically displayed to show the seasonal, weekly and even daily demands from a facility which will enable logical decisions to be made. In such cases deliberate attempts to manage demand is the way forward. A very simple example was a pharmacy in a hospital where other staff could get attention 'on demand' by pressing a bell. This created lots of interruptions for the pharmacists. A demand pattern analysis showed that the demands peaked at 9–10 a.m. and 1–3 p.m. each day. It was possible therefore to establish opening hours and for a pharmacist to be on duty to deal with requests. The overall result was a better use of pharmacy staff time with very little upset in the rest of the hospital. Even managers can be well advised to have 'regular availability' times for staff to see them so as to avoid constant interruptions.

If we consider the more commercial aspects of service demand, once demand patterns are well established either on a daily basis (e.g. meal times in restaurants), a weekly basis (e.g. people staying in hotels) or seasonally (e.g. holidays), then marketing strategies need to be used to make best use of the spare capacity. Such promotions as 'the happy hour' when cut price meals/drinks are available, special weekend rates in hotels and off-season holidays for such groups as Saga are familiar ways of dealing with this excess capacity.

The seasonal, weekly or daily patterns for service demands are not always adequately known. Some form of forecasting pattern should be established to help in establishing staffing levels, use of capital equipment and general market strategy.

Queuing or waiting line models

Waiting is seen as one of the main characteristics of the service sector since there is often either a number of people waiting to be served, e.g. at a bus stop or the hairdressers, or similarly a number of service facilities waiting for customers, e.g. hairdressers awaiting customers, taxis waiting for passengers. In establishing an optimum facility we need to know more about the interaction between the customer's arrival and the length of the servicing. This is quite critical when the service facility and the customers both belong to the same organisation, e.g. mechanics queuing to collect tools from a tool stores. The question that the analysis seeks to answer is 'Do we need to provide an additional services facility?' – that is will the cost of extra stores personnel be offset by a reduction of the mechanics' waiting time? Obviously other approaches would also be considered – opening another hatch at only specified times, anticipating demands, etc.

The type of queuing situation that we are all familiar with is that at the bank or post office. Many of the larger branches have created a single queue for all arrivals, so that choosing the shortest queue only to find that you are behind someone who has a massive transaction will not occur. However, supermarkets have multiple service channels, and although some do provide for cash only/basket shoppers (as against trolley shoppers), it is still difficult to judge which queue to join to be quickest.

In banks, post offices and supermarkets, the cost of the customers' queuing is not a cost to the organisation – unless people get frustrated and do not patronise the organisation. In a medium-sized supermarket at Saturday lunchtimes the queues may well be quite long, to the discomfort of those in the queue, the checkout staff and those trying to shop since the queues go down the aisles. So there is indeed a need to meet the customer satisfaction element and reduce the queuing time as much as possible.

Some organisations may have solved the queuing problem by turning a threat into an opportunity. Airports, railway stations, etc., now provide various ways for those waiting to amuse themselves – and, incidentally, spend more money – fruit machines, shops, restaurants, etc. This is taken to extremes by Morcego (1961) in which he states:

> The problem as originally stated by the managing director was:
>
> > 'Our three loading bays are obviously not enough. The queue of lorries at midday is twice as long as it ought to be. Prove that we need three more bays if the length of the queue is to be halved.'

189

The Operational Research department tackled the problem and proved that one more bay would halve the length of the queue.

However, another approach could be:

'The original statement of the problem included lorries and loading bays, but not the drivers. Waiting lorries cost money. They are the customers' lorries: they cost us nothing. Lorry drivers dislike waiting.'

The technique used was minimisation of cost (someone else's) instead of maximisation of profit (ours).

The sequel is by now too well-known to merit elaboration here – how, instead of loading bays, coffee-and-hamburger stalls for the waiting drivers were built; how Operations Research was soon turning its attention to office workers who started 'busking' in the lunch hour; how the manufacturing side of the business atrophied and was replaced by the great catering-cum-entertainment complex which serves queues of lorries all over the world.

Because queuing is so fundamental to the service concept we shall provide an example of how such a problem can be formulated and interpreted.

Definition

In general, queues may be defined as the flow of people, equipment or information through a bottleneck, where the arriving units sometimes pile up, waiting to get service before they continue on their way. More formally, we may say *units* arrive desiring to be *serviced*, wait in a *queue* if the *service channel* is busy, eventually enter the channel, are serviced and leave the system.

Systems differ in:

1. The average rate of arrival.
2. The average rate of service.
3. The number of service channels $(1, 2, \ldots, n)$.
4. The queue discipline (i.e. for people it is usually first come, first served, but for goods those on the top of the pile, i.e. last there, could be first served).

Arrival and service distributions

If the average rate of service is greater than the average rate of arrival and both are constant, the system will eventually settle down into a steady state. That is to say that the probability of finding a particular length of queue will then be the same at any time. If the values vary with time the system will not reach a steady state but may remain stable.

If, however, the average rate of arrival is greater than the average rate of service the system is unstable and the probability of a long queue steadily increases. Some systems may be unstable for a short time (e.g. rush hour traffic).

Tables 10.1 and 10.2 show the arrival times of customers at a single channel service facility over a short period. In Table 10.1 the service rate is set at 3 minutes per customer, but the arrival rate is based on a random distribution of an average of 12

Table 10.1

Arrival time of customer	Service begins at	Service ends at	Idle time of attendant (minutes)	Waiting time of customer (minutes)	Length of line excluding customer being served
10.02	10.02	10.05	0	0	0
10.09	10.09	10.12	4	0	0
10.13	10.13	10.16	1	0	0
10.19	10.19	10.22	3	0	0
10.34	10.34	10.37	12	0	0
10.36	10.37	10.40	0	1	1
10.37	10.40	10.43	0	3	1
10.38	10.43	10.46	0	5	2
10.39	10.46	10.49	0	7	3
10.42	10.49	10.52	0	7	3
11.02	11.02	11.05	10	0	0
11.03	11.05	11.08	0	2	1
11.05	11.08	11.11	0	3	1
11.05	11.11	11.14	0	6	2
11.09	11.14	11.17	0	5	2

Attendant's idle time = 30 minutes
Total clients' waiting time = 39 minutes

per hour. In Table 10.2 the service rate is 4 minutes per customer with a similar random arrival rate.

For Table 10.1 – random arrival rate with constant service rate – calculations are:

Average length of queue: $\frac{\lambda^2}{2\mu\,(\mu - \lambda)}$

Average waiting time: $\frac{\lambda}{2\mu\,(\mu - \lambda)}$

where λ = Average random arrival rate
μ = Service rate

Thus if the average arrival rate was 12 per hour and the service rate was constant at 20 per hour (i.e. 3 minutes per customer as in Table 10.1) these equations would give:

Average length of queue $= \frac{144}{2 \times 20 \times 8}$
$= 0.45$ people in line (excluding person being served)

Average waiting time $= \frac{12}{2 \times 20 \times 8}$
$= 0.375$ hours/person
$= 2.25$ minutes/person

Note: When arrival rate and service time equal theoretically waiting time becomes infinitely long, as shown in the equation: $\frac{\lambda^2}{2\mu\,(0)}$

since any number divided by zero yields infinity. In practice this would not occur as people would be discouraged by a large queue or service would be speeded up.

If, however, the service rate is as in Table 10.2 then the attendant has less idle time but the customer's average waiting time goes up from 39/15 = 2.6 minutes to 64/15 = 4.3 minutes.

Table 10.2

Arrival time of customer	Service begins at	Service ends at	Idle time of attendant (*minutes*)	Waiting time of customer (*minutes*)	Length of line excluding customer being served
10.00	10.00	10.04	0	0	0
10.09	10.09	10.13	5	0	0
10.13	10.13	10.17	0	0	0
10.19	10.19	10.23	2	0	0
10.34	10.34	10.38	11	0	0
10.36	10.38	10.42	0	2	1
10.37	10.42	10.46	0	5	2
10.38	10.46	10.50	0	8	2
10.39	10.50	10.54	0	11	3
10.42	10.54	10.58	0	12	3
11.02	11.02	11.06	4	0	0
11.03	11.06	11.10	0	3	1
11.05	11.10	11.14	0	5	2
11.05	11.14	11.18	0	9	3
11.09	11.18	11.22	0	9	2

Attendant's idle time = 22 minutes
Total clients' waiting time = 64 minutes

This is a relatively simple example. With more randomness in the service time (i.e. it is not constant) and with multiple channel service, the model gets much more complex. However, suffice it to say that by using data which can be easily gathered by observation or getting attendants to record, it is possible to provide useful information to judge whether or not to change the system.

Table 10.3 lists a number of typical situations that are suitable for the application of queuing theory. However, the development of a mathematical model of queuing is not always the best way to solve the problem – at least not at first. This is demonstrated in the short case study given below.

Some queuing situations are not always observable by having people waiting. Sometimes piles of documents awaiting processing or goods to be put away are just as much a queue as people or cars.

CASE STUDY

On taking up his appointment as Head Librarian at a college library John Sharp was surprised at the apparent disorganised crowding in the small entrance hall that occurred most mornings. Sometimes it was so bad that the people spilled out into the road outside and in front of adjacent buildings.

The reason for this was that the library operated a two-week loan period, allowed

Table 10.3 Typical situations for application of queuing theory.

1. In a shop, booking office, bank, hairdressers, etc., the customers arrive for service and wait for the counter to be free. The assistant, teller, etc., serves the customer.
2. At bus stops and taxi ranks the customers arrive and wait for a bus or taxi until it arrives.
3. In a doctor's or hospital waiting room, patients arrive for treatment and wait their turn to be treated by the doctor.
4. In a factory materials handling system materials wait on equipment at various points until they are moved by the equipment.
5. At an airport planes arriving to land may have to wait in the 'stack' until they can land on the runways.
6. In a factory warehouse or stores goods are held in stock after arrival until they are used or purchased.
7. In a telephone system calls are received at the switchboard and held until a line is free.
8. In an estimating department contracts are held until a price has been estimated before they are tendered.
9. In a port ships arriving wait for a free berth before they can be unloaded.
10. In a machine shop operators may have to await the arrival and work of a setter before they can proceed with the next job.

up to eight volumes per borrower and imposed a 5p per day fine. Most borrowers wishing to return or renew their books tended to do so first thing in the morning, since the library building was on the periphery of the campus.

The system of returning books was relatively straightforward, involving only the use of a penlight barcode reader linked to a VDU, which indicated whether a fine was payable or not. For renewals, which occurred in 75% of transactions, the book needed to be cancelled and then reissued. The reissue process required the reader's number to be keyed into the computer system, which would indicate if the number of books on loan was not greater than the allowable eight. For both renewals and returns the date was stamped on the inside cover of the book.

The layout and system were originally designed so that this activity was separate from those who wished to go directly into the library to study, browse or select books and other learning materials, and from the exit point which allowed new borrowings to be checked out. The effect was, however, to create a considerable interference to those customers wishing to use the library but not returning or renewing materials.

The return/renew desk had only one VDU, and after only a few transactions the area quickly got covered in piles of books. Two people were occasionally assigned to this activity but they tended to get in each other's way and there was little improvement in the speed of the operation.

People returning or renewing books got very anxious about waiting in queues, but the alternatives were to return later, which was not always convenient, or come back on another day, which had the potential penalty of a fine, and for both alternatives the customer had to carry the books for a considerable period.

The net effect was a somewhat bad tempered crowd and a very harassed library assistant.

Discuss:

1. In what respects was the present system giving unsatisfactory service to the customers?

2. Try to locate the weaknesses of the system now operating and the measures taken to cope with pressure on the return/renew counter.
3. Suggest means of getting the best out of the present system.

Simulation

The use of computers has enabled experimentation with mathematical models to test the effects of change away from real life. Many months or years of real-life trials could be dealt with in this way. The queuing problem looked at above is relatively short term but suppose a local authority wanted to judge the long-term effects (over, say, five years) of different policies regarding the admittance of people to an old people's home. It would be able to simulate the potential clients seeking admission on the basis of the probability of different groups requesting admission. In this particular example, the variables to be limited are the creation of vacancies and the generation of needy and deserving cases. In a real-life case, the procedure would be to determine, either from past records or from observation over a period of time, the type of pattern each of these followed.

CASE STUDY

With the objective of obtaining the maximum utilisation of all vehicles and personnel, a study of the group transport system was carried out for a hospital management committee.

The hospital group consists of a mental hospital of some 2,000 patients and a general hospital of 550 beds which share the same extensive grounds about a mile outside the town. In addition, the mental hospital has three annexes – one being 10 miles north-east, one 8 miles west and the other 4 miles north-west. All these annexes are dependent for supplies, e.g. stores, clean linen, shoe repairs, etc., on the main hospital and therefore a large number of journeys have to be made each week. In addition, journeys have to be made to transport patients and resident and non-resident staff.

The transport system at the time of the investigation comprised 10 different vehicles divided into two distinct groups:

  3 small vehicles
  7 large vehicles

Log sheets were kept for the majority of vehicles to record all journeys outside the hospital area, specifying all places which adequately indicated the extent of the journeys and the times of starting and finishing.

Log sheets for 4 sample periods of one week were taken and analysed in the form of a simulation chart which highlighted peak periods, regular and irregular journeys. This chart was closely studied to see if a greater utilisation of the vehicles was possible.

Then using the data from past use, and incorporating considerable 'experience' from the users, it was possible to simulate future use when some of the vehicles were not available. As a result it was found possible to rearrange journeys in such a manner that all the work of the 10 vehicles could be undertaken by 5 large vehicles.

It was therefore proposed that the number of vehicles be reduced to 5. However, in view of the need to provide cover for vehicles during maintenance or in case of accidents and because otherwise there might have been difficulty in always having a roadworthy vehicle available, it was recommended that one small vehicle be retained for·this purpose.

Thus an overall reduction from a total of 10 vehicles to 6 was possible, and the simulation enabled a high level of confidence to be invested in the revised model.

OPTIMISING MODELS

Amongst this type of models, where the level of unpredictability is less apparent than in other models, are those for controlling the level of stocks which were mentioned briefly in Chapter 7. Also included are a whole range of models which are entitled *linear programming*.

Linear programming

Linear programming (LP) is a technique for specifying how to use limited resources or capacities in an organisation to obtain a particular objective such as least cost, highest margin or least time when these resources have alternate uses. It is a computational technique which draws upon background mathematics to work out problems. When the problem is defined the mathematical model can be worked through in a series of iterations which require only simple arithmetic and algebra. Needless to say, as with all OR techniques the difficulties occur in problem definition and model building.

Basic concepts

Alternatives

Since we have defined LP as a method for allocating limited resources, there must be alternatives of one kind or another, such as vehicles or people, that can be employed to achieve the desired objective. For example, the vehicles could compete for alternative routes or the people could compete for alternative tasks.

Linearity

This means that a change, for example, in the number of hours worked will bring a proportional change in costs. This is essential for the use of the LP technique. For cases where this linearity does not exist, other OR techniques are available.

Programming

This involves the step-by-step calculations or iterations for solving the equations or inequations.

Method

We shall use a transport example to illustrate the method since it is a common problem in operations management. Note that the problem of the deployment of the transport fleet given above as an example of simulation is not suitable for LP since linearity does not exist. The need for homogeneous resources is an essential feature of LP.

Step 1: State the problem in terms of an objective

A bus company has three garages G1, G2, and G3 in which there are 2, 6 and 7 buses available respectively. There is a need to get buses to 4 parts in the company's district, A, B, C and D, which each require 3, 3, 4 and 5 buses respectively. Time information on travelling between each garage and each part respectively is given in Table 10.4. The objective is:

> What distribution of buses will minimise the time involved and what is the total bus time involved?

Table 10.4 Time information (in minutes).

| Sources | Destination | | | | |
	A	B	C	D	Available
G1	26	22	30	40	2
G2	34	28	24	26	6
G3	36	36	30	24	7
Required	3	3	4	5	15

Step 2: Determine the information that is likely to be used in solving the problem

This problem will require some comparative data – in this case the number of minutes to travel from each garage to each point.

Step 3: Go through the process of solving the problem

This type of problem, because of its obvious nature, is known as the transportation problem. To reduce costs the minimum time of travelling is sought. The end result is shown in Table 10.5.

Table 10.5 The relief bus solution.

| Sources | Destination | | | | |
	A	B	C	D	Available
G1	1	1			2
G2	0	2	4		6
G3	2			5	7
Required	3	3	4	5	15

CONCLUSION

This chapter has given a very brief look at methods available to solve the types of problems that could be of relevance to the operations manager. It deliberately does not become involved with the detailed mathematics, as for those who enjoy this aspect there are many books which give a much fuller treatment of the processes. What is most important is that the manager should be able to recognise the type of problem he or she is faced with and so is able to contribute towards determining the type of data that needs to be collected so that the appropriate model can be developed.

Managers should be able to explain the nature of their problems to the technical specialists, and generally understand the work of the specialist in the development of appropriate models to solve those problems. While this will not be possible as a result simply of reading this chapter, undoubtedly as the use of computers becomes more widespread, there will be a need for sharper training of managers in quantitative methods so that OR packages can be used.

However, the real test of effectiveness is in correctly identifying the problem in the first place.

References and suggested reading

Battersby, A. (1966) *Mathematics in Management*. Harmondsworth, Middx: Penguin.

Buffa, E. and Dyer, J. S. (1978) *Essentials of Management Science/Operations Research*. Santa Barbara, CA: Wiley.

Carlsberg, P. G. (1967) *Quantitative Methods for Managers*. New York: Harper & Row.

Churchman, C. W., Ackoff, R. L. and Arnoff, E. L. (1957) *Introduction to Operations Research*. New York: Wiley.

Day, B. and Prabhu, V. (October 1977) How to manage by numbers. *Management Today*, pp. 84–87, 162.

Department of Trade and Industry (1973) *Delphi Forecasting*. Technolink No. 1312.

Duckworth, E. (1965) *A Guide to Operational Research*. London: University Paperbacks.

Gass, S. I. (1970) *An Illustrated Guide to Linear Programming*. New York: McGraw-Hill.

Keay, F. (1969) *The Numerate Manager*. London: Allen & Unwin.

Lamsac (Local Authorities Management Services Advisory Committee) (1978) *Quantitative Methods for Use in Local Government*. London: Lamsac.

Lovelock, C. (1984) *Services Marketing*. Englewood Cliffs, NJ: Prentice-Hall.

Magee, J. F. (July–August 1964) Decision trees for decision-making. *Harvard Business Review*, pp. 126–138.

Makower, M. S. and Williamson, E. (1967) *Operational Research*. London: Teach Yourself/EUP.

Morcego, C. S. (May 1961) Mathematics – the science of opposition in industry. *The Manager*.

Multimedia (1975) *Decision-making Tape/Slide Kit*. Multimedia.

Smith, J. A. (August 1970) Operational research – a service to management. *Workstudy and Management Services*, **14** (8).

Whitmore, D. (1979) *Management Science*. London: Teach Yourself/Hodder & Stoughton.

11

DECISION-MAKING AND CREATIVITY

There is no sadder or more frequent obituary on the pages of time than:

We have always done it this way.

Black-bordered card reputedly printed by British Rail executives in the Beeching era.

INTRODUCTION

The original title for this chapter was 'using latent creativity', but on reflection the need was felt to link the creative process to effective decisions, since creativity is primarily used to identify clearly all the alternatives available and, in some cases, enable decisions to be taken which show great foresight, imagination and courage. Many of the decisions which tap creativity involve a level of participation in the decision by those affected, or at least some element of consultation. This then indicates that the decision is more likely to be accepted by all and therefore have a greater chance of success. Even individuals when wrestling with decisions need to be able to identify clearly and calmly the various alternatives, rather than jump to the first, apparently 'reasonable' decision.

The manager has to balance two conflicting challenges:

1. 'Any decision is better than no decision', and thus defer the decision until more information is available.
2. The recognition that as a manager the job requires decisiveness in the face of insufficient and inadequate information. Any attempt to 'defer the decision' could be construed as weakness and lead to inaction.

Thus the manager needs to make a clear value judgement on the effect of deferring a decision and only use this if there is adequate time and opportunity to collect useful information which will inform the decision. Sometimes more information may only be 'opinions' which can confuse the picture even more.

Decision-making and problem-solving

In previous chapters we have discussed many approaches to the implementation of decisions in the application of various techniques. The section on problem-solving and problem definition in Chapter 4 is similar to the approach taken in decisions. In fact the difference between problem-solving and decision-making is very little – perhaps the major difference is *who* is conducting the process. An advisor would be problem-solving and presenting solutions to the problem owner, who would select and thus decide. However, if the problem owner deals with his or her own problem to the point of implementation then this is referred to as decision-making.

Of course the level, futurity and element of risk associated with a decision is another differentiating factor. To rearrange your own time schedule would be a low level decision or just a problem, whereas a decision on staffing levels or even a change of activities within a unit would contain an element of risk and have an impact on the future role and purpose of the unit/department.

If we accept the similarity of problem-solving and decision-making we need to consider two aspects:

1. The various facets of the approaches to decision-making/problem-solving.
2. The degree of creativity within the process.

Both of these will help the operations manager to view the process objectively and to understand his or her own role.

THE PROCESS OF DECISION-MAKING

A definition of decision-making given by Buffa (1968) is:

> The decision process is judging desirability of alternatives in relation to purpose or aim.

The critical words here are *judging desirability of alternatives*, and the ways of generating alternatives requires a degree of creativity.

Thus a very simple three stage approach could be:

1. Search environment for conditions calling for decisions (*intelligence*).
2. Inventing, developing and analysing possible courses of action (*design*).
3. Selecting best possible course of action from those available (*choice*).

However, there is an omission here in that decisions need to be related to objectives. Step 1 (intelligence) above needs to be amplified as in Figure 11.1, which indicates that from the outset we should be questioning our unit objectives relating to performance and the problem/decision area could involve a revision of these. Here we see the constant need to spend time in really *defining the problem*.

The second stage is obviously where the creativity arises in the development of alternatives, but again before a choice can be made a number of criteria have to be developed against which this choice can be made. For example, when selecting a candidate for a post in your unit, in addition to the job specification you should produce a *person specification*, if not on paper at least in your own mind. The job specification will contain a number of essential criteria, e.g. age range, experience and qualifications, which will be used to select a short list. When the candidates are interviewed a number of desirable criteria are introduced (i.e. the 'person specification'), for example ability to fit into team, development potential and additional experience, and these are used to help in the final judgement – often very difficult when you have candidates with different strengths in the desirable criteria. Sometimes to help this problem of choice the desirable criteria are weighted by the organisation so that the selection is more likely to favour, say, ability to fit into team,

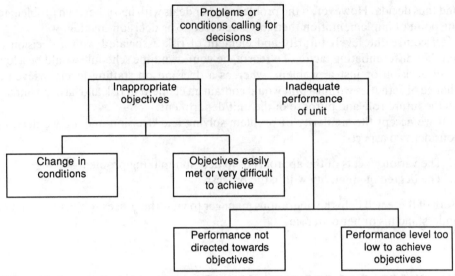

Figure 11.1 Step 1 in the decision-making process

as against development potential, or IT experience. This process is well illustrated in Chapter 6 when looking at alternative layouts.

The third stage, whilst now clearly much easier, requires the conversion of choice to action. This does not always occur smoothly. Delays can arise and people can still get doubts about the decision that has been made. This is a particularly difficult point in group decisions which may not have full support of everyone, since between announcing the decision and its implementation, the doubters can be more vociferous than those who supported the decision. Clearly a well-defined process for dealing with conflict in group decision-making needs to be established.

Also some form of feedback on the quality of the decision, once implemented, is required so that the organisation and individuals benefit from the learning process so that future decisions will be better informed. In selecting a candidate for a post, the top team of a leisure organisation selected a 'high flyer' who had a good track record, was well qualified and was even prepared to take a slight reduction in salary. They congratulated themselves on their skill at netting such a good manager, only to regret it when after two months he left for a higher salary. The feedback will probably have an effect on the criteria weighting so that 'likelihood of staying at least 12 months' gets a higher value than 'potential development' – though perhaps they should simply upgrade the post and offer a higher salary in future!

Having, then, taken the simplified approach as a starting point, we are now able to develop the more comprehensive model in Figure 11.2.

DECISIONS AND THE ORGANISATION

We briefly indicated that because of the type of work that is done at different levels in an organisation, the type of decisions will differ. Paterson (1972) indicated this clearly, and Table 11.1 provides an interpretation of his hierarchy.

Further aspects of decisions at any level are:

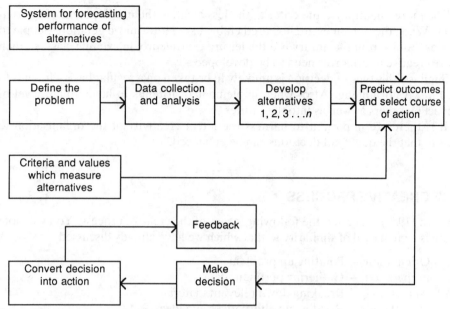

Figure 11.2 The decision-making/problem-solving process

Table 11.1 Decisions and the organisation.

Type of decision	Title	Example
Policy making	Top management	Chief executive
Programming	Senior management	General manager
Interpretive	Middle management	Unit manager
Routine	Skilled	Supervisor
		Technologist
Automatic	Semi-skilled	Chargehand
		Operator
Defined	Unskilled	Porter

Adapted from Paterson (1972).

1. Degree of futurity.
2. Impact on other functions.
3. Number of qualitative factors that enter into it, e.g. principles of conduct, ethical values, social/political beliefs.
4. Whether the decision is periodically recurrent, rare or unique.

The first two are easily understood but the third indicates that all decisions have a different number of measurable (i.e. quantitative) criteria and less easily measurable (i.e. qualitative) criteria, many of which introduce values and beliefs of some sort.

Some decisions can be judged on a single criterion, e.g. cost or profit. Many of these were demonstrated in Chapter 10 in which mathematical models were introduced to help in the decision-making process. In addition to the cost/profit features, the decision needs to be considered in terms of its effect on people, particularly the customer/client, but also the staff currently in post.

The more quantitative the criteria, the less creative the development of alternatives. When the outcomes are less predictable like 'How can we get more people to borrow books from the library/use the leisure centre/enrol in evening classes', then more creative alternatives need to be developed.

Similarly this type of decision is unlikely to be taken on a regular basis – it tends to be rare, if not unique. Also, when implemented, it tends to have a high level of impact on others as well as into the future.

It is therefore important to harness the latent creativity of the organisation to ensure that the quality of decisions can be enhanced.

THE CREATIVE PROCESS

Osborn (1957) suggested the following stages of the creative process. You will note there is a great deal of similarity to that which we have already discussed.

Orientation	– Pointing up problem.
Preparation	– Gathering pertinent data.
Analysis	– Breaking down relevant material.
Hypothesis	– Building up alternatives and ideas.
Incubation	– Letting up to invite illumination.
Synthesis	– Putting pieces together.
Verification	– Judging the ideas.

Although these stages apply to all creativity, from the individual artist to the problem-solver at work, we need to look at the process of creative thinking to see how it can be harnessed effectively.

Creative thinking

In Chapter 4 we looked briefly at methods of critical examination in which a specially devised sheet was used to encourage the development of alternatives. Here we intend to take this a little further, particularly where the boundaries of the problem are not so limited.

We have also differentiated between the easily measured quantitative problem and that which is more qualitative. In some books these types of problem are shown as *analytical* and *creative*. The analytical problem tends to be logical and predictable and uses 'convergent thinking' in which we focus on the problem. The creative problem needs imagination, is unpredictable and uses 'divergent thinking' in which we go out from the problem. This is also known as lateral thinking and Edward de Bono has produced many excellent books in which this thinking process is described (see, for example, De Bono (1972)).

Perhaps one of the difficulties we inherit from our culture and educational process is that the uninhibited ideas we had as a small child are gradually discouraged, so that when we are in the later stages of education our thinking is channelled into the more logical 'expected' approach. The thinking process used for mathematics, languages and most games is not likely to encourage creativity or imagination. Sometimes society itself puts all the 'artists' into a separate category and considers some of their ideas as slightly crazy, whereas the logical steady types move into management.

Yet we have need to harness these two extremes. We need to improve our creative abilities and use them when appropriate. We must not consider that the answers to problems are all likely to be solved by logical computer-like methods.

A definition of creative thinking is:

The relating of things or ideas that were previously unrelated.

This requires an ability to let the mind freewheel and drift. Many of us may have experienced this when faced with a difficult problem. The more we attempt to deal with it specifically, the more elusive is the answer. Then, when we are concentrating on something else – or even in the middle of the night! – a solution occurs, since the mind is now unfettered by the problem. The aim of developing skills in creative thinking is to recreate that unsought for link more speedily. It forces us to develop all sorts of possible solutions to problems, many of which we can use to overcome, creatively and with imagination, many open-ended problems.

This book indicates areas of development but is not the ideal vehicle for actually developing the innate creative ability we all have. For that you are advised to read Rawlinson (1970). Rawlinson identifies several barriers to creativity which are briefly summarised in Table 11.2. These barriers need to be broken down before people can be creative. The *brainstorming* procedure is designed to help in this process.

Table 11.2 Barriers to creativity.

- *One right answer*: The 'analytical' man is always searching for one right answer and is happy and relieved when he finds it. At this point he switches off.
- *Self-imposed barrier*: All sorts of obstacles or constraints are incorrectly assumed, which limit the range of opportunities presented to the mind.
- *Conformity or giving the answer expected*: An inability to think outside established conventions.
- *Failing to challenge the obvious*: 'We've always done it this way.'
- *Evaluating ideas too quickly*: 'That won't work' or 'That's silly.'
- *Fear of looking a fool*: 'I had better suggest some sound sensible stuff or my ideas may be laughed at.'

Adapted from Rawlinson (1970).

Brainstorming

Brainstorming is a method to get a large number of ideas from a group of people in a short time. A group of people are brought together to help develop ideas relating to a specific problem. The problem selected should be one which is *current* and important enough to justify the group's time, and one with many solutions and where imagination is needed to think of them. Examples range from developing better ways of delivering service – attracting more clients, increasing revenue or the reverse – how to cope with work loading, reduced budgets, staff absences or non-replacement of staff. These problems are frequently to be faced – in some cases the problem is ignored and people have to 'muddle through' whilst in other situations a solution is 'imposed' which then requires creative ideas to be made workable.

Suppose a college faced with financial problems wishes to close down one site and accommodate those courses in the main site. This may well create space and time difficulties. If a solution to overcome these problems were imposed – say an increase in the working day or year – resistance from staff and students may well be expected.

The problem first needs to be clearly stated so that creative alternatives are sought. It is important that the problem is not stated in such a way that the solution is only 'one site', e.g. 'In what different ways can we accommodate additional classes on the main site?' It needs to be more open so that real creative ideas can be developed, e.g. 'In what different ways can we most effectively use the existing sites?'

The brainstorming group should be no larger than 16 nor less than 6, with 12 as an ideal number. The leader will have a flip chart and write down all the ideas as they are shouted out. The idea is to go for quantity, evaluation is left till later. Since the ideas are called out this enables members to 'hitch-hike' on other people's ideas. Again to pick up from Rawlinson (1970):

Brainstorming rules

These should be in prominent view during a brainstorming session.

> *Suspend judgement*: Evaluation is not permitted at the brainstorming stage.
> *Let yourself go*: Freewheel the mind.
> *Quantity*: Go for lots of ideas.
> *Cross-fertilise*: Pick up someone else's ideas.

When ideas begin to dry up the leader may spur people on to get a specific number (say 100 ideas), and encourage a two minute silent incubation period. In some instances the wildest idea may be selected and used as a springboard for more ideas.

After all the ideas have been listed then evaluation takes place – not necessarily on the same day. The first stage is to sort the ideas into three groups:

1. Instant winners.
2. Instant failures – for reasons of being physically impossible, illegal, etc.
3. The middle grey area which will need more careful evaluation. The ideas should be sorted into groups of manageable size.

Analytical reasoning may be required at this stage to reduce a large number of ideas to a short list.

Financial, technical, environmental, social, human, political, economic, administrative, etc., criteria may be relevant in the evaluation stage. More specifically, criteria such as annual savings, payback time, effect on service and prices, number of hours saved, ease of implementation, etc., may be appropriate. Management must choose its own criteria, according to the problem and the objectives to be achieved.

Having reached a solution perhaps the next phase is to try *reverse brainstorming* in which the question 'In how many ways can this idea fail?' is asked. This identifies its weaknesses and the likely obstacles to implementation.

It is necessary to retain a sense of perspective about brainstorming – it is a useful management tool for the solution of *some* management problems. It is not a panacea. Although it cannot be guaranteed to be successful every time, it does *involve* people who feel they are making a positive contribution to the organisation. Such creative thinking does not replace analysis but is complementary to it. Together, creative and analytical thinking can lead to more effective management decisions.

TEAMWORK

The need for effective teamwork is now well established in the folklore of management. Most organisations recognise this and many training programmes will commence with activities designed to foster this. Because creativity is so central to effective teamwork it is felt important to review some of the mechanisms to improve the effectiveness of teams, so that the creative element is seen in context.

Characteristics of effective teamwork

Understanding and commitment to group goals

1. Goals should be clearly defined.
2. Members must *understand* the goals.
3. Members must be committed to working effectively towards their achievement and have belief in the solution being developed.

Maximum utilisation of members' resources

1. Involve all those with expert points of view.
2. Involve all those who will have to implement the decision. (People are more likely to carry out decisions in which they have had a part.)
3. Ensure the right people are in the group – and consider the balance of membership. Most effective teams have a balance of individuals with very different contributions to make (see Belbin (1981)).

Flexibility, sensitivity to the needs of others and creativity

1. 'Two heads are better than one' is not always true. Sometimes a problem can be thought through better on one's own.
2. Often (especially with a complex problem, or a situation affecting large parts of an organisation) more effective solutions are obtained by a group.
3. Many people have their best thoughts when stimulated by others.
4. People need to become skilled at stimulating others. (Too many conferences etc. are sterile, with a rigid agenda, tight procedures and poor interpersonal relationships.)
5. Encourage mutual support (by removing hostility and indifference). Each member can then be more himself, with no need to 'fight for his rights' or be defensive.

6. There is an obvious place for brainstorming.

Shared leadership

1. If the object of the group is to communicate information from a superior to his subordinates, say so. This is not a work group.
2. In a work group, encourage a 'team-type' of leadership. Different individuals will lead at different times as appropriate.

Effective procedures to resolve differences

1. Human differences present both a major asset and a major liability in team action.
2. *Vote*? Minority group can pose problems later on.
3. Try for *unanimity*? Unanimity will not occur very often. A great deal of time and patience needed.
4. *Compromise*? A decision is taken from two opposing points of view. The result is something different from either and thus pleases no one.
5. *Consensus*? This is the best method. The group agree next *steps*. Those not in agreement agree to have the tentative decision tested and evaluated.

Ability to examine its task and maintenance functions and to learn constantly

Many groups spend all their time concerned with the *task* and little or no time asking how effective they are as a team. This maintenance function is as critical for a team as for a car or bus. The need for proper methods (agreed) for doing this is essential.

A conducive organisational climate

Most people behave in accordance with the example set by their superiors. If the organisation feels that the only good decisions are individual decisions, then junior managers may not be able to use groups. If teams are used then the team must be recognised by their efforts and should get appropriate feedback.

Trust and open communications

1. Trust exists when a member can say: 'I know you will not take unfair advantage of me. I can put everything in your hands with complete confidence.'
2. Trust takes a long time to build. But it can be quickly and devastatingly destroyed.
3. Through trust comes open and frank communications, and a high tolerance for differences of opinions and personalities.

Individuals have a strong sense of belonging to the group

1. Each member will be committed to the goals and to the group.
2. Each member will respect the others and will want to work with them. (This does not necessarily mean 'liking' everyone.)

3. The need to ensure that isolated members are included.

ACTIVITY

There is a great deal of research on teams and their effectiveness, much of the results of which are contradictory. A view which is fairly well supported is that the decision whether or not to work as a team is one of the major determinants of an individual manager's overall effectiveness.

In order to help focus attention on the effects of team processes read the two lists below, one of the advantages, the other of the disadvantages of teamwork (reproduced with the permission of John Bothams). Choose any two advantages and write down some specific instances of them operating in your organisation and experience. Similarly write down two specific examples of the disadvantages operating.

Advantages of teamworking

1. More minds are better than one.
2. There is a removal of the blinkers from the eyes of the individuals.
3. Greater information, knowledge and experience brought as a result of combining membership.
4. Development of an idea by someone other than the originator.
5. Improved communication and understanding of a problem.
6. Stimulation, education and unification of members.
7. Greater scrutiny for adverse side-effects of possible solutions.
8. Conflict shows up where there are areas of agreement.
9. Opportunity for the development and training of individuals.
10. The people who put ideas into practice are frequently different to the originators of those ideas, but can be involved from the start in a team.
11. The allocation of tasks to 'trained', 'competent' individuals should result in more rapid execution of the overall task.
12. Group support will be available for the actions of the individual in carrying out a team decision.
13. The individual is open to team criticism and pressure to give a good performance because his responsibilities within the team are clear.
14. Co-ordination of different sections or work groups is made possible by the involvement of individuals in different teams.
15. If the team imposes a decision on itself it is more likely to work on it than if it had one imposed on it from above.

Disadvantages of teamworking

1. Any individual may fear opposing the rest of the team members.
2. Any individual may fear making him or herself look a fool in front of the team.
3. Status or power differences prevent subordinates contributing.
4. Some members are regarded as unacceptable, so that their ideas are not listened to or are disregarded.

5. Individuals often do not listen to others in teams because they are preparing their own case.
6. Greater time is used, as well as other resources.
7. A dependence on the team develops, leading to attempts to preserve the team when it has outlived its usefulness.
8. Lack of innovation due to the 'conservation of the team'.
9. Sabotage attempts by a minority.
10. Status seeking or other sub-goals become important.
11. A compromise may emerge which is less effective than the individual making the decision.
12. There is a strong tendency to reject outside help.
13. It can be used to avoid individual responsibility.
14. There can be a 'focus effect' when the first ideas put to the team get all the attention regardless of their merit.
15. It can be very disadvantageous to try to solve a problem with a team when only one person can have all the facts, say, for security reasons.

In dealing with the above activity you will see how creativity and brainstorming fit into teamwork. Even though it is suggesting how effective they are, there are always some drawbacks which should be understood. Although there are disadvantages as listed, part of the role of the manager as 'team leader' is to help reduce the disadvantages as much as possible, by drawing out individuals, overruling the saboteurs, etc. Thus some of these disadvantages may be more noticeable when the team leadership is weak or not present.

MEETINGS

Meetings are very similar to 'teams'. In fact one definition of a meeting is the 'formal coming together of a team' – say a top management group, a social work team, a school staff, etc.

Often meetings are formal and sterile and do not provide encouragement for ideas. Two films are available which explain how easy it is to change this by getting ideas down on a flip chart or board. In 'Meetings – Isn't There a Better Way?' the idea of a facilitator from another department is used to help obtain ideas which are then written down. Also in the Video Arts film 'More Bloody Meetings' this idea is used to good effect in both defining the problem and getting involvement and commitment in its solution.

VALUE ANALYSIS: THE APPLICATION OF CREATIVITY

Whilst creativity can be used anywhere there is one technique which has the creative process as a fundamental part of its application: *value analysis*. The BSI definition of value analysis is:

> A systematic interdisciplinary examination of design and other factors affecting the cost of the product or service, in order to devise means of achieving the specified purpose most economically at the required standard of quality and reliability.

Table 11.3 lists the basic concepts of value analysis.

Table 11.3 Basic concepts of value analysis.

1. Value analysis sets out to analyse the *functions* which a product or service performs and to develop a cheaper way of performing them, rather than considering initially the methods by which a product is made or service delivered.
2. Value analysis sets out to maintain or improve the quality of the products or service.
3. Value analysis is a *team* effort and as such enables closer liaison and involvement of people concerned with the product or service and bringing about change.

Value analysis (VA) has been applied with spectacular results to industrial products where the identification of alternative designs, materials and methods of manufacturing are all possible via an interdisciplinary team. In products which are manufactured in large quantities a small saving per item can save several thousand pounds per annum.

It is also reasonable to say that, although 'product or service' is included in the BSI definition given above, there is not very much documented on the use of value analysis in a non-industrial setting. However, this need not deter us, since there are many opportunities when it can be used in the service sector. First, we must recognise that parts of the service sector have a massive purchasing power, and if any equipment is bought in large quantities then it is an ideal subject for value analysis – either by yourselves or by your supplier. Government departments in the USA often include a clause in contracts to suppliers that VA must be used and that savings must be shared. Similarly, the approach can be used for the output of service organisations – rather than the procedures etc. – to look at how the service is marketed and delivered.

It must be emphasised that value analysis is not just 'cost reduction', although it must also be recognised that this is a great incentive for its initial adoption by firms. It does involve systematic examination of designs (product and service) and can lead to the following improvements:

1. Satisfaction of customers' requirements more precisely.
2. Reduction in costs.
3. Same or even better performance at lower costs.
4. Use of less difficult, less complicated, more convenient methods of delivery.

Table 11.4 Steps in value analysis.

1. *Information* – gather together all the facts and figures relating to the product or service.
2. *Define the function* – of the product or service and components or sub-services.
3. *Compare the cost of providing each function with the value of that function.*
4. *Apply creative thinking* – to generate alternative ways of providing the required functions.
5. *Evaluate ideas generated* – to arrive at the optimum alternative for providing the required functions.
6. *Develop best idea* – to ensure that it is a 'working proposition'.
7. *Report back* – to higher management.
8. *Implementation* – of 'selected alternative', which may produce lower costs, better customer service, better performance and/or better delivery.

The basic stages in value analysis are listed in Table 11.4. These are explained further below.

1. Information

This needs to be related to a suitable financial breakdown of the cost of service or services. This may be possible in, say, a bus company where such factors as cost per passenger mile are available, and similarly in a hospital with the cost of in-patient stay. Whatever method is used there is a need to identify how that cost is arrived at.

2. Define function

For a 'product', say a torch, the purpose is to 'provide illumination'. Similarly, there is a need to define the purpose of the service, and the sub-parts of the service are also important. In many cases a reconsideration of objectives is essential. For example, a library may have as its function: 'To facilitate book borrowing'. A cost per borrower/user/book can be established and unless you wish to reduce this by getting in more borrowers, the VA approach needs to be used to provide the same level/quality of service but at less cost, or to provide a better satisfaction of customer requirements.

3. Cost and function

Continuing the previous example, the 'book borrowing' is only part of the total activity. For this to be effective the following also need to be done:

1. Purchasing
2. Receiving
3. Cataloguing
4. Restacking shelves
5. Issuing
6. Tidying
7. Providing information
8. Enrolling new borrowers

Nowadays libraries also have subdivisions, i.e. children's, fiction/non-fiction, tapes, videos, records. Data on these also need to be collected before the procedure can be followed.

4 and 5. Creative thinking and evaluating ideas

This is brainstorming, the central focus of the technique.

6. Develop best idea

Note the optimum solution provides an opportunity to exploit other advantages, not *just* cost savings.

7 and 8. Reporting back and implementation

These are the stages for getting authority for change and then implementing it.

It must not be forgotten that the VA approach utilises a project team from different parts of the organisation, representing different functional responsibilities. This approach in itself has a valuable impact on the organisation.

CONCLUSIONS

Creative approaches need to be harnessed effectively in order to improve the decision-making capability of any organisations. In this chapter the way in which creative thinking is linked to decisions and how both inform teamwork has been demonstrated. A specific technique – value analysis – emphasises how analytical problems concerned with cost, performance and delivery can be helped by the use of creative thinking and brainstorming.

Finally, most organisations and individuals within them are capable of rejecting other people's ideas too quickly since they do not fit in with their own ideas. The comment 'Don't confuse me with facts, my mind is made up' is typical of the problem. The manager has to use all sorts of approaches to get others to look at problems logically and creatively. To help in the process, Table 11.5 (overleaf) provides a list of tongue-in-cheek ways to kill an idea so that you can recognise them in practice.

References and suggested reading

Belbin, R. M. (1981) *Management Teams – Why They Succeed or Fail*. London: Heinemann.

British Standards Institution (1974) *Glossary of Terms Used in Work Study and Organisation and Methods*. BS 3138. London: BSI.

Buffa, E. S. (1968) *Modern Production Management*. New York: Wiley.

De Bono, E. (1970) *Lateral Thinking – A Textbook of Creativity*. London: Ward Lock.

Francis, D. and Young, D. (1979) *Improving Work Groups*. San Diego, CA: University Associates.

Janis, I. L. and Mann, L. (1977) *Decision-Making*. New York: Free Press.

Juniper, D. F. (1976) *Decision-Making for Schools and Colleges*. Oxford: Pergamon.

Miles, L. D. (1961) *Techniques of Value Analysis and Engineering*. New York: McGraw-Hill.

Osborn, A. (1957) *Applied Imagination*. New York: Charles Scribner's Sons.

Paterson, T. T. (1972) *Job Evaluation* (2 vols). London: Business Books.

Prescott, B. D. (1980) *Effective Decision-Making*. Farnborough, Hants: Gower.

Rawlinson, J. G. (1970) *Creative Thinking and Brainstorming*. BIM Occasional Paper No. 7. London: BIM.

Tarr, G. (1973) *The Management of Problem-Solving*. London: Macmillan.

Table 11.5 Twenty-two ways to kill an idea.

1. *Ignore it.* Dead silence will intimidate all but the most enthusiastic proposer of ideas.
2. *See it coming and dodge.* You can recognise the imminent arrival of an idea by the growing unease and anxiety of the would-be originator. Change the subject or – better still – end the meeting.
3. *Scorn it.* The gently lifted eyebrow and a softly spoken 'You aren't really serious! You are?' works wonders. In severe cases make the audible comment 'Utterly impracticable.' Get your thrust home before the idea is fully explained, otherwise it might prove practicable after all.
4. *Laugh it off.* 'Ho, ho, ho, that's a good one, Joe. You must have sat up all night thinking that up.' If he has, this makes it even funnier.
5. *Praise it to death.* By the time you have expounded its merits for five minutes everyone else will hate it. The proposer will be wondering what is wrong with it himself.
6. *Mention that it has never been tried.* If it is new this will be true.
7. *Prove that it isn't new.* If you can make it look similar to a known idea, the fact that this one is better may not emerge.
8. *Observe that it doesn't fit company policy.* Since nobody knows what the policy is, you're probably right.
9. *Mention that it will cost.* The fact that the expected saving is six times as much will then pale into insignificance. This is imaginary money; what we spend is real. Beware of ideas that cost nothing though, and point out 'If it doesn't cost anything, it can't be worth anything.'
10. *'Oh, we've tried that before.'* Particularly effective if the originator is a newcomer. It makes him realise what an outsider he is.
11. *Cast the right aspersion.* 'Isn't it a bit too flip?' or 'Do we want this clever-clever stuff?' or 'Let's be careful we don't outsmart ourselves.' Such comments will draw ready applause and few ideas will survive collective disapproval.
12. *Find a competitive idea.* This is a dangerous one unless you are experienced. You might still get left with an idea.
13. *Produce twenty good reasons why it won't work.* The one good reason why it will is then lost.
14. *Modify it out of existence.* This is elegant. You seem to be helping the idea along, just changing it a little here and there. By the time the originator wakes up, it's dead.
15. *Encourage doubt about ownership.* 'Didn't you suggest something like Harry is saying when we first met, Jim?' While everyone is wondering, the idea may wither and die quietly.
16. *Damn it by association of ideas.* Connect it with someone's pet hate. Remark casually to the senior man, 'Why that's just the sort of thing John might have thought up.' The senior man loathes John. Your idea man doesn't and will wonder for weeks what hit him.
17. *Try to chip bits off it.* If you fiddle with an idea long enough, it may come to pieces.
18. *Make a personal attack on the originator.* By the time he's recovered, he'll have forgotten he had an idea.
19. *Score a technical knock-out.* For instance, refer to some obscure regulation it may infringe. Use technology as a bludgeon. 'But if you do that you'll need a pulsating oscillograph coupled with a hemispherical interferometer, so you see there would be a negative feedback on the forward rheostat – and you wouldn't want that, would you?'
20. *Postpone it.* By the time it's been postponed a few times, it will look pretty tatty and part worn.
21. *Let a committee sit on the idea.*
22. *Encourage the author to look for a better idea.* Usually a discouraging quest. If he finds one, start him looking for a better job.

12
CHANGE AND THE OPERATIONS MANAGER

THE SPEED OF CHANGE

Alvin Toffler (1971) in *Future Shock* says the following:

> If the last 50,000 years of man's existence were divided into lifetimes of approximately 62 years each, there have been 800 such lifetimes. Of these 800, fully 650 were spent in caves.

Against these statistics there is a need to consider even the last ten years and judge the speed of change brought about by technology, economic pressures, social and political forces, etc. Most would agree that there has been a considerable increase in the speed of change in our own lifetime.

The manager, in dealing with people, has got to be able to react positively in coping with change. In cases such as the introduction of technology the change could be regarded as evolutionary. However, there are also sudden changes to cope with, for example the departure of a member of the team for a new job, the organisation of a contract, different demands on the unit, etc. Changes can also be imposed, such as a change in the organisational structure or a forced relocation, which whilst not 'sudden' are not evolutionary either. The two extremes are illustrated in Table 12.1.

Table 12.1 Speed of change.

Speed:	Sharp or sudden	Gradual or evolutionary
Examples:	An announcement	Increased workload
	Change of political control	Reduced budgets
	Loss of power base	Drift of task activities
	Resignation, illness, death of people	New philosophies gradually embraced
	Takeover, merger	
	Bankruptcy	
Response:	Little control over this	Subtle/barely perceptible

It is quite likely that gradual change will be 'managed' by staff who wish to follow a particular ideology. It is, of course, easier where staff have discretion over the use of their time. Where methods are prescribed this is less likely and change is more imposed.

FACTORS THAT CREATE CHANGE

No list could be exhaustive but it is reasonable to categorise these into the basic causes of *imposed change*, i.e. circumstances act as a change agent and demand change, or alternatively *sought change*, where an organisation does some self-analysis which is used to indicate what change is necessary. These extremes will form a continuum as in Figure 12.1, with much change occurring with some agreement of those affected and a limited degree of coercion or manipulation by change agents – even a fully participative group will need to deal with internal conflicts.

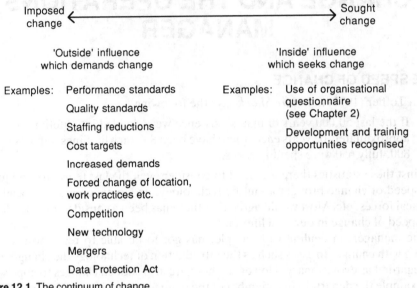

Imposed change		Sought change
'Outside' influence which demands change		'Inside' influence which seeks change
Examples:	Performance standards	Examples: Use of organisational questionnaire (see Chapter 2)
	Quality standards	
	Staffing reductions	Development and training opportunities recognised
	Cost targets	
	Increased demands	
	Forced change of location, work practices etc.	
	Competition	
	New technology	
	Mergers	
	Data Protection Act	

Figure 12.1 The continuum of change

The differences between the ends of the scale shown in Figure 12.1 are not quite so great as might appear at first glance, since there are many subtleties involved. For example, the 'inside' influence might lead to seeking advice through a consultant, who might be perceived by some as imposing change at a later date. Similarly the seeking of change itself may not only be because it is a 'good thing', but may be in anticipation of threats of the kind listed under imposed change.

This can be further developed by considering the attitude of people (at all levels) towards change. It could be *passive* in which people affected by change 'become different' and resigned to change, or it could be *active* in which people influence the direction of change. Again this may be represented as a continuum as in Figure 12.2. In management terms this represents a change in the characteristics of an organisation from a *rigid hierarchical mode* where policy is settled and a lot of attention is given to conformance and drill, to a *learning mode* where the innate capacity of the staff is realised creatively with high levels of involvement.

Become different (passive) → Make different (active)

Figure 12.2 Attitudes to change

Usually there is a root cause of change which can be traced back to one of the following broad categories:

1. Structure
2. Task

3. Technology
4. People
5. Environment

Examples of these are listed in Table 12.2.

Table 12.2 Types of change.

Structure	Job responsibility
	Relationships between jobs
	Key results
	Numbers of people
	Accountability
Task:	Methods of working
	Physical layout
	Volume of work/number of clients
	Variety in work
Technology:	New machinery
	Change in objectives/philosophy
	Opinion leaders
People:	New appointments
	Staff training and development
Environment:	Economic and financial climate
	Government influence
	Local authority influence

That change has a beginning helps to identify it, but it is more important to be able to recognise the effect that one type of change will have on other factors. This interrelationship is in Figure 12.3.

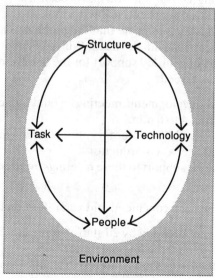

Figure 12.3 The task/structure/technology/environmental model
Source: Broussine and Guerrier (1983)

ACTIVITY

Refer to the task/technology/structure/people/environment model in Figure 12.3. Now write down a change which has taken place in each of these factors in turn in your recent experience.

For each item on your list indicate the consequent changes which had to take place in at least (in each case) two of the other factors. Were these resultant changes anticipated or not? What problems did they cause?

Before looking at other aspects of change we shall pause at this point to illustrate the subtleties of the change process so far mentioned. Read the following case study and identify the following features.

1. How much is change sudden or gradual?
2. Was change imposed or sought (or a combination of both)?
3. What were the attitudes of the people in the case, passive or active?
4. What was the root cause of change: structure, task, technology, people, environment? To what extent would it affect the others?

The case is shown in the form of two 'briefs' – one for a headteacher and the other for an investigator/consultant/change agent. (For a definition of these terms see page 225.)

CASE STUDY

The investigator's perspective

This school has about 40 staff, and as a result of falling rolls is suffering from a decline in morale. As a training consultant you have been asked to provide a training programme by the LEA advisor, ostensibly to look at the problems of the slow learners, but your own instincts indicate that the problem is more fundamental than that. After an initial discussion with the head, Wilfred Fenner, who is in his early 60s and gives the impression of guarded support for the involvement of an outsider, the following arrangement is agreed:

1. A series of six 'skills development' meetings would be held at fortnightly intervals, each running from 4 to 6 p.m.
2. Attendance at these would be voluntary, but a senior master, Andrew Leslie, Head of Maths, would act as co-ordinator.
3. The Head would give his support to these meetings by attending as many as he was able.

Four meetings have now been concluded and you reflect on the following:

1. The initial meeting was attended by 20 staff, but the latter three averaged at 14.
2. The Head appeared at only the first meeting.
3. Of those attending there was a great interest in many of the skills topics: meetings, use of time, appraisal and team building.
4. It transpired that there was resentment by the group that the key staff, i.e. heads

of departments, were not attending. There also appeared to be very little opportunity for the staff to influence decisions in the school.

You are so concerned about these problems that you spend some time in the fourth session filling in an 'organisational questionnaire', the results of which are attached (see Figure 12.4). (Organisational questionnaires are discussed in detail in Chapter 2.)

Potential blockage	No. of times aspects identified as a problem for the school	No. of times aspects identified as a positive within the school
	(High = Poor)	(High = Good)
Recruitment and selection	16	22
Organisational structure	34	13
Control and information flow	30	12
Training	26	13
Motivation	36	3
Creativity	34	13
Teamwork	35	20
Management philosophy	7	18
Management development	22	13
Aims	28	11
Rewards	15	8
Personal growth	27	12

Figure 12.4 Results of organisational questionnaire for an inner city secondary school

You have arranged to see the Head to give an interim report on the progress of the programme, but as a result of the information now available, realise that the programme is only likely to exacerbate difficulties and divisions within the school.

Your task is to attempt to persuade the Head as to an appropriate strategy to cope with the problem as it appears.

The Headteacher's perspective

You are a headteacher of the old tradition who is not happy with the idea of comprehensive schools, abolition of corporal punishment and the more relaxed and friendly disposition of younger staff towards the pupils.

Partly to combat these alien influences, you have surrounded yourself with a senior staff who think much on the same lines as yourself. The only head of department who is under 40 is Leslie who is a constant critic of your style of leadership. You got him to have a term off last term at the polytechnic, but he has returned full of bright ideas. Your strategy of getting him involved in this programme is to get him off your back a little.

In your heart of hearts you realise that the management style that you have developed has evolved from expediency. You are often very lonely as a decision-maker, and feel that it is a sign of weakness to change your mind or consult with the younger members of the school.

You enjoy teaching, and regret having to spend so much time on administration. The apparent threats of falling rolls with its consequences are of limited concern to you since you can opt for early retirement, and yet you are concerned for other staff – but you are unable to find a suitable way to get the problem properly articulated.

REACTIONS TO CHANGE

> There is nothing more difficult to carry out, nor more doubtful of success, nor more dangerous to handle than to initiate a new order.
>
> The performer has enemies in all those who profit by the old order and only lukewarm defenders in those who would profit by the new order. This lukewarmness arises partly from fear of adversaries – and partly from the incredulity of mankind who do not believe in anything new until they have had actual experience of it.
>
> (*Machiavelli*, The Prince)

From what has already been said it should be evident that people are going to react to change with varying degrees of resistance. Again it should be evident that much resistance can either be overcome or, better still, the energies that might go into resistance can be harnessed to further positive change by effective management of the change process.

Table 12.3 lists the possible range of reactions to change. We need to add to the table the following dimensions that all have implications for managing change:

1. The impact which the change may have upon individuals on how far the proposed change is seen as an improvement upon present practice.
2. The way in which it is presented (including the degree to which it can be tried and tested on a limited basis).
3. The general feelings and attitudes of those affected in particular towards the innovator.
4. The degree of risk involved.
5. The quality and education of the people involved.

These are further explained below.

1. How does change affect the individual?

Anything which threatens an individual's security (financial or otherwise), habits or status will tend to be resisted. To overcome this resistance requires time, intelli-

Table 12.3 The spectrum of possible behaviour towards a change.

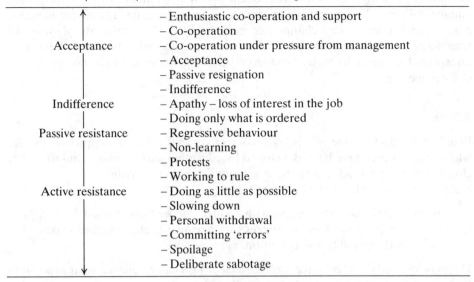

Acceptance	– Enthusiastic co-operation and support
	– Co-operation
	– Co-operation under pressure from management
	– Acceptance
	– Passive resignation
	– Indifference
Indifference	– Apathy – loss of interest in the job
	– Doing only what is ordered
Passive resistance	– Regressive behaviour
	– Non-learning
	– Protests
	– Working to rule
Active resistance	– Doing as little as possible
	– Slowing down
	– Personal withdrawal
	– Committing 'errors'
	– Spoilage
	– Deliberate sabotage

gence, skill and patience in breaking down old habits and techniques and replacing them with new ones.

2. Method of presentation

The way in which the change is presented is all-important. A sudden, possibly threatening, instruction is bound to create hostility and resentment. The better way is to present the proposed change in a planned manner, allowing adequate time for people to understand, raise objections and have these answered, and become involved in the successful implementation of the change.

3. Feelings and attitudes

People who positively like and trust the innovator will also be more ready to accept and adopt his ideas. If, on the other hand, they dislike or mistrust the innovator, they will be more likely to misinterpret his ideas and resist their introduction. If therefore management has consistently shown concern for people's welfare, kept them informed of relevant information about the organisation's activities, and shown itself worthy of trust and respect, people are likely to accept new ventures relatively easily (always assuming, of course, that these have been properly thought out). Those who feel that their justifiable needs have been consistently ignored and that they have been kept in the dark about plans are likely to release their hostility and mistrust through stubborn opposition to any change.

4. Risk

All change entails risk, and the risk takes many forms. The risk of redundancy causes a great deal of the opposition to change which can be minimised by improved manpower planning. The risk of redundancy (of management as well as men) may equally well arise, however, from the failure to change in time. The risk of failure is always present with every change and must be limited by adequate planning of resources. The risk of success also has to be considered – to avoid if possible unexpected and undesirable by-products arising from the successful accomplishment of a change.

5. People

People with alert, active minds, clear objectives and a flexible approach to life, whose basic talents have been developed by education and training, tend to accept change much more readily than those without these characteristics.

As a corollary to the above it is stated that:

> If an organisation is to cope with change successfully it must have a significant proportion of employees with personality characteristics associated with flexibility and commitment to change.

Having identified the various reactions to change how can we ensure as far as possible that the attitudes are more positive than negative?

1. *Aims*. A clear idea of aims that you wish to be accomplished, couched in specific terms that are easily understood, is essential. For example 'To improve the workload of a specified group from 70% to 80% of that theoretically possible.'
2. *Stages*. Identify the stages that need to be accomplished to achieve the goal above.
3. With a clear knowledge of the people in your organisation, mobilise individual contributions to achieve organisational effectiveness.

Later on we shall look at some specific approaches to achieving the above. Figure 12.5 indicates the personal characteristics related to change within organisations and indicates those which are more successful.

Finally, there are many reasons that are put forward as to why change should not take place. Table 12.4 lists the standard objections to change. It is suggested that if you wish to confront resistance this list could be issued.

Technology and change

Because technology is one of the most likely causes of change then some guidelines for organisations and individual operations managers are useful. The first guidelines are from Lawlor (1970) for the whole organisation:

1. Plan the future by engaging in some kind of technological forecasting.
2. Try to ascertain the nature of the technology gap in the appropriate sector.
3. Determine the rate of change taking place; crude measurements might include: number of new services which did not exist, say, two years ago; number of new departments or functions created within the last two years; and significant changes in employed strength, also in the same period.
4. Is there a need to change the way in which the service is delivered?
5. Ascertain if the present type of organisation structure is suitable for change.

The individual operations manager should:

Less successful	More successful
Orientation	
Towards equilibrium As before Safety and security	Towards growth and change Desire for new experience Risk-taking
Sentiments	
Preoccupation with means Belief in 'one best way'	Greater attention to ends There is always a better way
Work aspirations	
Regularity and order Financial security Prestige and status	Responsibility Achievement and challenge Interesting work
Technical skills	
Boss is the expert on all subordinates' jobs	Boss no longer an expert
Dimensions of leadership	
Efficiency and human relations are separate Reactive Directive and authoritative	Efficiency and human relations are merged Authority according to contribution Equality in relations with others
Decision-making	
Use of previously successful solutions ('What did we do last time?')	Less dependence on experience and more on systematic evaluation of the evidence

Figure 12.5 Personal characteristics and performance in organisational change

1. Try to adopt a strategic orientation and avoid fragmentation of effort. A need to focus on the 'how' of organisational purpose.
2. Be constantly aware of potential problems and try to anticipate and avoid them.
3. Be aware of the types of approaches to adopt towards others which will ensure that a change strategy is successful.
4. Develop teamwork at all levels.

The above will require the development of skills in problem definition and solving, interpersonal behaviour and team building, as well as a 'political awareness' of the organisation.

PREPARING FOR CHANGE

The manager's approaches in preparing for change will include elements of the following:

1. Organisational development
2. Team building
3. Installing an organisational 'culture'
4. Consideration of management style and leadership

Table 12.4 Standard objections to change.

1. We've never done it before.	25. It's too long-haired and theoretical.
2. Nobody else has ever done it.	26. You can't teach an old dog new tricks.
3. It has never been tried before.	27. Teaching grandmother to suck eggs?
4. We tried it before.	28. It's too radical a change.
5. Another place tried it once.	29. It's not my responsibility.
6. Our place is different.	30. It's not my job.
7. We've been doing it this way for 25 years.	31. It will make our present method obsolete.
8. It won't work in a small station yard, office, depot, works.	32. We haven't the time.
9. It won't work in a large station yard, office, depot, works.	33. It's contrary to policy.
	34. It will increase overheads.
10. It won't work in our station yard, office, depot, works.	35. The staff will never accept it.
	36. I don't like it.
11. It is not being done in other	37. You're right, but . . . (fill in as required).
12. Why change it? It's working all right.	
13. The boss will never accept it.	38. We're not ready for it.
14. It needs a further investigation.	39. It needs more thought.
15. It's too much trouble to change.	40. We can't take the chance.
16. The . . . department says it can't be done.	41. We'd lose money on it.
	42. It would take too long to pay off.
17. The . . . department won't like this.	43. We're doing all right as it is.
18. The chief clerk is against it.	44. We must appoint a committee to consider it.
19. My foreman says it can't be done.	
20. It can't be done.	45. It needs sleeping on.
21. We haven't the money.	46. It won't work in this office.
22. We haven't the staff.	47. It's too hard-headed for words.
23. We haven't the equipment.	48. I'm scared of it.
24. You'll get trouble from the unions.	49. It's impossible.
	50. You're impossible.

Reference has been made to many of the above points in Chapters 2 and 9, but for the busy operations manager there is a need to ensure that these aspects are put together in an effective way for implementation. Implementation will not be any quicker, or easier, but it will contain elements of all of the above in a fully integrated way.

The technique is called *structured task management development* (STMD). The basic objective is to gather together a group of managers from different functions within an organisation as a project team to develop an answer to a real organisation-wide problem. They also have to gain acceptability of the solution and undertake responsibility for its implementation. The major objective of the task is management development, but the solution to major problems is an advantageous spin-off. So when a group of managers from an organisation is brought together for 'in-plant' development courses, there is a golden opportunity to use the real-life problems of that organisation as the practical basis for the developmental process.

Developing a training programme

All sound development programmes require that senior managers conduct some form of appraisal which will elicit the training requirements of managers to carry out their present and future duties and responsibilities. Additionally techniques can be identified that would be 'nice to know' but these will be subordinate to the major development exercise. In many cases the techniques that managers require will relate to ongoing problems, such areas as payment structure development, costing, capacity, more effective capital investment, quality problems, etc. So at the same time that senior managers are defining training requirements the major problems facing different managers are being brought into sharp focus.

At this point the person responsible for training should be in a position to discuss with the management of the unit the types of task which could form the basis of the practical follow-up in a development course. In some organisations the problem areas will be the major concern of one functional manager, who by recognising the interdependency of problems realises that an acceptable solution is more easily and quickly resolved by a project team representing other associated functions. However, an organisation-wide problem is much better if one can be selected. For example, a stores manager could be concerned with layout, a local authority manager could be concerned with a shrinking budget, a headteacher could be concerned with integrating curriculum changes, and so on.

Having identified a suitable task or tasks the next stage is to define clearly the terminal objectives of the development course. For example, in a local authority the objectives were:

> To present a report to the chief executive on the effect of new technology within the authority and to outline the requirements of a New Technology Agreement which will lead to speedy and trouble free implementation. There will be an oral presentation on site to all senior executives.

In some cases to facilitate this a training agency may be employed – for example, the local college or a consultant. A 'neutral' individual with some management development experience from the organisation could also be used.

The normal format for a training programme to fit the above is given in Table 12.5.

Table 12.5 General format for structured task management development.

Phase 1	Formal inputs relevant to task as specified.	Normally 3–4 days off site.
Phase 2	Team works on task analysis with further inputs either as requested by team or as identified by trainee/consultant.	6–10 weeks, ½ day per week, plus internal meeting as necessary on site.
Phase 3	Identified inputs in:	
	(a) project network techniques (to assist in implementation stage).	1 day on site.
	(b) report writing and presentation techniques (to assist in professional reporting).	2 days on site.
Phase 4	Presentation to senior site staff.	1 day on site.
Phase 5	Implementation.	As required.

Comments on the programme

The objective of this first phase is to give sufficient knowledge to the participants so that they can commence their task. This will include problem-solving and analytical techniques relevant to the task plus other techniques which will have a bearing on the problem. For example, in a recent programme for a retail and distribution organis-ation the problem was concerned with payment systems, particularly with devising a suitable structure. Inputs were made on aspects of job evaluation and similar structures, though not in too much depth, just enough for people to know how to set about this problem.

Another very important aspect is 'team working'. Time is devoted to exercises with the objective of building effective teams.

As the teams move into the second phase they have ready access to a consultative group. This should ideally comprise experts from the training agency in the specific task areas (plus others as required) and company personnel – usually from training but often including other functional managers, particularly where the problem is of prime importance to that functional area.

All the teamwork must have an end result and so a goal is set, completion being marked by a suitably impressive presentation to senior staff, who as sponsors of many of the team members will be keen to review the results. A further feature of some programmes has been to use the sponsoring senior managers as a 'control group' to monitor the progress of the teams, and also to get complete rather than partial commitment by those managers to the development programme so that support for attendance at formal team meetings is not withheld.

Experience with many organisations in both private and public sectors has shown this approach to be well worth while for the effective promotion of change, so that those most affected are committed to ensure it is properly implemented. In this type of detailed investigation the problems are clearly identified and dealt with.

CASE STUDY

A research and development organisation manager wished to make quite consider-able organisation structure changes to a group which would be likely to resist an imposed solution. He also felt he was unlikely to have enough data to ensure an effective end result model. The managers (15) were divided into three teams, each with a specific subtask to investigate the way the organisation operated. The end result enabled everyone to contribute and be enthusiastic about the changes they recommended.

From an individual participant's viewpoint the following specific advantages occurred:

1. Knowledge gained of specific techniques relevant to an organisation problem.
2. Knowledge gained of unit's organisation and information systems.
3. Knowledge gained of other functions (via other team members).
4. Understanding gained of group dynamics, team working and the role of the individual in the team.
5. Ability acquired to write pertinent, action-centred reports.
6. Ability acquired to present proposals in a professional manner.

If this methodology is followed as specified above it does provide a very effective means of coping with change when this change can be anticipated.

THE OPERATIONS MANAGER AS CHANGE AGENT

All managers when they bring about change are acting as *change agents*. Change agents may be defined as:

> A resource person whose job it is to help a system in the process of deliberate planned change and who attempts to influence the adoption of decisions in a manner that they feel is desirable.

Already we have seen the need for involving others but change agents who occupy senior positions are wont to feel that responsibility for change lies exclusively with them. If recipients of change can be made to accept some responsibility for changing themselves, the resulting change can be more lasting.

It is suggested by Lamming (1986) that the skills required to bring about major change are different from day-to-day management and therefore, as with STMD, the manager may decide to involve a 'project manager' as change agent. This could be an outside consultant, management trainee, personnel or management services specialist, etc. There have been problems in the past, however, in using staff specialists: 'Managers and management specialists are operating as two separate cultures, each with his own goals, languages and methods ...'. This is now being changed by teamwork development and a recognition of the 'change agent' as a member of that team (Butcher and Mountford, 1977).

Change agents themselves need also to recognise the different styles they need to adopt in their consultancy role. This can range from being simply reflective through fact-finding, joint problem-solving and training to 'expert' and 'advocate'. Details of these roles are given in Lippitt and Lippitt (1978). There is also a need to recognise the different roles of consultant and consulted.

CONCLUSIONS

Change has many facets. It manifests itself in many ways and once commenced as a result of one factor, will have an effect on all parts of the organisation. These are a number of points worth considering about change which are summarised by Neale (1970):

1. There must be a massive investment of time in discussion and communication. Conditions of trust and confidence must be developed.
2. In working with groups one must understand and, to the extent that this is possible, take account of the reasonable aims and aspirations of the group. Theories about group behaviour can help in clarifying management's ideas.
3. There must be leadership and support from the top and this includes by example.
4. Difficulties encountered – and there will be – should be seen as problems to be solved.
5. The changes envisaged should be thought out, risk and consequences considered and action steps planned and reviewed systematically and flexibly.

Finally, as a little humorous aside, this is an oft-quoted example of attitudes towards change generally:

> A man named Joshua Coppersmith was arrested in New York for

attempting to extract funds from ignorant and superstitious people by exhibiting a device which he says will convey the human voice any distance over metallic wires so that it will be heard by the listener at the other end. He calls this a 'telephone' which is obviously intended to imitate the word 'telegraph' and win the confidence of those who know the success of the latter without understanding the principles upon which it is based.

Well informed people know it is impossible to transmit the human voice over wires as may be done with Morse Code and that, were it possible to do so, the thing would be of no practical value.

ACTIVITY

Before we can decide on how to manage change we must assess which changes we wish to instigate. One approach is to make judgements about an organisation in order to ascertain its 'strengths and weaknesses':

1. *Strengths*. Those aspects which you feel should be retained and utilised in the future. Those characteristics and facets which will benefit the organisation and will promote successful change.
2. *Weaknesses*. Those parts which are identified as being the least desirable facets of the organisation and will probably hinder successful change.

It is also possible that you may become aware of elements that are needed to generate and sustain successful change, but are not yet features of the organisation. These should be recorded as 'innovations to assist change'.

You are asked to write down between five and ten 'strengths and weaknesses' of an organisation with which you are familiar, which presumably has major implications for the management of change. The organisation must provide the real context for this exercise. You should also record any perceived 'innovations'.

References and suggested reading

Boettinger, H. M. (1971) *The Impact of Rapid Change*. London: BIM.

Broussine, M. and Guerrier, Y. (1983) *Surviving as a Middle Manager*. London: Croom Helm.

Butcher, P. and Mountford, F. T. (November 1977) Problems of productivity. *Management Services*, **21** (11), pp. 4–9.

Dempsey, P. J. R. (1973) *Psychology and the Manager*. London: Pan.

Harris, N. D. (Autumn 1978) Are you getting the most out of management development? *Commerce, Industry, Finance* (Journal of Tyne and Wear Chamber of Commerce and Industry).

Hickman, C. and Silvia, M. A. (1985) *Creating Excellence*. London: Unwin.

Judson, A. S. (1966) *A Manager's Guide to Making Changes*. New York: Wiley.

Lamming, R. (1986) Managing change in the factory is no easy matter. *Works Management*.

Lawlor, A. (1970) Technological change and management. *Works Management*.

Lippitt, G. and Lippitt, R. (1978) *The Consulting Process in Action*. La Jolla, CA: University Associates.

Mangham, I. L., Shaw, D. and Wilson, B. (1971) *Managing Change – A Practical Guide to Organisation Development*. London: BIM.

Neale, B. A. (April 1970) Developing a change strategy for an organisation. *Workstudy and Management Services* **14** (4).

Nunford, E. and Ward, T. B. (1968) *Computers – Planning for People*. London: Batsford.

Oldfield, F. (March 1967) People and change. *Workstudy and Management Services*, **11** (3).

Oldfield, F. (April 1970) People, participation and productivity. *Workstudy and Management Services*, **14** (4).

Toffler, A. (1971) *Future Shock*. New York: Bantam.

Woodcock, M. and Francis, D. (1979) *Unblocking Your Organisation*. La Jolla, CA: University Associates.

13
MOTIVATION

INTRODUCTION

Motivation can be viewed from the perspective 'How can I motivate others?', i.e. direct their behaviour in a specified way, and also from the perspective 'What motivates me?', i.e. what are the features of a job or task that make me strive for an objective or satisfy a need? These two viewpoints clearly show the dilemma facing many managers since much attention has been paid to those extrinsic features of working life which *tend* to motivate people – pay, fringe benefits, style of management, etc. However, it has been recognised that, whilst such rewards are important, there is a need also to recognise the intrinsic motivators such as the work itself and the satisfaction gained from applying skills, working in a harmonious team, etc.

Even this brief description is not wholly satisfactory since motivation is highly complex and personal needs differ greatly from one person to another, and can also vary at different times of life for the same person. To put this into perspective we shall try a somewhat reverse approach.

ACTIVITY

Make a list of those factors in *your* job that could dis-motivate you.

Now although your list will be very specific, it is likely that all of these factors can be placed in one of the following three groupings:

1. *Remuneration/reward systems*. Whether your pay is enough overall to meet your needs or perhaps you don't feel you get enough in relation to others in your organisation or those you know who do a similar job. This can also include other pay-related factors such as fringe benefits, holidays, etc., and covers time off when required, opportunity for promotion, and so on.
2. *The job itself*. Is it boring and repetitive with little challenge? Is it very time demanding or stressful? Are the conditions under which you work poor or uncomfortable?
3. *The management you get*. Is your manager very demanding or do you not get adequate leadership? Are decisions fudged or are unacceptable demands made on you? Do the managers say 'Well done, thanks' when it is deserved so that you feel appreciated? (See section on organisation in Chapter 2.)

These three aspects of the concept of motivation as perceived by people at a very personal level are illustrated in Figure 13.1. All three need an equal amount of effort spent on getting them right, otherwise the imbalance will still depress the level of motivation. For example, many organisations pride themselves on having a well

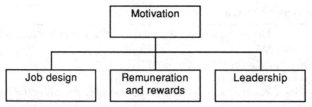

Figure 13.1 Motivating factors on a personal level

designed and carefully developed payment system which is seen as fair to everyone. They then begin to wonder why signs of frustration occur within the ranks – only to discover later that the effort put into supervisory training is very low with the result that staff are not being treated effectively by their managers. In another firm in which pay and supervision were good a series of very routine 'machine minding' tasks caused great concern amongst staff because of the boring nature of the jobs, so much so that they kept on 'inventing' excuses for improvements in working conditions, e.g. lighting, ventilation, etc. The real cause, however, was the way that the job was designed.

In this chapter we are going to use this simple model to identify those aspects of motivation improvement over which the operations manager can exercise control. It is very easy to oversimplify motivation, but it is equally a problem when it is overcomplicated with theory which does not necessarily have any meaning for the manager. So at the risk of offending the motivational purists, comments will be confined to those practical aspects that the manager can influence.

LEADERSHIP

In motivation terms this is concerned with the way the staff perceive the manager and is fundamental to management in any sphere. Do staff see the manager as an autocrat, a bully, a wimp, a pushover, someone who cannot make up their mind? Even worse is the manager seen as someone who is unpredictable – nice and friendly one day and like a bear with a sore head the next. Such inconsistency in behaviour in reaction to events is perhaps one of the most difficult factors for staff to cope with. An autocrat is at least predictable, and whilst as an approach it is not always effective, consistency is perhaps more valued by staff.

Leadership style cannot be discussed in detail without reference to the research that has been conducted over the years, and we will attempt to isolate those features of behaviour which can be differentiated so that some means of identifying 'style' can be approached. To underpin the earlier comment that motivation is a very personal thing, how staff perceive a manager is also very personal. For some it is sufficient that they are 'left alone', despite the fact that this is not conducive to the department achieving its targets. So management style has to link together the 'people management' and the 'task management' aspects of work.

Before we explain the above ideas in more detail consider a manager that you know. Ask the questions in Table 13.1 about the manager. These are not by any means conclusive or exhaustive but show the many aspects of a manager's behaviour that affect 'style'.

Table 13.1 Some questions about a manager's performance.

1. How flexible and adaptive? Is evidence available to show that the individual has grown with the organisation?
2. Ability to make realistic, effective decisions?
3. Clear-sighted in thinking and planning?
4. Is the impression given that knowledge is possessed as to what is going on in the organisation?
5. Are other people kept informed of what is going on?
6. Initiator – someone who gets things going or simply reacts to events?
7. Gets on easily with people?
8. Gains respect on a first meeting?
9. Able to consider alternative approaches to a problem?
10. Inspires confidence – *real* confidence?
11. Relevance of training and experience?
12. Good judge of people?
13. Able to listen effectively as well as to express thoughts clearly?

Leadership theories

There are many theories on leadership – and as many interpretations of them. Only three will be discussed here so that a flavour of the approach can be appreciated:

1. Blake and Mouton's *managerial grid* which demonstrates the task/people link.
2. Tannenbaum and Schmidt's *leadership continuum* which is a model from which a choice of leadership pattern can be selected according to the type of decision called for.
3. Hersey and Blanchard's *situational leadership theory* in which the notion that the most effective leadership pattern not only depends on the demands of the situation but also the level of maturity of the followers.

The managerial grid

Blake and Mouton (1964) showed that managerial style can be plotted on a two dimensional grid as illustrated at Figure 13.2. The two dimensions are *concern for task* and *concern for people*, and are measured by asking the manager questions of his perception of his style. These are then cross checked with his subordinates as to *their* perception of his style.

Some indications of points along these scales are as follows:

1.1 The manager who has little concern for people or the job. He exerts the minimum effort to get the job done.

1.9 The manager who concentrates on having a friendly workforce to the detriment of operations.

5.5 Compromise position where the manager balances the necessity of producing work with the upkeep of staff morale.

9.1 The manager who has little concern for people and arranges work so that human elements have minimum impact.

9.9 Maximum concern for people and the tasks. The interdependence

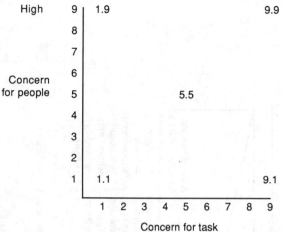

Figure 13.2 Outline of Blake and Mouton's managerial grid

of people having a common stake in the organisation leads to mutual trust and respect.

You can probably draw your own conclusions about these but this analysis is designed to help managers to look carefully at how they perform and to adjust their style to the benefit of the organisation if necessary.

Leadership continuum

Tannenbaum and Schmidt (1958) showed that, as part of the proposition of choosing a leadership pattern, a successful leader is one who is keenly aware of the factors in his own behaviour: that he understands himself, the individual subordinates and the work group, and the way they interact. This then allows for the selection of an appropriate leadership style relating to the type of decision called for as illustrated in Figure 13.3. No manager can operate entirely at the right-hand side of the continuum, nor would it be desirable, and there are times when an autocratic decision of the left-hand side is called for so that managers can use their experience. It is desirable that some element of involvement in decisions that affect them should be given to staff. The effective leader will know when to engage in full participation, and when consultation is both acceptable and provides for a high quality decision.

Situational leadership theory

A further dimension introduced by Hersey and Blanchard (1982) is the recognition that the maturity of the team and the demands of the situation must interact to provide for the most effective leadership style. Their theory is based on a relationship between these factors:

1. The amount of task behaviour which the leader exhibits (providing direction and emphasis on getting the job done).
2. The amount of relationship behaviour which the leader provides (consideration for people, level of support).

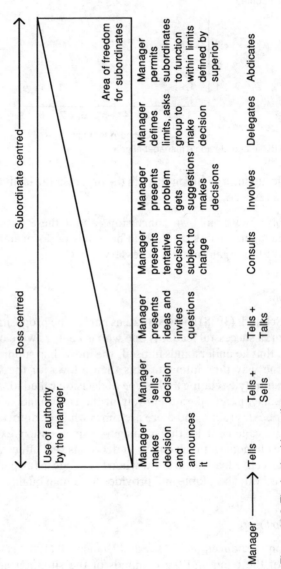

Figure 13.3 The leadership continuum

3. The level of task-relevant maturity that followers exhibit toward the specific goal, task or function that the leader wants accomplished.

The key concept of this leadership theory is the level of task-relevant maturity of the followers. Maturity is not defined as age or psychological stability but as

1. A desire for achievement (level of achievement motivation) based on the need to set high but attainable goals.
2. The willingness and ability to accept responsibility.
3. Education and/or experience and skills relevant to the particular task.

This is particularly pertinent if you are managing a group of professional staff, e.g. teachers or social workers, as they would normally be self-motivated and have a high level of discretion in the use of their time.

What the theories mean in practice

From the discussion above of various leadership theories it should be apparent that there is no one style of leadership that is equally effective for all circumstances. The best leadership style is the one that fulfils the needs of the group the most whilst at the same time satisfying the current needs of the organisation.

The manager has to provide in leadership:

1. *Direction* – the elimination of uncertainty of what has to be done and the co-ordination of all effort to pull in one direction.
2. *Drive* – the commitment of the group to want to move forward which will include satisfying the intrinsic needs of group members.
3. *Representation* – represent the purpose of the group to the outside world, which includes consultation and involvement as appropriate.

Whatever the situation or group, to be successful the leader must have:

1. *The impulse to lead* – but it must not be so strong that the leader must lead rather than just wish to lead.
2. *Self-awareness* – the ability to evaluate the effect of the style being used on the group and the task.
3. *Intelligence and knowledge* of the task so that judgements are right most of the time.
4. *Human sympathy* – authority is given by the group and is not a divine right. A leader who regards people as a nuisance or as his only interest is doomed to fail.
5. *Tough mindedness* – to be single-minded and do what is required in a situation in spite of side-effects. To overcome opposition and also any personal disappointments.
6. *Integrity* – a wholeness in all of the above so that the group feels the leader rings true and can be trusted.

The variables that define the successful style are:

1. *The personality of the leader* – probably the most rigid of the variables which define the most effective leadership style (see above).
2. *The situation of the group* – can vary from calm to crisis, simple to complex, severe threat to security, and will drastically affect the successful style. The task,

technology, structure and environment in which the group is working will have similar marked effects.

3. *The situation within the group* – can be co-operative to militant which will also affect the successful style.
4. *The people within the group* – will vary in intelligence, education, interest and motives. They may be loyal and longserving, aggrieved, casual or troublemakers. This is obviously independent of the other variables.

These variables and their interactions are illustrated in Figure 13.4.

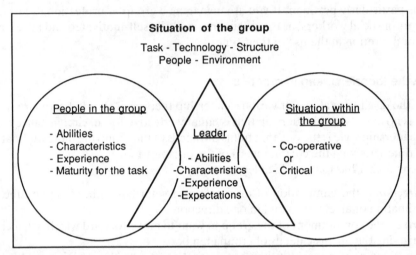

Figure 13.4 Variables which define the successful management style

Management skills

Because of the importance of this aspect of motivation it is essential that managers have some effective development covering these interpersonal skills which involve them in face-to-face situations with their staff – either individually or as leader of groups. This is one of the fastest growing areas of management development and one which should not be covered just once but needs continual maintenance.

These skills are dealt with in detail by Torrington (1982), Johnson (1984) and Goodworth (1984). A skills development programme was conducted for a group of managers whose organisations are brought within the umbrella of the National Association of Care and Resettlement of Offenders (NACRO). At the conclusion of the programme a list of 'achievable objectives' was drawn up and is included as an appendix to this chapter. This is not intended to be exhaustive since it was built on the programme of activities that the participants themselves helped devise.

Current research in management development is looking at a related facet to skills – *competence*. If we are to judge the effectiveness of a manager, it is the degree to which he or she is demonstrably competent. These competencies do not *just* relate to the face-to-face skills, but involve a balanced set which combines the task and people dimensions. An inventory of a possible range of competencies is given in Table 13.2.

Table 13.2 Classification of the competencies of supervisors and managers.

1. Competence of a *general* nature pertaining to:
   - Communication – of all kinds
   - Numeracy
   - People orientation
   - Goal orientation
   - Self-awareness/development orientation
2. Competencies pertaining to *people*:
   - Those for whom one has responsibility
   - Peers, clients and customers
   - Those to whom one reports
3. Competencies concerned with *managing activities*:
   - Systems control
   - Financial control
   - Techniques – as appropriate to sphere of activity
4. Competencies reflecting a *sensitivity to environment* with respect to:
   - Customer expectation/needs
   - Legal considerations
   - Organisational, social, economic and political environment including technological change

JOB DESIGN

In Chapter 4 we used the term 'systems design and redesign' in which the facility was to be reviewed in the light of corporate objectives particularly resource productivity and customer satisfaction. Part of this investigation might identify lack of motivation as a problem, and whilst we did not deal with that in Chapter 4, it is certainly relevant here.

The aspect of motivation that concerns us is that of *job design* or *work design* (or redesign). These two expressions are used synonymously and the intention behind each one is very similar. It is an emerging discipline drawing upon the social sciences and industrial engineering in order to design *healthy work systems*.

Louis E. Davis (1972) defines job design as:

> Specification of the contents, methods and relationships of jobs in order to satisfy technological and organisational requirements as well as social and personal requirements of the job holder.

As you can see the concern is for the individual worker in terms of how the balance between productivity and job satisfaction can be achieved. This is now very much an issue of the Department of Employment Work Research Unit in which research is conducted into the quality of working life.

The development of the current awareness of job design has resulted from a number of individual research structures and interest movements in both the USA and Europe from 1910 onwards. This includes work concerned with the following:

1. Social aspects of work, bureaucracy and alienation
2. Method study/work simplification
3. Psychology of work and research into fatigue
4. Human engineering and ergonomics – design of workplace to fit job to worker,

looking at such aspects as heat, light, glare, seating, posture, controls and dials, etc.
5. Job enlargement
6. Job enrichment
7. Group dynamics and teamwork

Perhaps a good example of the approach is examplified by the work of Frederick Herzberg (1968). Herzberg and his associates distinguished two groups of motivational influences which appeared to have very different effects on behaviour and performance. The first group consisted of influences which produced reactions which ranged from extreme 'dis-motivation' to neutrality. They never produced positive enthusiasm. Herzberg concluded therefore that all management could hope to do was to eliminate the dis-motivating factors in this group – it was not possible to use them to provide positive motivation. He therefore coined the expression *hygiene factors* to describe them on an analogy with public health legislation which aims to remove causes of ill-health rather than to make people healthier. Among the elements which Herzberg categorised as hygiene factors were many previously regarded as positive motivators such as pay, social benefits, management styles, company policy and physical working conditions.

The second group were called *motivators* because they did appear to produce positive satisfaction with and commitment to the job. These factors included those which were associated with the employee's sense of competence, accomplishment and responsibility.

The best-known application of Herzberg's work has been in the *job enrichment* (as distinct from job enlargement) experiments carried out in the ATT Company in the United States and ICI in Britain. These have involved redesigning jobs in such a way as to eliminate or at least reduce the amount of time spent on dull, unstimulating tasks. Related tasks previously separated into several jobs are incorporated into a single job so as to provide clear responsibility on the part of each individual for a definable unit or subunit of work. In addition, each individual has been given more challenging responsibilities related to the work such as scheduling, setting priorities and making on-the-spot decisions relating to the product or process.

Among the benefits which have been found with such job enrichment experiments have been reductions in labour turnover and absenteeism, and increased quality and efficiency, resulting from greater pride in the work. Further developments have included the setting up of *autonomous work groups* which have responsibility for quite complex production (as in the production of Volvo cars).

From Herzberg's point of view enriching the job is critical, *but* the hygiene factors cannot be dismissed. They still need to be there, and when they are not, e.g. when pay is too low or the management style is intrusive, the job design is flawed.

The role of operations management

A number of factors are known to influence the degree of satisfaction people derive from their work. These include a sense of achievement, recognition where there is achievement, responsibility in the making of judgements and the taking of decisions, and scope for developing skills and capacities. A further factor is the pleasure which people get simply from working together successfully.

People are more likely to accept a work situation and try to operate effectively within it if they have some say in the way it is organised. Each individual may not agree on how much a particular job does allow for autonomy. For instance, a job which entails short-cycle, paced work in which the worker is tied to the machine may be made tolerable to one individual if he can work automatically with his mind elsewhere. It may equally be more tolerable to another because he or his colleagues have the power to stop the line, and do so from time to time. Strong feelings of autonomy are likely to be created if groups of workers themselves decide there shall be changes, and on the basis of full participation help to formulate and implement them.

Principles of job design

A well-designed job is one which has as many as possible of the following characteristics. It will:

1. Use an individual's skills and abilities.
2. Provide scope for learning and development.
3. Provide a defined area of responsibility and the opportunity to exercise discretion and make decisions.
4. Provide opportunity for social relations with colleagues.
5. Make an identifiable contribution to the eventual product made or service provided.
6. Be reasonably demanding and present some degree of challenge.
7. Provide for variety in the range of tasks performed.
8. Be thought of as worthwhile and meaningful by the person doing it.

REMUNERATION AND REWARD

These two words have been used since they mean more than just *pay*. *Remuneration* includes the development of an acceptable pay structure and also includes other pay-related factors such as pensions, opportunity for additional earnings, insurance schemes, etc. The term *reward* is used since in many work environments the effort/reward bargain is the subject of much negotiation.

In his book *How to Motivate People* Michael Le Boeuf (1986) suggests that reward is the greatest management principle in the world. He then goes on to show different types of rewards and the type of behaviour to which they should be linked (see Table 13.3). Looking at this list we see that some of them should be covered when attention is paid to leadership style and job design (recognition, time off, piece of the action, favourite work, freedom, personal growth, time). However, that still leaves money, advancement and prizes, and even parts of the other rewards can often be linked to money, payment structures and opportunity for additional earnings and include certain factors concerned with fringe benefits.

So again the message comes through loud and clear that remuneration cannot be looked at in isolation, but is part of a complex system. We have already seen how it links to motivation, leadership and job design, but taking this further we can show remuneration as part of system as in Figure 13.5. In this we recognise that in addition

Table 13.3 Rewards and their associated behaviours.

Use these rewards...	To reward...	Instead of...
1. Money	1. Solid solutions	1. Quick fixes
2. Recognition	2. Risk taking	2. Risk avoiding
3. Time off	3. Applied creativity	3. Mindless conformity
4. A piece of the action	4. Decisive action	4. Paralysis by analysis
5. Favourite work	5. Smart work	5. Busywork
6. Advancement	6. Simplification	6. Needless complication
7. Freedom	7. Quietly effective behaviour	7. Squeaking joints
8. Personal growth	8. Quality work	8. Fast work
9. Fun	9. Loyalty	9. Turnover
10. Prizes	10. Working	10. Working

Source: Le Boeuf (1986). Reproduced with permission.

to the factors we have covered in this chapter, the remuneration system must also be linked to objectives, and these are not just managerial but include employee objectives. The box indicating 'circumstances of the organisation' is meant to indicate that every organisation is different in terms of its technology, industrial relations history, manpower and structure – all of which can affect the selection of the remuneration system.

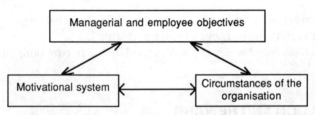

Figure 13.5 Remuneration as a system component

Objectives

The types of objective that any management group might have when considering remuneration could include all or some of the following:

1. Retaining manpower.
2. Obtaining consistency in labour performance.
3. Reducing time and cost of labour disputes.
4. Controlling labour costs.
5. Improving service quality.
6. Improving delivery times.
7. Improving equipment utilisation.
8. Obtaining a lower level of service failures.
9. Gaining control over pay structure to reduce wage drift and differential issues (see below).
10. Improved methods, flexibility, etc.

The employees will also have a number of objectives, different from, but not necessarily in conflict with, those of management. The factors that influence the level of employee contentment with pay are as follows:

1. Adequate in relation to colleagues with similar levels of skill and responsibility.
2. Adequate in relation to superiors in authority chain.
3. Adequate in relation to subordinates.
4. Do employees receive a fair reward in relation to that the shareholders receive?
5. Is treatment fair in relation to price levels?
6. Is pay in line with outside job market?
7. Is additional pay to basic pay available, e.g. commission, incentive bonus?
8. Is there suitable reward for danger and hazards?
9. Does trade/profession via the union keep its proper place in the hierarchy of pay levels?
10. Other benefits (pension, etc.) commensurate with cash payment.
11. Personal career prospects – for experience, meritorious promotion, etc.
12. Job security, job enlargement.

It is clear that this is not a situation in which management want maximum output for minimum wages whilst employees want minimum output for maximum wages. By understanding the objectives of both groups it is possible to structure a payment system which can satisfy both.

Payment structures

Most payment systems are very complex and contain many components. It is not possible to illustrate all such systems here, but a general model of the payment structure is given in Figure 13.6. The following sections explain further some of the components of Figure 13.6 to illustrate the care with which this aspect needs to be considered.

Job evaluation differential

Many of the employee objectives were concerned with fairness of pay in relation to others, and often disputes over pay are not so much on absolute pay but on comparative pay in relation to other groups, usually within the same organisation. Therefore, as a preliminary to any development of variable pay relating to contribution or effort, it is imperative to get the payment levels right between groups in an organisation.

Job evaluation is defined as the systematic process of determining, without regard to personalities, the comparative worth of one job with the worth of others. Most job evaluation is conducted for a specific group of workers in isolation – e.g. office staff, technical staff, manual staff or supervisors and managers. However, the difference between 'white collar' and 'blue collar' work is becoming more and more blurred, and the reduction in size of organisations combined with changing technology has led many to embark upon an organisation-wide job evaluation scheme.

Regardless of the size of the group the procedure is as follows:

1. Consensus as to method, approach, time, weightings, etc.

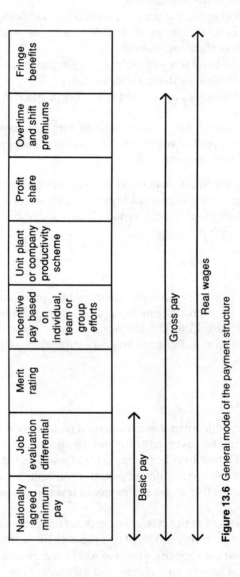

| Nationally agreed minimum pay | Job evaluation differential | Merit rating | Incentive pay based on individual, team or group efforts | Unit plant or company productivity scheme | Profit share | Overtime and shift premiums | Fringe benefits |

Basic pay

Gross pay

Real wages

Figure 13.6 General model of the payment structure

2. Job analysis/description.
3. Job comparison.
4. Arrange jobs in rank order.
5. Determine a grade structure.
6. Convert to money.
7. Install and maintain.
8. Appeals procedure.

There are many job evaluation systems available, all of which have applicability in the appropriate circumstances. A method for making this selection is dealt with in an article by Harris and Bothams (1981).

Merit rating

This is the systematic assessment of the behaviour and ability of workers in their work. This is much more subjective than job evaluation, and is concerned with the merit of each individual worker. When in operation it must be continually carried out and used as a means of improvement.

Incentive pay and productivity schemes

This is usually the major part of the variable pay and whilst in the past this has applied mainly in manufacturing, many such schemes in various guises are being used to great benefit in the service sector. To explain these quickly and without too much unnecessary detail we will return to consider our third box in the model shown in Figure 13.5.

Circumstances of the organisation

Research in the 1960s indicated that the most critical factor in payment selection was to take account of those organisational variables that influenced the type of payment system used. This then influenced whether some form of flat rate pay, incentive pay on a weekly basis or an incentive which is paid on (say) a four-weekly basis was introduced.

Some form of analysis is certainly to be recommended to avoid having a mismatch between the organisation and the pay. Whilst it is not possible to go into detail about all methods of pay, suffice it to say that we can identify the methodology that should be used:

1. Define payment system objectives (managerial and employee) – see above.
2. Classify all payment methods by procedures relating effort and reward – see Table 13.4.
3. For each unit, department, section, etc., conduct a profile analysis which takes account of some 21 dimensions grouped into 4 divisions – see Table 13.5.
4. Interpret the results of this to indicate either:
   (a) Which payment system is acceptable, and/or
   (b) What features of the organisation need to be changed to limit the breakdown of a payment method.

Table 13.4 Payment systems classified by the time relationship between effort and reward.

Immediate	*Deferred*	*No relationship*
Shift and overtime premiums	Productivity bonus schemes (individual and team)	Daywork
		Measured daywork (consolidated)
Weekly incentive schemes (individual and team) based on output	Group productivity bonus schemes (e.g. added value)	Contract prices
Multi-factor schemes	Group collective long-term schemes based on output, costs, etc.	
	Profit-sharing	
	Stepped measured daywork	

Table 13.5 Circumstances of an organisation that can influence pay policy.

1. *Technology* – Machinery and equipment, methods, quality, etc. Strong influence on choice as to how a job is done.
2. *Labour markets* – Turnover, scarcity of supply, overmanning.
3. *Disputes and dispute procedures* – Control and drift erosion of pay system.
4. *Structural characteristics* – Where are pay levels decided; number of TUs in organisation; age and sex distribution; absenteeism.

Profit-sharing

This is a means whereby an organisation makes available a percentage of profits for distribution to all employees on some acceptable basis, yearly or twice yearly. Although thought by some to be an incentive, since profits are dependent upon economic and other outside factors, such a scheme can only be regarded as a fringe benefit.

Overtime, night and shift rates, etc.

This is extra payment for working other than normal hours. For night work and shift work this is usually a flat addition to the basic wage. Overtime is paid at varying rates for different days of the week. In some industries the amount of overtime available is important from the employee's point of view as an incentive potential.

Fringe benefits

Fringe benefits can cost some organisations up to a quarter of their wage bill. These have come under close scrutiny by the government and taxation is to a large extent controlling the extent of such benefits. In the higher salaried strata where high taxes make mobility between jobs hardly worthwhile, fringe benefits have a large part to play in making a job attractive.

The type of benefits covered by this include the following:

1. Additional employment conditions, e.g. more holidays, restaurants, etc.
2. Additional financial benefits, e.g. pension schemes, insurance schemes, low interest loans, etc.

In reviewing remuneration and reward, these are very important areas to be included within the total system.

Success in payment scheme design

A participative approach to the development of payment systems of whatever type is probably the most important factor in success. The journals are full of disasters in the implementation of payment systems. In a most exhaustive study carried out by Bowey and Thorpe (1986) the conclusions were (amongst others):

1. It is a mistake to introduce a payment scheme without some primary aim of influencing performance.
2. Extend the information that is taken into account, i.e. a high level of consultation is required with all parties affected.
3. Ensure the scheme is not modified or subverted in its implementation. It must be linked to strategies rather than tactical objectives.
4. Be participative. This can lead to greater trust, understanding *motivation* and commitment.

References and suggested reading

Blake, R. R. and Mouton, J. S. (1964) *Managerial Grid*. Houston, TX: Gulf.

Bothams, J., Harris, N. D., Marran, A. and Orchard, H. (1983) Management skills for residential and day care staff. *Business Education*, **4** (3).

Bowey, A. and Thorpe, R. (1986) *Payment Systems and Productivity*. Basingstoke: Macmillan.

Davis, L. E. and Taylor, J. C. (1972) *Design of Jobs*. Harmondsworth, Middx: Penguin.

Department of Employment (1975) *Making Work More Satisfying*. London: HMSO.

Goodworth, C. T. (1984) *How to be a Super-Effective Manager*. London: Business Books.

Grayson, D. (September 1982) *Job Evaluation and Changing Technology*. London: Work Research Unit, Department of Employment.

Harris, N. D. and Bothams, J. (May 1981) Selecting an appropriate job evaluation scheme. *Management Services*, **25** (5).

Hersey, P. and Blanchard, K. H. (1982) *Management of Organizational Behaviour*. Englewood Cliffs, NJ: Prentice-Hall.

Herzberg, F. (1968) *Work and the Nature of Man*. London: Staples Press.

Johnson, R. (1984) *How to Manage People*. London: Business Books.

Le Boeuf, M. (1986) *How to Motivate People*. London: Sidgwick & Jackson.

Lupton, T. C. and Gowler, D. (1969) *Selecting a Wage Payment System*. London: Kogan Page.

Tannenbaum, R. and Schmidt, W.H. (1958) How to choose a leadership pattern. *Harvard Business Review*.

Torrington, D. (1982) *Face to Face in Management*. Englewood Cliffs, NJ: Prentice-Hall.

Torrington, D., Weightman, J. and Johns, K. (1985) *Management Methods*. London: IPM.

Whitmore, D. A. and Ibbetson, J. (1977) *The Management of Motivation and Remuneration*. London: Business Books.

APPENDIX: NACRO Management Skills Course

Some objectives that should be achievable

Management and organisation

1. Recognise that management involves functions (accounting, public relations, personnel management), elements (planning, motivating, controlling) and activities engaged in by the manager (figurehead, dispute handler, negotiator, etc.).
2. Recognise that 'organisational blockages' can reduce the effectiveness of management and identify strategies for unblocking organisations.
3. Identify clearly the aims of your organisation or unit and relate these to the key results of individual members of staff.
4. Ensure that key result areas are established which are specific, measurable and time bounded.

Decision-making

1. Recall the main stages of the decision-making process – define aims, collect facts, list choices, predict outcomes and make decisions.
2. Recognise the different styles of decision-making and where each is appropriate.
3. Recognise the differences between group and individual decision-making.
4. Use suitably weighed criteria in evaluating alternatives to ensure that effective decisions are made in such vital areas as staff selection.
5. Use brainstorming to generate alternatives for open-ended problems.
6. Recognise the need for preparation of contingency plans as all decisions carry risks.

Groups

1. Recall those factors that can contribute to greater effectiveness of group working.
2. Utilise measuring instruments to monitor the maintenance function of groups and thus improve the working of groups in which you are a member.

Meetings

1. Recall the main faults of meetings as depicted in the film and recall that effective

meetings need to be organised as follows: planning, agenda, preparation, control, recording.

Time management

1. Recognise that effective time management requires a knowledge of how time is spent, a critical appraisal of this and an ordering of priorities.
2. Use time logs to identify your own and others' use of time.

Interviewing

1. Recognise effective approaches to interviewing for selection, ensuring information is obtained additional to that on the application form.
2. Recognise the need for appraisal interviewing to have an emphasis on future staff development. Be able to ensure that this is suitably agreed by staff and not imposed.
3. Plan interview to investigate behaviour as well as results.

14

THE TIME RESOURCE

Time is like money under the mattress – it is not sufficient to possess it, we must use it.

Anon.

INTRODUCTION

Throughout the book we have been concerned with resource productivity, and one of the most important resources managers have at their disposal is their own time. This chapter will be addressing ways in which managers can more effectively utilise their time, thus giving them the opportunity to apply many of the ideas presented.

In some service activities, individual members of staff have a great deal of discretion as to how they use (or misuse) their time – social workers, many office staff, college lecturers, etc. Many of the ideas presented here can be equally applied to such groups, enabling the manager to increase capacity. Time management applied to a job by the incumbent is the ultimate in work study.

The term used above is critical. You cannot impose time management, and individuals – whether professionals or managers – have genuinely got to feel strongly that there is a real problem that they wish to address.

An indication of the pressures that cause certain groups to be concerned about 'overwork' is shown in the short extract which follows:

Teachers say their day is never done

Infant school teacher Mrs Ann Martin clocked up her usual 70 hours at work last week. Sometimes she works 85 hours. She is, in her own words, 'just an ordinary classroom teacher' – one of many in a National Union of Teachers' survey to demonstrate how hard their members work.

Mrs Martin, from New Earswick, near York, is busy even in the weeks off in the summer. She has been teaching for 29 years and has responsibility for music and for children with special educational needs.

She says that pressures on teachers have increased enormously over the past decade: 'I've never sought promotion. My workload is no greater than that of my colleagues. It is sometimes difficult not to go under, and some people do.'

She is one of 1,000 teachers featured in the union survey to be published at the end of the month which shows that they work a 50-hour week on average and that some work as many as 100 hours.

Tomorrow the union will publish a booklet explaining why teachers' workload has increased in the past 10 years.

The reasons suggested by teachers last week for the change were:
- new curriculum initiatives, such as computing;

- attendance courses to keep abreast of change;
- more evening meetings and time spent with parents;
- more hours dealing with police, social services and with disruptive pupils.

The survey will be treated with scepticism by Ministers who feel that teachers are well-compensated by long holidays, during which they cannot claim to be working a 50-hour week.

Mr Bob Morris, education officer of the Labour-controlled Association of Metropolitan Authorities, which employs teachers, also doubted that the work-load was now greater than in the past. 'Teaching has always been a hard and demanding job, particularly in term-time. To demonstrate that it is getting harder you need firm evidence to compare what it is now with what it used to be, not just impressions about morale and stress.'

The view taken by some employing authorities is that a 50-hour week is not unusual in many jobs and that working in the evenings and the holidays is as old as the profession itself.

The contention that teachers' burdens have increased was accepted, however by the Conservative-controlled Association of County Councils. A spokesman doubted the 50-hour-a-week figure but felt that 'a responsible teacher is more likely to be doing 40-plus hours than 30-plus. In terms of working hours it does not compare unfavourably with other professions.'

The one sour note, he said, was that in some areas teachers today undoubtedly did less than in previous decades. 'In earlier years you could be roasted alive for not doing dinner duty. Now it is deemed voluntary.'

The growing demands on teachers were emphasised by teachers outside the NUT. Mr Michael Hayhurst, 33, head of curriculum development at Ongar comprehensive school in Essex, said he worked every break and lunchtime because of his pastoral responsibilities, every evening but Friday, and at least four hours each Sunday.

He said youth unemployment had created time-consuming activities: his curriculum had been altered to include more vocational preparation, mock interviews for all fifth formers, work experience and stronger links with industry and the community.

(Source: The Observer, 13 January 1985)

It would be wrong to suggest that all of the above problems will be solved by application of time management, but many could be made more manageable.

THE IMPORTANCE OF TIME MANAGEMENT

There are a number of reasons for the need to take time management seriously:

1. Time has a variable quality – sometimes it 'drags' and sometimes it 'flies'. When you are at work it is amazing how it can ooze away resulting in either poor quality work or the need to work longer hours to catch up.
2. Time has a cost. If a person earns £10,000 p.a. and works a 238-day year at 7 hours per day the cost is 10p per minute.
3. Much has been written about job satisfaction (see Chapter 13) and this is unlikely to be achieved if time is not managed properly. Terms that are sometimes used to describe this are 'crisis management' and 'management by chaos'.
4. The corollary to the above is the development of *stress* which is damaging to the individual, family, friends and the organisation itself.
5. The most important part of time management is to differentiate between

efficiency and *effectiveness*. This means that all people should be doing right things, not just doing *things right*. There is a need to ask fundamental questions such as whether some things should be done at all (see Figure 14.1).

In this chapter we will not just be producing a series of hints and methods about time management, but will provide a number of frameworks which can be of value to you in analysing your own time, thus enabling the real problem to be identified. The application of strategies of time management thereafter is not easy. There has got to be a conscious effort on your part to apply your strategy, to avoid alienating staff or colleagues and in so doing to recognise that you will backslide and need continually to reapply these skills.

Getting more effective use of time for any individual has similar features to giving up smoking or attempting to lose weight. It too can be helped by a group meeting regularly to provide support (cf. quality circles).

A job well dun!

A newly hired travelling salesman in the United States wrote his first sales report to the home office. It stunned the brass in the sales department because it was obvious the new 'hope' was illiterate, for he wrote:

> 'I never seen this outfit which they ain't never bought a dimes worth of nothing from us and I sole them a couple of hundred thousand dollars of guds. I am now going to Chicawgo.'

Before the illiterate could be given the heave-ho by the sales manager along came this message from Chicago:

> 'I cum hear and sole them haff a millyon.'

Fearful if he did, and fearful if he didn't fire the man, the sales manager dumped the problem in the lap of the president. The following morning the ivory tower members were amazed to see the two letters posted on the bulletin board - and this memo from the president tacked above:

> 'We ben spending two much time trying to spel instead of trying to sel. Let's wach thoes sails. I want everybody should read these letters from Butch, who is on the rode doin a grate job for us, and you should go out and do like he done.'

Figure 14.1

ACTIVITY

As a preliminary to the next part Table 14.1 provides a useful checklist. Spend a few minutes only considering this before we take these ideas further.

Table 14.1 Checklist for use of time.

1. Am I giving adequate attention to current activities, past review and planning for the future?
2. Is my time divided correctly between aspects of my job?
3. Have I allowed for changes which may have occurred?
4. Am I certain that I am not doing work that I ought to have delegated?
5. Am I spending the correct amount of time with the right people?
6. Do I organise the working day/week according to priorities?
7. Am I able to complete a task or am I interrupted?
8. What have I done recently to further my own development?

How is my time being used?

Before many of the questions in Table 14.1 can be answered we need to know how our time is actually used. Only then can we examine our use of time systematically and devise suitable strategies. Figure 14.2 is an example of a time log that has been used effectively with a variety of professionals and managers. Table 14.2 gives instructions on how to fill the log in.

ACTIVITY

Photocopy 5 copies of Figure 14.2 and, following the instructions in Table 14.2, keep 5 days' worth of time logs.

CASE STUDY

Determination of need for study of social workers

Initially involvement was through the mounting of a training course on 'The Use of Time by Social Workers' based largely upon time management books and made pertinent to the social worker group by discussion and observation over a period of weeks. In the initial session of the course when the group were asked to comment on the difficulties of the job as they saw it, considerable variation in 'time spent on crises' was recorded and it soon became obvious that some factual data as to how time was spent was going to be necessary. There was of course a natural spin-off in that once this data was known it could be used to change the system to give greater utilisation of social worker time, since in the current economic climate they are likely to be restricted in numbers but increasingly in demand by their clients.

It was recognised that social workers are very similar to managers as a group since they have a great deal of control over their time but are continually under pressure. The term 'task management' most correctly sums up the situation.

There was a need to develop an adequate self-recording sheet which would:

Column 1 Time		Column 2 Brief description of activity		Column 3 Fleeting contacts																			
1/4-hour intervals				Contact Please indicate P=Personal, T=Telephone																				
		1		11	Supervisor																			
		2		12	Clerical staff																			
		3		13	Colleagues																			
		4		14	Other agencies																			
		5		15	Clients																			
		6		16	Others																			
		7		17	Was this an interruption?																			
		8																						
		9																						
		10	Other please indicate briefly																					

Name: _____ Day and date: _____

Figure 14.2 Time log

Table 14.2 Notes on completion of time log sheets.

1. *Identity.* Please ensure each sheet is marked with your name/code.

2. *Activities.* Identify up to 9 major activities that you engage in as part of your job. There is a total column for 'other'. Write these clearly on the log sheet. Use the same headings for all days of the time log record.

3. *Time.* Put on the time started and then mark the time in 1/4 hour intervals down the page. Clearly tick the appropriate column for each 3/4 hour. (Rest time should be recorded as coffee breaks, lunch, etc., but this will not be used in final calculations.) If you are working a long day continue on a second sheet.

4. *Fleeting contacts.* If your 1/4 hour is interrupted by a telephone call or a talk with someone in the office which is only short, indicate this in the appropriate column against the appropriate time slot.

5. *Comments.* Any additional comments you may wish to make please do so on the reverse of the sheet.

6. *Method of completion.* For greater accuracy try to get into the habit of completing the sheet every hour so that memory does not fade.

---

1. Fit the work pattern of the social worker.
2. Be easy to understand and use.
3. Be able to record interruptions and fleeting contacts which are often a source of irritation.
4. Be not too much of a straitjacket bearing in mind the work is highly variable (remember the 'time on crisis situation' mentioned).

Pilot study

After discussion and consultation at area office level (most social services departments have several geographically separated area offices) a pilot project was developed with the following activities:

1. Seek volunteers for the exercise.
2. Initial briefing and introduction to the time logging sheets.
3. Follow-up whilst data is collected (a two week period).
4. Debriefing discussion on the significance of the results with volunteers.
5. Report to Social Services Department Management Planning Group.
6. Meeting with first-line supervisors to discuss results and gain approval for the extension of the project.

A group of five social workers volunteered for the above exercise and kept logs for a total of 41 working days. Two log sheets were used – one to keep a quarter-hourly log of activities under predetermined columns (travel, writing/dictating, interviewing clients, etc.) and the other to record by dashes the type of fleeting contacts which occurred during the day.

The main purpose of the pilot exercise was to validate the log sheets but the results were of interest. At the conclusion of the pilot study an extract from the report to the Planning Group is of significance.

A further more extensive study would be of great value to make compari-

sons between area offices and different activities and this will be facili-
tated by the use of the revised time log sheet.

(The revised sheet is that presented in Figure 14.2.)

The main project

The activities in the main project were:

1. Contact area managers to arrange for meetings with themselves and first-line
   supervisors.
2. Selection of volunteers.
3. Individual area briefing of volunteers.
4. Obtaining estimates of 'will be' and 'should be' figures.
5. Follow-up whilst data is collected.
6. Analysis of data.
7. Production of figures, charts, etc., for concurrent feedback to volunteers, Planning Group and team leaders.
8. Debriefing session.
9. Final report and action plan.

Two points of interest arose from this.

Item 3
Since each area office was asked to provide at least four persons it was essential that
the 'consultant' establish a good relationship with each and every one of them by
explaining in detail how the study was to be conducted, what data they will get at the
conclusion and the hoped for results of the whole study. Many people had complained in the past that they had involved themselves at considerable personal cost in
time recording studies, only to hear nothing further. Individuals were to get a full
copy of the report plus (in confidence) their own results.

Item 4
Since the eventual aim was to change the balance of work it was useful to know what
expectations social workers had about their work pattern. They were, therefore,
each asked to estimate the 'will be' figures based on their work experience, and the
'should be' figures based on their expectations. Comparison between these two sets
of figures and the actual results were considered helpful in the final analysis.

Seventeen social workers agreed to keep work logs for a 10 day period each
(October/November 1975) and the results are shown in Table 14.3. The data
includes:

1. Pre-exercise estimates
2. Actual values main study
3. ± 'Will be' and ± 'Should be' estimates
4. Pilot study results
5. Overall results based on 22 persons

Debriefing and recommendations

For the sake of completeness the comments of the group and the major recommen-

Table 14.3 Comparison of results.

Activity	'Will be' estimate	'Should be' estimate	Actual values Nov. study	± Will be	± Should be	Pilot study Mar–April	Grand average 22 social workers
Travel	12.4	8.6	15.70	+3	+7	15.0	15.6
Writing/ dictating	21.4	16.2	21.06		+5	20.0	20.8
Supervisor	5.6	7.6	6.95	+1½	−1	5.5	6.7
Formal meetings	6.8	5.4	8.47	+1	+3	5.5	7.9
Colleagues	7.8	6.6	7.62		+1	11.0	8.3
Clients	31.0	41.4	28.83	−2	−12½	28.0	28.7
Reading	3.2	5.0	3.44		−1½	4.0	3.5
Telephone	6.0	4.8	4.13	−1		5.0	4.8
Other	5.8	4.4	3.15	−2½	−1	7.0	3.9

All the above figures are expressed as a percentage of the working day. The working day does not include rest time.

dations are included. From the figures it would appear more time should be spent with clients and less travelling, writing and dictating and in formal meetings. But after discussion it was concluded that time savings could only be made by reducing the time spent writing/dictating since more time with clients (either in number of cases or frequency/duration of visits) could lead to more travel and formal meetings.

The discussions after both projects indicated that considerable time was wasted and individuals were dismotivated because of some or all of the following features:

1. *Office information* – size, noise, decor, etc.
2. *Telephones* – availability, access.
3. *Job description* – problems of duplication of effort due to lack of clear delineation of duties.
4. *Training* – requirements noted in following:
   (a) Dictation
   (b) Chairmanship
   (c) Interviewing.

These conclusions lead to further specific studies to be undertaken by management in office layout and accommodation, in telephone provision and by the Social Services Training Group in job descriptions and verification of training requirements. It may be significant to note that all of this did take place against the background of training seminars on 'the more effective uses of time', since there must be a willingness on the part of those being investigated to recognise their own efforts in this direction. These seminars, for this organisation, are now a current feature of training and in particular are being used as part of induction courses.

TIME ROBBERS AND TIME WASTERS

Whether or not you have kept a time log record you will have some idea of those features in your working life – and even in that part of your life which is not paid employment – which cause you concern. (One of the writers in time management, Alan Lakein, uses this idea in the title of his book *How to Get Control of Your Time and Your Life* (1973).)

A useful question (or a variant of it) is:

> Do you use your time effectively? Whatever your answer list reasons and examples.

Whether this is answered individually or in groups inevitably the list identifies those things that may be called *time robbers*, i.e. ways in which our time is eroded by other people or the organisation. Examples are:

1. Information
   (a) Lack of
   (b) Unclear
   (c) Incomplete
2. Too much to read
3. Meetings
4. Telephone
   (a) Lack of ability to get people
   (b) Too many interruptions
   (c) Other people speaking too long
5. Lack of support staff
6. Filing systems
   (a) Poor
   (b) Complex
   (c) Incomplete
7. Mechanical and electronic failures
8. Other people's laziness, absences, latenesses
9. Staff turnover

These are very easy to identify and they must be tackled in various ways, but it is also necessary really to answer the following questions:

1. What am I doing that does not need to be done at all – by me or anyone else?
2. What am I doing that could be handled by someone else just as well – if not better?
3. What do I do that wastes other people's time?
4. What do I do that wastes my own time?

Question 2 is dealt with later in the section on delegation, but apart from people recognising that they do not delegate effectively often *time wasters* are:

1. Attempting too much at once.
2. Procrastinating over difficult tasks.
3. Creating too many interruptions.
4. Failing to listen.
5. Being unable to say no.
6. Failure to set priorities.
7. Involving everyone.
8. Too much attention to detail at expense of main thrust.
9. Lack of planning/organisation.

10. Lack of reflecting on the job as a whole and reviewing objectives.
11. Failure to take rest/relaxation periods thus becoming tired and more likely to make mistakes.
12. Having a highly fragmented job.

Probably we all are guilty of some of the above to a lesser or greater extent. Perhaps we can sum all of this up by the question:

> *Do you manage time or does time manage you?*

In the next two sections we look at ways in which the job can be analysed to answer some of the questions posed above.

MANAGERIAL ROLES

Although the cycle of management elements planning, initiating (providing and guiding), controlling and communicating is a comprehensive description of management, it is very difficult to observe managers actively planning, initiating and controlling. This is possibly because the average manager is planning several activities at the same time and often has to switch from one problem to others almost instantaneously. It has been suggested that the average timespan of a manager (i.e. the length of time spent on each individual activity) is six minutes.

Recognising that to understand management more fully Henry Mintzberg conducted some extensive research in 1973. In this he suggested that managerial activities and managerial roles could be observed. He identified 10 separate roles which in turn could be grouped into three categories which are concerned with:

1. Interpersonal relationships
2. Information processing
3. Making significant decisions

The roles concerned with *interpersonal relationships* are figurehead, liaison and leader, which all derive from the manager's formal authority and status. These lead to *informational roles* – monitor, disseminator and spokesman – which in turn enable the manager to perform the *decisional roles* – entrepreneur, disturbance handler, resource allocator and negotiator. A description of each of these roles is given below.

Interpersonal roles

1. The *figurehead role* identifies the manager as a symbol obliged to carry out a number of social, inspirational, legal and ceremonial duties. In addition, the manager must be available to certain parties that demand to deal with him because of his status or authority.
2. The *leader role* identifies the manager's relationship with his subordinates. He defines the climate in which they work, motivates them, enquires into their activities and takes responsibility for their development. The manager attempts to bring subordinate and organisational needs into a common accord to promote efficient operations. The power of the manager is most clearly manifested in the leader role.

3. In the *liaison role* the manager develops a network of contacts outside the unit in which information is traded for mutual benefit. Managers spend considerable amounts of time performing this role, first by making a series of commitments to establish these contacts, and then by carrying out various activities to maintain them.

Informational roles

1. As *monitor* the manager seeks and receives information from a variety of sources in order to develop understanding of the unit and its environment. Information arrives on internal operations, external events, ideas and trends and in the form of analyses and pressures.
2. As *disseminator* the manager sends external information into his unit and internal information from one subordinate to another. This information may be of a factual nature or contain 'values' introduced by the manager.
3. As *spokesman* the manager must transmit information to various external groups. He must act in a public relations capacity, lobby for his unit, keep key influences (board of directors or boss) informed, inform the public about his unit's performance, plans and policies, and send useful information to his liaison contacts. Furthermore, the manager must serve outsiders as an expert in the field in which his unit operates.

Decisional roles

1. As *entrepreneur* the manager initiates and designs much of the controlled change in his unit. He continually searches for problems and opportunities. When a situation requiring improvement is found, the manager initiates an 'improvement project', a series of related decisions and other activities, sequenced over a period of time that leads to the actual improvement.
2. The manager must take charge when his unit meets with an unexpected stimulus for which there is no clear programmed response. In effect, he assumes the role of *disturbance handler*. Disturbances may arise from conflicts between subordinates, conflicts between the manager's unit and another, and losses of resources or threats thereof.
3. In his *resource allocator* role the manager overseas the allocation of all forms of organisational resources (such as money, manpower and reputation). In scheduling his own time the manager implicitly sets unit priorities. What fails to reach him fails to get support. Thus his time assumes a significant opportunity cost. The manager also takes responsibility for establishing the basic work system of his unit and programming the work of subordinates – deciding what will be done, who will do it, what structure will be used.
4. As *negotiator* the manager takes charge when his unit must engage in important negotiating activity with other organisations.

ACTIVITIES

1. Using the above description as a guide, from your own experience write down one example of how each of the roles are carried out by *one* person in an organisation of your choice. If you are a manager this can be for yourself; otherwise choose a single manager.

2. Different types of manager spend more time in some roles than others. Estimate in percentage terms how much of the working time of the manager chosen for the previous activity is spent on each of the roles above. When you have this time estimate you may see some obvious omissions, or recognise that some roles absorb a disproportionate amount of time.

3. Compare the examples and time estimates you have produced for the activity above with the 'Eight Managerial Job Types' given in Table 14.4 which is based on Mintzberg (1973).

Table 14.4 Eight managerial job types.

1. *The contact man.* Spending a lot of time outside the organisation in the primary role of liaison and figurehead.

2. *The political manager.* Spending a lot of time in formal activities. Primary role of spokesman and negotiator.

3. *The entrepreneur.* Spending a good part of his time seeking opportunities and making changes. Primary role of entrepreneur and negotiator to implement changes.

4. *The insider.* Mainly concerned with the maintenance of the smooth running of the internal organisation. Building structures, training and development subordinates. Primary roles of resource allocator and leader.

5. *The real-time manager.* Like the insider concerned with inside operations, but operating primarily in the present. Highly fragmented activities, often a foreman or a production manager, or a manager of a small business dealing with quite a large number of crises. Primary role of disturbance handler.

6. *The team manager.* Preoccupied with the creation of a team. Perhaps somewhat concerned with a project like R&D. Major role that of leader.

7. *The expert manager.* Usually head of a specialist staff function such as management services. Does a lot of desk work alone and provides advice. Primary roles spokesman and monitor.

8. *The new manager.* Fairly obviously new to the job, lacking contacts and information. At the beginning he concentrates on the liaison and monitor roles. When he has got established he would tend to concentrate on the entrepreneurial role.

Based on Mintzberg (1973).

DELEGATION

When a definition of management refers to such activities as guidance, motivation and supervision, it implies that people are trained to assume responsibility for activities. Thus a driver is trained to operate a lorry/bus/tractor and take any decisions relative to its operation. A senior manager will communicate decisions to his subordinates or work with them in a team in reaching decisions. Afterwards putting the decision into effect is delegated to one or more people.

Delegation is a complex task and all managers should carefully review what they can delegate and what they cannot. Not all get it correct and perhaps the biggest danger in poor delegation is *not* delegating enough. To help indicate this Table 14.5 provides a checklist for you to complete on your own delegation practice.

No doubt the checklist in Table 14.5 will have given you much food for thought. There are no immediate feedbacks in the checklist, except what you make of the honest answers you gave, and, perhaps, what you are prepared to do about them. It is also worth looking at two other useful checklists: BIM Checklist No. 62 *Are You Delegating?*, and Management Action Checklist No. 1 *How to Delegate*.

CASE STUDY

Jack Freemont had recently received a promotion to the position of laboratory manager within a test department of a water authority. The laboratory was responsible for undertaking a variety of water tests concerning the purity of waterways, being particularly concerned with the outpourings of effluent from local factories. Jack had been with the authority for more than five years, after having graduated in chemistry from a local polytechnic.

Jack's record as a chemist was excellent. He had developed a number of ways of speeding up tests and contributed considerably to the development of a computer-based information system. He was widely respected in his department, since not only was he an effective chemist, but was popular with almost everyone on site. Throughout his five plus years with the water authority, Jack had kept 'up to date' in his field by reading chemical journals and attending seminars and conferences. He had been asked several times to contribute to in-organisation training courses, explaining to the others the work of the test laboratory.

Because of his technical expertise and experience with the organisation and his ability to get along with people, top management felt very confident in promoting Jack to the position of laboratory manager.

Jack's early experience in supervising the ten staff (mainly all graduate chemists) proved to be a real challenge. He experienced considerable difficulties with being a manager compared to being a chemist. He continued to be very involved with research and test design, and worked very long hours (sometimes up to twelve hours per day) in order to 'keep up' with technical development. As a result of this situation Jack did not provide the overall direction and co-ordination of the department that top management believed was necessary in order to achieve maximum effectiveness.

Jack began to feel pressure from some of the chemists, who likewise believed he was overinvolved in performing 'routine chemistry' rather than in 'managing' the department.

Since Jack wanted to improve as a manager, he decided to discuss the problems with his boss.

QUESTIONS

1. What is the basic problem confronting Jack Freemont as a manager? What is the cause(s)?
2. How does being a manager differ from being a chemist? Be specific.
3. Did top management make a mistake in promoting Jack to the position of laboratory manager?

Table 14.5 Activity/delegation checklist: Do you need to delegate more?

1. Do you have to take work home almost every night? Why? *Yes/No*

2. Do you work longer hours than those you supervise? *Yes/No*
   Steps you could take to change this to a 'No' are:

3. Are you frequently interrupted because others come to you with questions *Yes/No*
   or for advice or decisions? Why does this happen?
   Plans for cutting down these interruptions are:

4. Do you spend some of your working time doing things for others which *Yes/No*
   they could do for themselves?
   Actions you might take to avoid this are:

5. Do you have unfinished jobs accumulating, or difficulty meeting deadlines? *Yes/No*
   The jobs could be finished in time by:

6. Do you spend more of your time working on details than on planning and *Yes/No*
   supervision? Why?
   For better balance you could:

7. Do you feel that you must keep a close watch on the details if someone is to *Yes/No*
   do a job right? Examples?
   Different plans for control of results would be:

8. Do you work at details because you enjoy them, although someone else *Yes/No*
   could do them well enough? Such as?
   What you can do about this is:

9. Do you lack confidence in your staff's abilities so that you are afraid to risk *Yes/No*
   letting them take on more responsibility? Examples?
   New plans for action are:

10. Are you too conscientious (a perfectionist) about details that are not *Yes/No*
    important for the main objectives of the job in hand? Examples?
    New plans for actions are:

11. Do you keep job details secret from staff, so one of them will not be able to   *Yes/No*
replace you? Examples?
New plans for action are:

12. Do you believe that a manager should be rushed in order to justify his   *Yes/No*
salary?
13. Do you hesitate to admit that you need help to keep on top of your job?   *Yes/No*
Examples of help you could use are:

List subordinates who could be trained to give this help.
14. Do you neglect to ask staff for their ideas about problems that arise in their   *Yes/No*
work? Examples?
To change this you could:

---

4. What skills are important for Jack as the manager? Why?
5. Does being a good chemist guarantee success as a manager? Why or why not?

Remember that, although Jack in this example is a chemist, he could be instead a teacher, architect, social worker, administrator, fireman, etc.

DEMANDS, CONSTRAINTS AND CHOICES

Further analysis of one's job may be carried out by following the research work done by Rosemary Stewart (1967; 1982) in which the manager's job can be divided into three categories:

1. *Demands* – those kinds of work which are essential to meet minimum standards of performance, i.e. spending time with boss, subordinates, meetings.
2. *Constraints* – those factors which limit the job: resources, technical, location, organisation.
3. *Choices* – how work is done and in some cases what is emphasised and what rejected.

Analysis along these lines gives an indication of the discretion a person has. This naturally leads to seeing ways of either getting more discretion or, better still, using the choice element to provide for more effective use of time.

PRIORITIES, SCHEDULING AND RATIONING

Having discovered how your time is used, the next stage is to:

1. Fix priorities
2. Schedule activities
3. Ration time

There are a number of approaches to this which have been found to be of value. One is *routine v. key tasks* as illustrated in Figure 14.3.

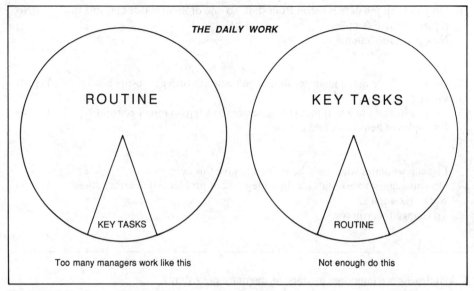

Figure 14.3 Routine versus key tasks

However, of more help is the classification of work as *urgent v. important*, illustrated in Figure 14.4. In this figure, the time demands quadrant is self-explanatory. It is also worth while just commenting on those tasks in the bottom right-hand quadrant: high importance but low urgency. Such activities would include staff development interviews with staff which, if not properly planned, will not get done until it is late and therefore they are rushed, i.e. they move into the quadrant above.

Figure 14.5 gives an extract from a desk diary that might help people organise their jobs into proper priorities.

CONCLUSIONS

The activity trap

There are many good books and films on the subject of time management. The message from all of them is much the same – avoid the *activity trap*:

> Most people get caught in the Activity Trap. They become so enmeshed in activity that they lose sight of why they are doing it and the activity becomes a false goal – an end in itself. Successful people never lose sight of their goals.
>
> *(Odiorne, 1974)*

If you don't know where you are going any road will get you there.

Checklists

There are many of these in the literature on time management and no apology is made for adding a further one in Table 14.6. There are also many books on time

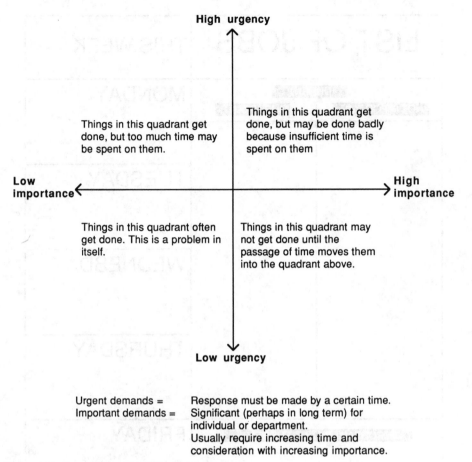

High urgency

Things in this quadrant get done, but too much time may be spent on them.

Things in this quadrant get done, but may be done badly because insufficient time is spent on them

Low importance

High importance

Things in this quadrant often get done. This is a problem in itself.

Things in this quadrant may not get done until the passage of time moves them into the quadrant above.

Low urgency

Urgent demands = Response must be made by a certain time.
Important demands = Significant (perhaps in long term) for individual or department.
Usually require increasing time and consideration with increasing importance.

Figure 14.4 Urgent versus important tasks

management. Those not specifically referred to in the text are included as a separate list.

Over to you ...

Enough has been written and read and reflected upon for you to do something about your own management of time.

ACTIVITY

Having considered those aspects of your job that affect the use of time, write down at least three things that *you* will do to make your time management more effective.

References and suggested reading

British Institute of Management (1975) *Are You Delegating?* Checklist No. 62. London: BIM.
Davidson, J. (1978) *Effective Time Management*. New York: Human Sciences Press.

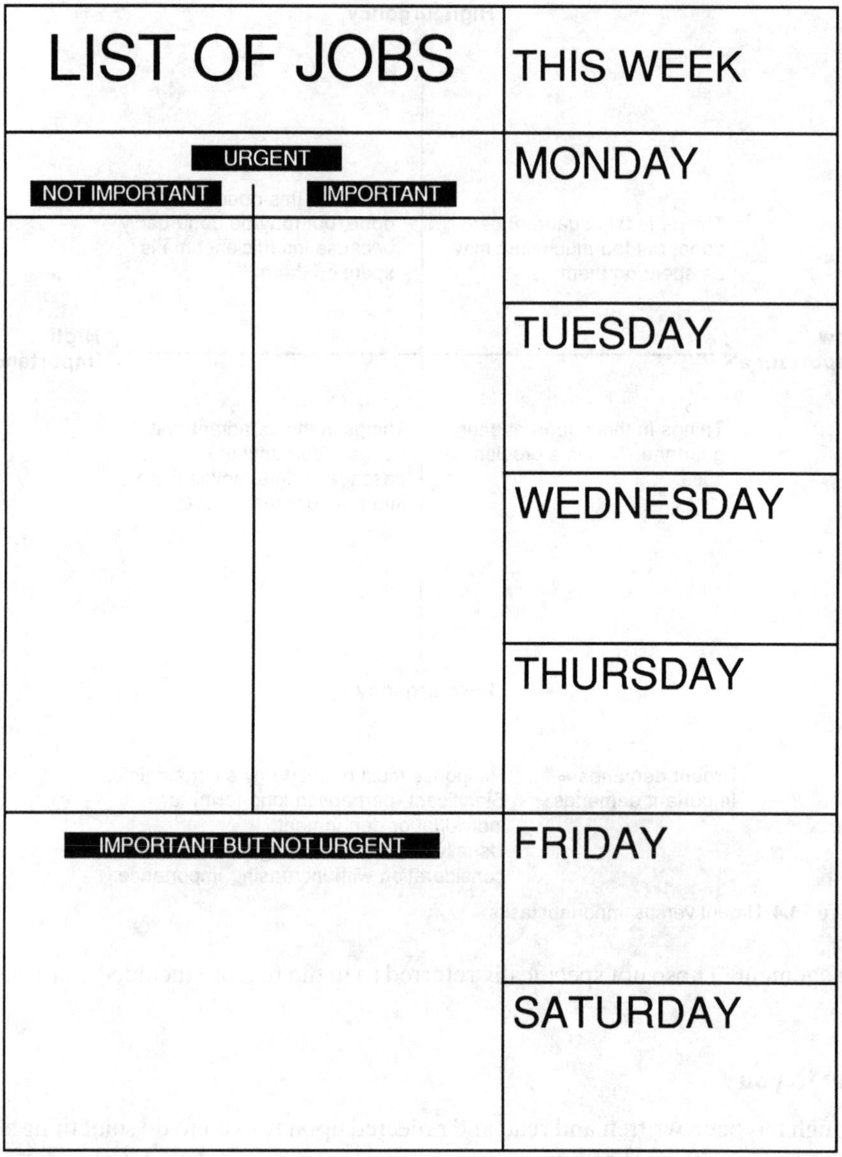

LIST OF JOBS	THIS WEEK

	URGENT	
NOT IMPORTANT		IMPORTANT

MONDAY

TUESDAY

WEDNESDAY

THURSDAY

IMPORTANT BUT NOT URGENT

FRIDAY

SATURDAY

Figure 14.5

Drucker, P. (1981) *The Effective Executive*. London: Pan.
Feldman, E. (1968) *How to Use Your Time to Get Things Done*. New York: Frederick Fell.
Garrett, S. (1985) *Manage Your Time*. London: Fontana.
Grove, A. (1985) *High Output Management*. London: Pan.
Harris, N. D. (May 1975) A question of organisation. *Industrial and Commercial Training*, pp. 402–409.
Harris, N. D. (December 1976) Management services and professional staff. *Management Services*, **20** (12), pp. 34–37.
Lakein, A. (1973) *How to Get Control of Your Time and Your Life*. New York: Signet.
Mackenzie, R. A. (1972) *The Time Trap*. New York: Amacom.
Management Action (January 1985) How to delegate. Checklist No. 1. *Management Monitor*, **3** (3), pp. 28–34.

Table 14.6 Some ideas for better time utilisation.

1. Value time – it is a scarce resource.
2. Challenge your tasks.
3. Aim to complete jobs in one go.
4. Learn to speak and shut up.
5. Devise drills for recurrent situations.
6. Checklists.
7. Read effectively:
   (a) Quicker reading.
   (b) Selective reading.
8. Train staff to save your time:
   (a) Shut that door!
   (b) Have regular availability and reporting times.
9. Plan work and appointments well ahead.
10. One diary with you.
11. Make lists for tomorrow.
12. Time for telephone calls.
13. Filing – when in doubt, chuck it out.

Marshall, J. and Cooper, G. L. (1979) *Executives under Pressure*. London: Macmillan.
Mintzberg, H. (1973) *The Nature of Managerial Work*. New York: Harper & Row.
Odiorne, G. (1974) *Management and the Activity Trap*. London: Heinemann.
Peter, L. J. and Hull, R. (1969) *The Peter Principle*. London: Pan.
Reynolds, H. and Tramer, M. (1979) *Executive Time Management*. Aldershot: Gower.
Stewart, R. (1967) *Managers and Their Jobs*. London: Pan Piper.
Stewart, R. (1982) *Choices for the Manager*. Englewood Cliffs, NJ: Prentice-Hall.
Townsend, R. (1970) *Up the Organisation*. London: Coronet.

INDEX